PRIVATE DETECTIVE

PRIVATE DETECTIVE

From the Files of the World's Greatest
Private Eye

WILLIAM C. DEAR

BLOOMSBURY

First published in Great Britain 1992

Copyright © 1992 by William C. Dear

The moral right of the author has been asserted

Bloomsbury Publishing Ltd, 2 Soho Square, London W1V 5DE

A CIP catalogue record for this book is available from the
British Library

ISBN 0 7475 1235 3

10 9 8 7 6 5 4 3 2 1

Typeset by Cambridge Composing (UK) Ltd, Cambridge
Printed in England by Clays Ltd, St Ives Plc

CONTENTS

Foreword   1

CHAPTER 1: **Teenage Gumshoe**   8
  Bill Dear's Notepad: Jimmy Hoffa's Ticket   22

CHAPTER 2: **The Exhumation of Lee Harvey Oswald**   24
  **Bill Dear's Notepad: An Encounter with
  Robert de Niro**   43

CHAPTER 3: **The Glen Courson Case**   46
  Bill Dear's Notepad: Island Governor   71

CHAPTER 4: **Dade County Lawman**   73
  Bill Dear's Notepad: They Stiffed me!   92

CHAPTER 5: **The Gas Station Murders**   94
  **Bill Dear's Notepad: He Wasn't a Tough Guy,
  See?**   108

CHAPTER 6: **A Brush with Politics**   110
  Bill Dear's Notepad: Hotel Dick   116

CHAPTER 7: **Howard Hughes Had Nothing on
  Pete Coffield**   119
  Bill Dear's Notepad: The Big Hose   134

CHAPTER 8: **The Woman Who Kidnapped Herself**   136
  Bill Dear's Notepad: Too Domestic for Me   146

CONTENTS

CHAPTER 9: **Amber Cries No More**   150
   Bill Dear's Notepad: Crossed Wires   166

CHAPTER 10: **An Offer I Couldn't Refuse**   168
   Bill Dear's Notepad: My Kingdom for a Plane!   180

CHAPTER 11: **The Desperate Search for Christie Meeks**   184
   Bill Dear's Notepad: Just Sit Up and Take Notice!   199

CHAPTER 12: **The Great Impostor**   202
   Bill Dear's Notepad: The Tamperproof Bottles   210

CHAPTER 13: **'Please Help Her . . . She's Only Six'**   214
   Bill Dear's Notepad: Bill In One   229

CHAPTER 14: **The Deadly Date**   230

CHAPTER 15: **'What Are You Doing Now, Mr Dear?'**   238

Epilogue   242

Acknowledgments   244

DEDICATION

To my sons Michael and Adam Dear
and to those who are also so
important in my life, Gini Clement,
and my parents, James and Lucille Dear.

And to someone very special,
E.J. Witenhafer, my friend,
now and forever. Thank you.

AUTHOR'S NOTE

Asterisks after names indicate that a pseudonym has been used for legal reasons.

FOREWORD

'Ladies and gentlemen, we're very happy to have with us today a private investigator who has been inducted into the Police Officers' Hall of Fame as one of the top homicide investigators in the world . . . '

Hearing those words as I prepared to get up in front of five hundred members of the Texas Corrections Association, my mind ran back across thirty years of my life and career. The memories are as fresh as a fall morning in East Texas. So many cases. Hundreds of stories. Most of them unbelievable . . . but all true.

'Bill Dear lives a life most of us only dream about . . . ' the introduction continues.

He's probably right. Sometimes I wonder why I was chosen by fate to live this life; though at times I've been so close to death I've often thought of fate as having a very strange sense of humor as it toyed with me. It's been a long road and a library full of cases since that morning as a paperboy on a bicycle in Miami, Florida, when I came across two suspects from an armed robbery and helped the police catch the crooks. But it wasn't simply a 'local boy makes good' story. Before the case was closed, my life was threatened and I really believe I could have been killed.

It was the first time I had known the fear of being threatened like that, but it wouldn't be the last. Yet over time I learned to handle the fear; fortunately, death threats don't occur all the time, but when they do I just laugh at them for what they are . . . mental terrorism. After all, very few people are going to tell you in advance that they are about to hit you. Likewise, when I get the proverbial hushed call in the middle of the night, I laugh into the phone . . . though sometimes it really irritates me that someone woke me from a good night's sleep.

'The cases marked "solved" by Mr Dear have made worldwide headlines . . . '

Like the Dean Milo murder case in Akron, Ohio. Dean Milo was the head of the Milo Beauty and Barber Supply Company when he was murdered in the foyer of his suburban home in 1980. The family was, as is so often the case where there is a lot of family money involved, reluctant to be straightforward, though anxious to solve the case. I actually lived in the dead man's house and in his clothes for a few days, to understand better what he was like and may have felt that fateful night. I learned a lot of family secrets and uncovered numerous family skeletons.

When it was over and we went to trial, we took eleven murder suspects to court and obtained eleven convictions. That was the most convictions in one murder case in the history of the United States. It was a classic case of family greed and jealousy that caused the death of Dean Milo.

The case made almost as many headlines as the exhumation and autopsy of Lee Harvey Oswald, the alleged murderer of President John F. Kennedy. The exhumation was to dispel rumors of a Soviet spy in the grave marked 'Oswald'.

Or the investigation of the bizarre murder of one of Canada's most famous jockeys that led me to the most intriguing case of a conwoman with a list of aliases as long as my arm and a prison record she kept hidden from those across North America she had swindled out of millions of dollars.

The case of the death of Glen Courson, a prominent Dallas businessman, and the ineptness of a local suburban police department took its toll on my life and severely damaged my career. The police manipulated physical evidence and witness testimony so that Courson's death would be ruled a suicide. This would protect the personnel in the department who had botched the crime scene. It kept his family from receiving the insurance they were entitled, nearly implicated an innocent man as the murderer and got me crosswise with the department to a point where they began investigating *me*.

Then there was the case of a teenage girl I had to find and rescue from a father who was heavily involved in dealing drugs. The rescue and 'getaway' was a most harrowing experience, staying just steps ahead of our pursuer. Before it was over we were responsible for the temporary closing of the Jacksonville, Florida, airport and a daring escape that even Ian Fleming's James Bond wouldn't have thought of. Speaking of which . . .

'. . . *and of course, ladies and gentlemen,*' the introduction continued, '*you've all seen the media accounts of Mr Dear, the man many have called "the real-life James Bond"* . . . '

I was wondering when that would come up. Ever since that newspaper reporter did a big story back in 1982, virtually every interview or introduction has included the comparison. I'm not sure if I like it or not. It's the expensive clothes, the large home, the planes and helicopters, the guns, the cars and all the other trappings of my profession that shape that image, but I do like to go first class. I got tired of watching the rich in Florida have it all, while as a young police officer I had to eat my meals at the back door of restaurants because I couldn't afford any better. So I decided there was a better way to make a living. I value my privacy, so I need a large home with added security (that's part of my business). And what man doesn't enjoy being around beautiful women? I certainly do. Some of my cases have centered around some very interesting and beautiful women. I've never had a Lauren Bacall lookalike waltz into my office past my secretary (who also happens to be blonde and very attractive), but I have known, worked for and even investigated the woman from Dallas known as the Black Widow. Three times her husbands have died mysteriously, giving credence to what seems to be a very appropriate nickname.

I always thought Teresa Russell was beautiful . . . and played the role of the Black Widow quite well. But her mysterious femininity couldn't match that of the true 'Black Widow', who was a dangerously desirable woman, like a Godiva chocolate laced with arsenic.

Then there was the Careflight Helicopter nurse who, while working on her Master's thesis at her Dallas home, seemed to vanish into thin air with the paper still in her typewriter and a half-full cup of coffee on the desk. Police searched for her everywhere, including her home. Everyone just knew she had been kidnapped and possibly murdered. After an extensive manhunt and the anxiety of waiting to hear from a kidnapper, she turned up as suddenly and mysteriously as she had vanished. Her story made headlines, especially when I uncovered what really happened.

Exposing the truth is really what my job is all about. Many times it's just a matter of getting at evidence overlooked by others and presenting it to the right authorities. But sometimes, even with the evidence in hand, you can't seem to clamp the handcuffs on.

A great example of a real master was the man known to most, especially in law enforcement, as the Great Impostor; also as Jack Eubanks*, Jack Ritchie* and by a host of other names. By the time I exposed his true identity, this expert in karate and several languages had posed as a prison warden, a CEO of a major company – even a surgeon. Amazingly, he had performed some very sophisticated surgery during his 'tenure'. But the most incredible thing was the fact that the Great Impostor had posed as a Colonel of a United States military base in Guam! He forged the documentation and used his skills acquired while in the Civil Air Patrol some years earlier to fly every type of American military aircraft in the arsenal, and fly them all very well.

There was multi-millionaire H. H. 'Pete' Coffield, one of the nation's most powerful 'behind the scenes' men. We became very close in the four years I worked with him, protecting the man from attempts on his life, both from outside and from within his own organization. We grew so close he was like a father to me. He would fly to Dallas from his ranch every day so that we could lunch together. I don't believe I ever met anybody as flamboyant as 'Pete' Coffield. Steeped in money and power, and surrounded by beautiful women, he was the Texas wheeler-dealer personified, even though he was in his eighties.

To find a Chicago street bum and inform him of a vast inheritance awaiting him back home in Florida was no small task, complicated by family members who hated the rightful heir and had caused his exile from the family so many years before. It reopened old family wounds, though it closed a case with a father's love for the prodigal son.

Of course, there are those cases that may never be solved, and we may never even know the motive behind them. On July 20, 1978, a very sweet and attractive young woman called Mary 'Bobo' Shin disappeared from her small Arkansas town of Magnolia. She had been last seen with a man who got into her car at a convenience store. Mary was a part-time realtor and it was presumed the man wanted to see a house. Though her car was later found at a grocery store in Magnolia, Mary was never seen again.

A year and a half later I was contacted by her parents, since eighteen months of police work had turned up nothing. One suspect's name kept coming up as a strong lead, but when we checked it, it turned out the man had died three months after Mary's disappearance. He had a history of mental illness. It's believed he committed suicide, though the ruling is still in question. Was he actually murdered? Did he know anything about Mary's disappearance? Had he been Mary Shin's abductor and murderer?

Vic Feazell was a District Attorney in Texas who made the Texas Rangers and the FBI mad. The Rangers and the FBI had hung three hundred murders around the neck of Henry Lee Lucas. Lucas was a self-confessed mass murderer, but Feazell felt Lucas had killed only three of the three hundred claimed by the state and federal investigators. For sticking to his guns, Feazell was charged with corruption in office. I came into the case and helped prove his innocence before the Federal Court in Austin. It was very unsettling to see how people would perjure themselves and misuse facts just to get even and cover their asses.

In the case of Ian Smalley, a British arms dealer accused of smuggling a variety of firearms around the world, I watched two federal law enforcement agencies battle against each other and pit

5

informants against informants, all because of bureaucratic jealousies. In addition, my staff and I were set up in such a way, by a major television news network working on the Smalley story, that we were all almost killed.

While that case really makes me mad when I think about it, some cases touch me in other ways, like the story of Cherie Ann Kennedy. The newborn baby was literally kidnapped from her mother's arms by a woman posing as a nurse. I took the case for the sum of one dollar. It was then I learned how police departments love private eyes one minute and hate them the next. It was like watching James Garner on *The Rockford Files*. After we searched across Texas, New Mexico and into Mexico, having endless meetings with informants and going over the results of hours of surveillance in meticulous detail, the police took credit after we found the child and they then tried to discredit me in the press. Like death threats, that wasn't the first time, nor would it be the last.

One and a half million children go missing each year in the US. Two hit me personally. Seven-year-old Christie Meeks lived with her folks in East Dallas. One day a white male abducted her. The case dragged on for months of dead ends and unresolved motives before Christie Meeks's body was found floating in Lake Texoma. As far as most people are concerned, her murderer has still not been located. But because of facts I've uncovered, I feel I know exactly what happened to Christie Meeks that cloudy day.

Just as frustrating and sad was ten-year-old Christie Diane Proctor. We located a Jordanian national working at the University of Texas at Dallas as a suspect, but the police had no concrete evidence linking him to Christie Proctor's disappearance. As we closed in on him, he left the country and returned to his home leaving an American wife and three children behind. About eighteen months later, Christie's body was found three miles from her Dallas home.

In the case of two-year-old Amber Crum, an innocent child subjected to unimaginable forms of physical abuse, we tracked down her killer but couldn't do a thing. This guy had pushed the little girl's head into the toilet, and even scalded her with hot water, before killing her. I had him in my car when I looked at him and said point blank, 'I know you killed Amber.'

'But you can't prove it,' the bastard replied.

Sometimes the guilty fall through cracks in the system, leaving the victim's family to cope with murder. Telling parents that their child has been found – dead – is the unbearable curse of my business. I never get over it. If I said I never cried with them, I'd be lying. I'm a parent and I'm human. It's probably the cases involving the kids over these many years that has made me speak to any group of teenagers that will listen, trying to persuade them to say 'No' to drugs, strangers and deadly fads like the Dungeons and Dragons game. The case of James Dallas Egbert at Michigan State still haunts me.

'. . . and now,' the introduction concluded as I remembered James Dallas Egbert, 'may I present to you one of the top private investigators in the world, Mr William C. Dear . . . '

Applause carried me to the podium as I drew myself back to the present.

'Thank you, Tom. Ladies and Gentlemen,' I began, 'sitting there, I wasn't sure of what I was going to say to you today. Oh, I knew what I wanted to say, but how to say it . . . that was the obstacle I faced. You see, what I have to tell you is very important to you and the lives of your family – especially your children. Let me take you back to 1980 and to the campus of Michigan State University . . . '

Just recalling the case of James Dallas Egbert as I looked out across the room sent a chill up my spine. It must be the thought of those damn tunnels under the campus.

CHAPTER 1
Teenage Gumshoe

Hot, salty sweat poured down my forehead, stinging my eyes as they peered through the narrow steamy black hell of the tunnels beneath Michigan State University. It did no good to try to wipe away the sweat from my eyes. My hands, my arms, my body were soaking wet and covered with dirt and gravel from the tunnel walls and water pipes crisscrossing the pitch-black maze. As I hunched over and sometimes crawled through the slime that hung from these dungeon passages, I knew that no cave could be darker and no swamp more miserable. Water, condensed by the consuming heat, dripped constantly from a spider's web of hot pipes above. I was certain I would soon trip on some unseen fixture and hurl myself headlong into the wall or on to the puddled floor. I was also certain that at any moment I would walk straight into the very face of Satan himself. I remembered all too well my fear of the dark as a very young child and thought how this experience then would probably have sent me over the edge. My only fear now was that the devil already held in his arms the young genius I was searching for.

James Dallas Egbert III had graduated high school in Ohio at the age of thirteen and entered college at Michigan State University at fourteen. He was a master of the computer and an avid fan of Dungeons and Dragons, a game of fantasy roleplaying some took to violent and deadly extremes. I worried that his roleplaying in these passages had taken the game to a deadly level, and I prayed I could piece the puzzle together in time to save him. Yet I wasn't even certain he had been down here. All I knew for sure – all anyone knew for sure – was that Dallas suddenly disappeared. Vanished. Now I had to find him and the trail led me through these tunnels, where the heat reached 130 degrees. I sure as hell couldn't imagine staying down here for any length of time . . . especially for some damned game.

I was getting irritable. There was no air, and it was difficult to breathe as I inched along. I felt the debris of the filthy tunnels being sucked into my lungs with each hacking gasp. What the hell am I doing down here, was the relentless mental refrain somewhere in the back of my burning skull.

I had taken the case, despite wishing for a little time off, after hearing the despair and anxiety in the voices of Dallas's parents as they begged me to find their missing son. As I snaked my way through the ever-narrowing, rat-infested passages of filth, I tried to keep my mind focused on the search for the smallest of clues. I couldn't help but remember the conversation with Dallas's parents. They told me of their son's 'differences', his IQ of 180, his shyness and the unlikelihood of his leaving school without telling anyone where he was going.

I could also remember, as I wedged my body beneath several hot pipes and through a small opening, how I looked at the photograph of my son, Michael, during the phone conversation; I thought how desperate and emotionally shattered I would be if *he* had suddenly disappeared. There was no doubt how much I wanted to find Dallas; it had now become an obsession. And the fact remained that if I were waiting endless hours by a phone for an investigator to find Michael, I would want to know he was doing everything possible to locate him. No one but a parent would know the pain I would be going through.

Suddenly I thought I heard voices. No! I *knew* I heard them!

It was pitch black, save for the bouncing ray of light from my flashlight, but I didn't want to lose the direction of the noise. Brushing cobwebs from my eyes in the darkness, I was determined to catch whoever it was, maybe Dallas, maybe the people holding him. Dear God, let it be Dallas! Water from random puddles splattered all over me as I fought to miss fixtures and pipes I could see merely a split second before I hit them. I knew it was stupid to run faster through these dark, small, slimy corridors with only a flashlight, but Dallas was my only concern and I sensed he might be close. The hot steam and mist burned my face as I raced through the tunnels, and breathing seemed impossible in the humidity.

Then, without warning, my left foot lost its balance in the slimy water and I felt myself falling. The flashlight seemed to scatter its beam everywhere as it flew from my hand and I simultaneously groped in vain for something to catch on to in the darkness. There was nothing. Just the reverberating feeling of the solid floor meeting my head. All became abruptly still. The dark world fully engulfed me . . .

. . . Through the haze I can see the car coming by me. I'm fourteen years old and it's a cool, but humid early morning in Miami. Once again, I'm up at four a.m. tossing the *Miami Herald* to five hundred daily customers. Funny, that car doesn't look familiar . . . and it's heading for a street on my route. That just doesn't look right. As it turns the corner I begin pumping my newspaper-laden bike for everything I'm worth. A couple of turns keeps the car going slow enough to let me jump a few curbs and dash across several front yards and sidewalks to stay within sight of it . . . but they obviously don't see me. I watch them turn into the driveway of one of my customers . . . just a few blocks from my house. Oh well, I guess some family must be visiting. But something still doesn't seem right, so I jot down the license number. I always figured it was easier to write things down, especially a number, than trying to remember it later.

A few minutes pass and I'm delivering papers, again, when I see a couple of beat patrol cops. These guys have the greatest jobs. Catching criminals, riding around in cool cars with the power to stop anyone who looks suspicious. It sure beats pumping a bike. Everyone really looks up to them, especially me. Being a policeman . . . that's my dream. It's still dark, but they see me riding

10

through the neighborhood delivering the news, and they stop alongside me.

'Billy, you seen anything out of the ordinary, son?'

'No, why?'

'Lookin' for some bad ol' robbers,' he smiles.

'Well, I did see this old Chevy a few blocks from my house. Never saw it before.'

His smile fades a little. 'When was that, son?'

'Just a little while ago back on 39th Terrace. I got the license number.'

The cop's smile returns as I hand it to him. 'Thanks, Billy.'

It's fading again, the images are blurring, but a couple of days have passed as the recollection comes clear. I can see the newspaper . . . the *Miami Herald* . . . a big picture and everything about the *Herald* paperboy who helps the police nail a couple of robbers. But like a quick cut to the next scene of a movie, I'm back on my bike pedalling as hard as I can in the predawn morning. Someone in a car is following me. It's that same car from the robbery. They're trying to run me off . . .

My bike and I tumble as I edge too close to the curb. When I finally stop falling my arm hurts, and the man and woman the cops had arrested stand over me. I recognize them from the picture in the paper.

What are they doing out of jail? She was the sister of one of my customers. I don't really know who he is, and I really don't care.

'You open your mouth about what you saw the other night, kid, and you're dead . . . you understand me, boy?' His voice is gravelly. I don't doubt for a minute he would kill me. They leave me there, an acne-faced, skinny, scared teenager. Yesterday, I was a hero with my picture in the paper. Now, somehow, they're out of jail and threatening to kill me.

I don't really know what to do, except sit there. I'm scared. But I can't tell anyone. They'll kill me. And what about my Mom and Dad? My sister? I've got to do something. I just don't know . . . The cop! He'll help me.

'You bet we will, son.'

11

It's later in the morning and I'm standing next to his patrol car. I've just told him about the threat. He has a pretty mean look on his face, like this is something that's become sort of personal now.

'You just deliver your papers, Billy. We'll take care of the rest.'

It's early in the morning again . . . except this time it's a patrol car following me on my bike. It's the third time this hour he's passed by. I'm not scared any more. Man, it's humid this morning, sometimes it's so humid here on the Florida coast that I feel drenched, my clothes all wet . . .

I came to on the floor of the tunnels, soaking wet as I lay in a puddle of what I hoped was just water and not my lifeblood pouring from my head. It felt like a split watermelon. Boy, what I wouldn't give for an Excedrin right about now. I rubbed my neck as I recalled the dream I had while I was unconscious. But it was no dream. It was an actual case. My first, in fact. I helped catch two robbers, one of which was a sister of the lady who lived in the house there on 39th Terrace.

I've often wondered what made me stand up to those two, despite their death threat, and see to it they were put away. I was a shy, skinny kid, afraid of almost everything including the dark. But somehow I built up the nerve, and overcame them. Many times I've thought how out of character that was for me at the time. But it made me face a lot of fears, mostly in my own mind, and deal with them straight on. That's how I've faced life since then. And since then, I haven't lacked for confidence. Although I do still have this thing about small dark places. Like those damn Michigan State tunnels.

Filthy, wet and hurting, I managed to crawl back through the tunnels, find the opening and get to my car. I was staying at a Red Roof Inn near the campus. I thought, as I drove into the parking lot, how good a bath was going to feel. I think every muscle I had ached.

When I opened the door to the lobby of the motel, a horde of reporters, wielding microphones, cameras and lights, rushed my way and encircled me. I know I looked like death warmed over

12

and smelled even worse, but they crowded in as close as they could. Ever since I had arrived, reporters had been bothering me about the case. The story of the missing young genius had become big news and when the university denied the existence of any tunnels beneath the campus, as well as the idea they were being used for Dungeons and Dragons, the story became national news. Just the thought of college kids involved in such activity that many percieved as violent was scandalous for the school. But, with the information of a few anonymous students who knew how to get into the 'non-existent' tunnels, I had just proven the university wrong.

'There *are* tunnels under this campus,' I said. The journalists were quiet now. 'I don't care what MSU says, I've been in them. They're down there and college kids are definitely playing Dungeons and Dragons in them.'

The crowd of reporters suddenly began shouting questions and pushing microphones and cameras in my face. I answered very few after my initial statement, trying to get through the crowd and make my way to my room. I was mad. Mad at myself for not having found Dallas. The pressure was on now. The story had begun making news around the world, but that was good. I had asked the university about the tunnels and received a cold, flat denial, thank you very much. Now the media knew what I knew and there would be no denying the existence of these tunnels. I'd let the media put the pressure on the university to help me find Dallas at all costs. In a way I felt triumphant, but in a bigger way, as I said, I was mad at myself.

I opened the door to my room and felt the cool air surround me. My head hurt like a sonofabitch, and a knot above my eye was now raised and tender. At least it was swelling out and not in. All I needed now was a concussion.

The headlines, *Tunnels DO Exist Under MSU*, was the embarrassment to the college that I needed. The school was reluctant to grant me permission to search the tunnels, yet a maintenance man was provided in case I needed help finding my way around. I also

13

took my associate Dick Riddle with me to see if we could cover ground faster. A gnawing image of a trapped and hurt Dallas Egbert kept running through my mind.

Knowing what lay in store, I wore a jumpsuit for the second trip and took a new and much more durable flashlight. I also went into the tunnels through what you might call the front door this time. I had gained access before through a remote entrance that a couple of the students told me about. But front door or side entrance, I could immediately tell when I went back in that it was the same slimy hell as before. Some of the newspaper photographers and TV cameramen came down with us for the first few dozen yards into the tunnels, just to get a feel for things. But they didn't go very far and soon their bright lights were walking away from us as we eased further into hell. Before long Dick and I split up and my guide and I were soon crouching down and squeezing through yet more small and filthy passages.

As the maze grew darker and darker and seemed to close in around us, we noticed ambient light coming from somewhere down the tunnel. I worked my way toward it, amazed as I drew closer just how dark the passage really was.

We walked for what seemed like for ever, dodging hot pipes and slimy cobwebs. The humidity was taking its toll; I was already soaked to the skin and just as dirty as I was during my first stroll through the 'dungeon'. Even my shoes and socks were soaked from the countless puddles of stagnant, foul-smelling water. Each step sent slimy water squishing between my toes. God only knows how they smelled at that moment, but surely not as bad as the tunnels. Man, they smelled bad! I just kept reminding myself why I was down there, and how important it was to find something . . . anything that might lead me to Dallas.

A series of rather bizarre clues had led me to search the eight miles of tunnels beneath Michigan State, not the least of which was a small bulletin board in Dallas's dorm room. Stick pins were arranged on the bulletin board in the shape of a large blocked letter L with several other pins scattered around the main configuration. The 'design' made me wonder if the young man was leaving a map behind for someone to find. Was it part of the game? Was I being drawn into it?

Hot water condensing on the pipes above would occasionally grow into a single heavy drop and fall on my head, seeping into my hair or running like sweat down my neck or into my ears. There was no way to miss them and I dared not look up or one would surely hit me right in the eye like a hot-water version of the Chinese water torture.

I was miserable. My head still hurt from the fall, and my eyes strained to see in the limited light of our torches. I was trying to concentrate on getting around the hot pipes, missing the hot water drops and finding any hope of oxygen in the one hundred per cent humidity, when suddenly I felt something with claws land on my shoulder!

'Hey, wha . . . !' Without thinking I swirled and swatted it off in a startled panic. 'Damn. What was that?' I looked at my shoulder to see a huge rat glaring nose to nose at me.

My guide's flashlight found the phantom running like hell into some dark corner. What a jolt!

'Damn.' I bent over to catch my breath. 'I haven't seen too many dogs that big back in Texas.' My heart raced with every breathless pant.

I think my guide was too scared even to laugh at what had been a comical moment. And if he wasn't scared, he was sure as hell ready to leave. But the faint light at the end of the tunnel drew us both ever closer.

We hadn't traveled much further when I stepped into an intersection of two tunnels and a blast of freezing cold air shot like a jetstream across the passage. It must have dropped seventy degrees at least. I froze and quickly jumped back to the area just a foot or two away where the one hundred and thirty degree temperature was a quick and welcome relief. It was like being on the moon. The dark side is freezing and the sunny side is scorching hot. No happy medium.

'You'll hit those pockets a lot,' the guide instructed.

'Hey, thanks for the warning,' I replied, still shivering like a popsicle. The blast was bad enough, but in soaking wet clothes my body couldn't get warm. I wrapped my arms around myself and still felt like a giant goosebump. I wondered if Dick and his guide were having as much fun chasing after shadows and dodging arctic blasts in other tunnels.

By now my body was aching all over, but more importantly, my mind was beginning to feel the effects of fatigue. It had been a restless night before, and several phones calls from students wishing to remain anonymous had disrupted my sporadic sleep. We held our breaths and ran across so as to continue toward the light, but I kept thinking about the restless night.

The most surprising phone calls during the night came from two young women. They told me they had been raped on the campus. This was the first anyone had heard of anything like that going on at MSU. The case was growing more complicated. In the midst of all this, no one had ever mentioned or even hinted of rape. But apparently some of the girls at MSU feared walking the campus alone at night. Their close-knit network of girl talk had spread the word of several rapes on campus, though none of the young ladies could bring themselves to tell the authorities.

I just hoped that I wouldn't discover Dallas had been mixed up in this. He didn't seem, by everything I had discovered about him, to have the psychological makeup of a rapist. At the same time, his could have easily been the profile of a rape suspect. A loner, no longer challenged by school work, he had, once while in junior high school, been taken by the US Air Force to Wright Patterson Air Force Base to fix the base computer system when most of us had no idea what a computer really was. Too young to mix well with the college society, this slender, shy, short kid with horn-rimmed glasses didn't have many friends . . . I just didn't know – truthfully, there wasn't much at that moment that made sense either way, so realistically I figured anything was possible.

My thoughts had wandered but were quickly returned to the task at hand when my guide and I reached a fork in the tunnels.

'Hey, Jim,' I asked, 'which one should we take, the right or the left?'

'Your guess is as good as mine, Mr Dear.' The guide swallowed hard. 'I haven't been down here in many years . . . I don't even wanna be here now.'

'Well . . . let's try this.'

As I started to the right, I looked down at the slime-covered puddle of water I was walking through. I looked up as a drop of water hit my glasses.

'Damn, it's getting hot again. Where's that cold air when you need it?' Just as I uttered those words I looked back down and in front of me to see a small spurt of steam hissing from a pipe at head level less than ten feet away!

'Dammit!' My exclamation was almost as startling to my guide as the pressure release of steam. 'Somebody could get scalded to death. Is that normal?'

'Routine pressure release,' he said as he stared at the hot fixture. 'This is one of the damn reasons I don't come down here.' His words told me his better judgment could explain the incident. But his gaze at the fixture told me his constitution was yielding to the uncertainty of the whole situation.

'It's like trying to cross a minefield back in Korea,' the guide said. 'The valves go off from time to time. That's why it's so damn hot and humid down here.'

He was right. I had stepped perhaps fifty more feet when I saw another pressure valve beginning to vibrate. There was no doubt in my mind that the damned thing was about to release. I wanted out of there fast. We started to run, but just as we passed the valve, like it had eyes, it jettisoned a burst of flaming hot steam right into my torso.

'Ooouuuch!' I screamed at the top of my burning lungs. The heat felt like a blowtorch had cut through the jumpsuit and was burning away my skin. I doubled over as I fell back from this flamethrower disguised as a steam valve and ended up on my butt in a small puddle of water. I felt like Indiana Jones searching for the lost Ark of the Covenant; trying to dodge deadly booby traps and groping blindly like a mouse in a maze.

'Mr Dear, are you hurt?' His concern was genuine as he hurriedly sloshed through the water to me. But the pain made me want to answer, 'No, I feel absolutely great, let's do it again.' In fact, I was feeling a little sorry for the poor guy. He had not wanted to come into the tunnels, but the administration had made him.

I checked my burn and looked up as I tried to clear the sweat from my eyes. When they focused, I could see something overhead that looked like a grate or . . . it was a manhole cover! Now I could see the rungs of a metal ladder leading up to the manhole cover across the small tunnel from where I sat. Without thinking I scurried across to the ladder and up.

The opening came out in a remote area of the campus. Was this how the kids got into the tunnels for their fantasy games? The fresh air was a welcome relief like I had never experienced before. Then it dawned on me: could this have been the way the rapist(s) moved round the campus and abducted young girls without being detected? It hadn't slipped my mind that it had been while I was searching for the truth about the tunnels that the young ladies had contacted me. Maybe they were trying to tell me they thought the tunnels were where the attacker(s) hid. It would be as if Satan himself had reached up from hell and pulled a victim down for his own temporary and perverted pleasure, escaping through the manhole as the cover slid into place. I could better understand now why they sounded terrified over the phone. Who knows how many others had been victims?

I stayed there for a short while, turning the clues over in my brain and breathing in the intoxicating fresh air. I didn't relish the idea of going back, given what I had just been through, but I had no choice, because of Dallas.

Our lungs screaming for mercy, my guide and I started walking, again, toward the ambient light at the end of this section of tunnel. It wasn't that it was that far, just that I was taking my time now, walking with uncertainty in each step. I had no idea what lay in the darkness before me.

We continued to duck under ice-cold and fire-hot pipes and slide between narrow, slimy passages toward the light. After what seemed like an eternity of crawling through hell's own swamp, we came to realize the end of the tunnel was no such thing, but a jagged black hole in its side. I took my flashlight and directed its beam into the endless darkness. I knew damn well I was going to have to crawl in. I turned to the guide, who was already shaking his head.

'No, not me man, this is as far as I go.'

I took a deep breath, grabbed a hold of the broken concrete edges of the hole and lifted myself inside. On hands and knees, I crawled along the damp and humid tunnel that made the last section of tunnel seem like Grand Central Station. After I had crawled about ten feet something caught my eye just as I lost my balance due to a misplaced hand stretching too far past the tunnel. I could feel myself starting to fall head first into a black eternity, with nothing to grab. As I fell, the beam of my flashlight crossed a face!

'What th- . . . '

I slammed on to the hard floor that was, fortunately, only a few feet below. This time my flashlight stayed in my hand as I quickly scanned the area and regained my composure. A little to the left, then to the right . . . there!

There was a head sitting on a table. I inched closer, using my flashlight to look around at what appeared now to be a hiding place, but never keeping the light off the head for more than a split second. There was a table and six chairs with the head sitting on the table. Had the game resulted in someone's head being severed? A little closer, but the light was still too bad. This was unbelievable. This room was obviously not meant to be found. What the hell went on down here? Now as the flashlight's beam grew more intense on the object, with each step closer, I began to think . . . yeah, it's not . . . it's not a real head. It seems to be . . . it's made of paper.

A papier-mâché head? There was a sign next to the table that said, 'PLEASE WAIT TO BE SEATED, the show will begin shortly.' The first thing that occurred to me was the fact that there was no way the table could have been brought in through this maze and placed in the room. It reminded me of the old ship in the bottle routine. It only added another question to the long list for which I had very few answers. I stood there for a moment, with my mouth gaping. This was certainly one of the more unusual things

I'd come across as an investigator, to say the least. Then I thought of Dallas; a fifteen-year-old mixed-up kid. Was he part of this game? But what kid isn't confused at fifteen?

'Are you all right down there?' I had forgotten about the guide until he called out. 'Are you okay, Mr Dear?'

'You'll never believe it,' I answered.

I crawled back through the small tunnel that led back to the main tunnel and my guide. I began to laugh as I pulled myself out of the small opening.

'You know,' I chuckled, 'people pay five dollars to see a horror movie . . . this was better than anything Stephen King could come up with.'

'You're telling me!' he replied with a puzzled look. 'The funny things is, Mr Dear,' – he paused as he looked down the hole – 'there ain't no room supposed to be there.'

'What do you mean?'

'I mean I've got the engineering and architect's maps and there ain't no room shown right here.'

'Huh,' I replied. 'Then there are probably others.'

I was about to give up when we came across another opening about one hundred yards down the tunnel. This one was lower to the ground. I bent down to enter and looked back at my guide to make sure he hadn't changed his mind about sharing the adventure.

'Nope,' he replied, 'I already told you. No way.'

All around us we could hear the eerie sound of rattling and hissing pipes. Why me, I thought, as I entered the small opening with even more apprehension than the time before. I was amazed that it felt cool. I could raise up slightly as this hole was larger than the one before. I was beginning to feel claustrophobic. I tried to think . . . this wouldn't bother James Bond . . . but, hell, I'm not James Bond. I inched my way along the passage and I saw a light, a single bulb. I now got down on my hands and knees to crawl the rest of the way. I could see a blanket and laying on it were several half-eaten packages of crackers and a quart container of milk, long since soured. Looking around I saw a red milk crate which could have been used for a seat. What a hiding-place . . .

was it Dallas's? Maybe this was where he came to get away from the world and the parents who didn't understand him; his jump from the world of reality to the world beneath the ground . . . a world of fantasy.

Dallas had become a Dungeon Master in high school. Other students looked up to him. But now, a fifteen-year-old boy finds himself in college, and who wants to play with him? Who wants to date him? I couldn't help thinking how lonely he must have been on this campus of 35,000. Had he created his own version of the game? Was this short, subdued outcast now in his own world, a world that would accept him as he was? A boy who had mastered the game could become a man, making himself as strong as he wanted and as powerful as he wanted, all by entering the world of fantasy. He was Dallas Egbert, the Magic User . . . the most powerful of figures.

My next thought: had Dallas, out of desperation, designed the epitome of games, the Game of Death? Was Dallas Egbert the Dungeon Master? Was I being drawn into this final game? I sensed, as I looked around, that Dallas had been there . . . recently. Was this to be just another clue in the adventure? One thing I did know, as I crawled back out, was that he wouldn't be found during this trip.

BILL DEAR'S NOTEPAD: Jimmy Hoffa's Ticket

A big sedan pulled up and stopped right smack in the middle of a 'No Parking' zone at Miami International Airport. It was 1960 and I was, again, being punished for doing my job as a Dade County Sheriff's Deputy, for arresting someone who wasn't supposed to have been arrested. So, naturally, I was assigned to walk the airport beat for a while with a number of other unfortunates until the powers that be felt that I had repented. I really wasn't in the mood for a smartass that day and couldn't believe the driver was stupid enough to stop the car in the 'No Parking' zone, get out and walk to the terminal like nothing was wrong, especially with me standing right there.

'Sir,' I called, politely but sternly, 'you've got to move that car.'

He glanced at me, brushed his chin my way with his three middle fingers, flipped me the bird, and kept walking.

'Hey!' My politeness has its limits. 'I said, move the car.'

'I'm waiting on my boss,' the cocky little bastard replied.

'I don't care who you're waiting on,' I instructed, my eyes locked on his as I approached, 'move the car . . . *now*! Or I'll tow it!'

His brow furrowed and he had turned to face me head on. 'I'm waiting for Jimmy Hoffa,' he said, like I was supposed to be impressed.

'That's wonderful,' I replied as I pulled my citation pad and began writing up the car belonging to the powerful Teamsters Union leader. When I had just about finished with the citation I heard a booming voice from behind and below me.

'Hey! What the hell do ya' think ya' doin'?' The short, stocky guy had a truly surprised and upset look on his fat little face.

I turned toward him and without even batting an eyelid answered, 'I'm giving you a ticket, Mr Hoffa.'

'You ain't giving me shit . . . '

'Oh yes I am,' I interrupted, 'and I'd suggest you take it.'

He was pissed off! His face was flushed as he yelled, 'This is the first goddam ticket I ever got!'

'. . . and it probably won't be the last if you hang around here much longer.' I smiled as I ripped it from the pad and handed it to him.

'Goddamit! You sonofabitch!' He jerked it from my hand and got in the car.

I believe the fine for illegally parked vehicles at Miami International Airport, at the time, was five or ten dollars. He paid the fine, and I never saw his car there again. Maybe I taught him a lesson that kept him from a life of organized crime and parking tickets. Or maybe he just didn't get any more parking tickets.

CHAPTER 2
The Exhumation of Lee Harvey Oswald

'Paging William C. Dear.' I paused in the middle of the terminal as my name echoed over the public-address system at O'Hare Airport.

'Paging William C. Dear . . . please pick up the nearest yellow courtesy phone for a message.'

I let my carry-on slip from my shoulder a full step or two before reaching the phone. It had been a long day already and I was tired.

'Hello, this is William C. Dear.'

'Mr Dear, this is Howard Stevens . . . we're getting ready to go ahead with the exhumation.'

'Well, it's about time,' I popped off, 'you-all have been in touch with me for two years now . . . '

'We've finally obtained all of the releases,' Stevens interjected, 'and we want to do this within the next forty-eight hours.'

There was no hesitation on my part, I had been ready to go long before now. 'I can turn around and be back in Dallas immediately,' I said, 'if you're sure this is finally going to happen.'

'It's finally going to happen,' Stevens assured me, 'and maybe we can get to the bottom of some of these rumors.'

On board the plane back to Dallas, I thought about that day in November 1963. I'm never very comfortable when I fly, and usually walk around the cabin, but this time I sat and stared out of the window, slipping back to that cool, sunny day on the corner of Ross and Harwood Streets in downtown Dallas.

The crowds lined the barricaded curbs. Like every other spectator there, I was excited to be able to see President Kennedy. I was luckier than most. Not only would I see him here, but I had been invited to the luncheon at the Dallas Trade mart where he would speak.

The atmosphere on the street was like a carnival, and a surge of adrenalin seemed to rush through the masses as we heard the sirens of the motorcycle police a few blocks away, escorting the motorcade toward us. I could feel the groundswell of excitement moving toward me like 'the wave' you see at football games. I was glad I had arrived early to stake out my claim on history, as I got caught up in the fever of the moment. The screams of the sirens sliced through the roar of the crowded street, reverberating off the walls of the buildings until I couldn't hear myself.

Suddenly, to my left, just before the motorcade arrived at the corner of Ross and Harwood, some guy in a convertible, pulling a trailer with an outhouse on it, darted out from a sidestreet. A sign on the outhouse read IMPEACH EARL WARREN. The crowd gasped as the police quickly surrounded the vehicle and got it out of the way. But I wondered: how in the hell had he gotten through security?

There had been ill feeling among many of the conservatives toward Kennedy and Supreme Court Chief Justice Earl Warren for their stands on issues such as civil rights. A full page ad in the paper, laying the problems of the world at the White House doorstep, appeared in that morning's edition. But right then, at that moment in the noon hour, in that place, everyone loved President Kennedy. No matter how unpopular his politics he was, after all, the President of the United States and worthy of respect and admiration, not a cheap shot on a parade float.

But what bothered me even more was to know that security around the President, now less than a hundred yards from me, was so lax. Anything could have happened. That protesting convertible driver could have been out to do some serious harm and, by the looks of things, gotten close enough to do it without anyone able to stop him. Where was security? What about the barricades in the area? Where were they? Those questions tugged at me, but the excitement of seeing the Chief Executive, and the unbelievable noise in the street, wouldn't let them surface.

Suddenly, larger than life, there they were . . . President and Mrs Kennedy, moving slowly in front of me not a dozen feet away. The noise around me threatened to lift me off the ground. I wanted to wave, but I was a little bit embarrassed.

The President, in his blue pinstriped suit and neatly trimmed hair with just a hint of gray, waved back at the thousands crowding against the barricades. Then, all of a sudden, as I looked at Jackie, in her very fashionable pink suit and matching pill box hat, she turned and smiled back at me. Me! What a beautiful lady, more beautiful than the cameras had ever suggested. They were the perfect couple, leading a great nation. I wanted to reach out and touch them; feel the confidence they exuded to this new generation, this brave new world.

As the motorcade, and the noise with it, passed at a walking pace, I continued to watch until I could no longer see their car. Certain I had seen the last glimpse of the motorcade, I turned and headed for my car. I had about an hour before I had to be at the luncheon, so I thought I would run by Sears. I walked away, weaving through the excited spectators, but I could still hear, through my ringing ears, the sirens' echoes and the crowd's roar as the motorcade moved through the city streets. It coasted past many other street corners like mine before moving gracefully on to Dealey Plaza . . . and its destiny.

I never really paid much attention to those who touted conspiracy in connection with the assassination. Perhaps it was my training and faith in the system as a young policeman that made me believe no one that high in government could be hit. Or maybe my experience as a former officer convinced me that no city, county, state or federal investigator or law enforcement official I knew, including those at the Justice Department and the Central Intelligence Agency, could develop and execute a plan as precise as those that conspiracy buffs hawked all over the country in unrelenting news conferences, seminars and even gun shows. I didn't think a bunch of bureaucrats could find the brain cells between them to pull off the elaborate schemes these people presented. So when I was approached about being involved in the most riveting investigative event since the Warren Commission itself, to end speculation about one particular conspiracy theory, I was excited about it. I figured we would get to the bottom of this one once and for all.

The Warren Commission, charged by President Lyndon B. Johnson with investigating the Kennedy assassination, named Oswald as the lone assassin. He had been shot to death by Dallas nightclub owner Jack Ruby three days after the President's murder. And like the death of the President, Oswald's assassination had been caught by the cameras and shown across the world. There seemed to be no doubt that Oswald was the killer of both President Kennedy and a Dallas Police Officer named J. D. Tippit, who had been shot to death later the same day.

Of course, the rumors ran rampant for years that the Mafia had hit Kennedy; or that Lyndon Johnson arranged for the assassination. Certainly those rumors had a following. Attorney General Robert Kennedy had a personal feud with Teamster leader Jimmy Hoffa, and many suspected the union leader of mob connections. Lyndon Johnson had been handpicked by then House Speaker Sam Rayburn of Texas to be John Kennedy's running mate in 1960. But the Kennedys and Johnson did not get along; the vice President was of the opinion he was playing second fiddle to a bunch of 'wet behind the ears Ivy Leaguers'. It was a hard role for the former congressional leader to play with a straight face.

As the years passed and more conspiracy theories surfaced, so did speculation as to who was actually buried in Lee Harvey Oswald's grave. As a young man, the same young man who stood on that Dallas street corner waving at the President and First Lady, I would have never even considered such a question as valid. But as I got older, I had become familiar with the kinds of things that go on behind closed doors and in smoke-filled rooms. So, raising the question of who is really buried in Oswald's grave was not so far-fetched. I'll admit, the first time I heard speculation about the body in the grave, I thought of the old joke about who's buried in

Grant's tomb. It seemed just as silly and about as obvious. But in my line of work, obvious is seldom right and always suspect.

The funeral of Lee Harvey Oswald was not much more than a pauper's affair. At the time, Oswald was the most hated man in America; he was convicted without trial of the death of the President. So few wanted to have anything to do with the man or the funeral, at Rose Hill Cemetery in Fort Worth, that several reporters were asked to act as pallbearers. It was a brief, quiet affair, overshadowed by a nation in mourning for its fallen leader.

The night before the exhumation was a sleepless one. Mostly I just sat in my chair and remembered November 22, 1963. The image of the President and First Lady passing by a few feet from me ran over and over in my head like a slow-motion replay on television. The subsequent images of those horrible three days: the poor-quality Zapruder film of the President's head being blown off; the wrinkled squint of pain on Oswald's face as the TV cameras watched Jack Ruby gun him down in the basement of the Dallas City Jail; the funeral of the President flanked by a stone-faced honor guard; all these made sleep impossible. I wondered if I was on the verge of another page in that chapter of history. I wondered if the exhumation would prove or disprove anything. The wheels wouldn't stop spinning, so, around one o'clock on the morning of October 4, 1981, I decided just to get up, shower and get dressed.

It was a warm Sunday morning, though most people out partying at that hour were still calling it Saturday night. I left my DeSoto ranch to pick up my associate Dick Riddle, then we drove to Grapevine, a small northern suburb in the Dallas-Fort Worth Metroplex near D-FW Airport. There we met another of the investigators, Joe Villanueva, at the manufacturing company that had made the vault to hold Oswald's coffin. The manufacturer, Carl Lily*, showed us the type of vault they had used and how we would be opening the small tomb once we unearthed it. As I looked over the fairly simple concrete structure, Lily said, 'Now listen, whatever you do, if the Oswald vault is cracked, don't say anything to anyone.'

What? I looked back at him without saying a word. He really thought I was going to add to the cover-up if his vault was cracked, just to protect his reputation and maybe save a lawsuit? Isn't it ironic, I thought. Everyone's got an angle. Here I was under the impression all these years that these vaults really had a purpose, when all they did was help funeral directors jack up the price of one of the most expensive 'emotional buys' in life: the funeral. Of course they're guaranteed, usually for a century. But, if you think about it, who's going to go back and check?

Then, as we prepared to leave, the mortician told me something that both puzzled and scared me. He said he had 'overembalmed' Oswald's body. The reason? Just in case the body had to be exhumed in the future. The puzzling part was not the fact the mortician had such soundness of judgment during all the turmoil of those three days in November 1963. It seemed like the experience of a man who knew the body he prepared might be the key to some future investigation; a reasonable assumption when one is embalming the body of a Presidential assassin. What bothered me was that the mortician knew something might go wrong. Both men were acting as if they were preparing me for a worst-case scenario. But the question remained in my mind. Why 'overembalm' a body if it's supposed to be sealed against the elements and guaranteed?

We hadn't driven very far out of Grapevine, heading back to Fort Worth and the Rose Hill Cemetery, when another unsettling revelation came out. Again, it was from the mortician, now seated with his assistant in the back seat of my car.

'I'm glad I didn't do it,' the funeral director mumbled as he looked out the window. Dick, seated in the front next to me, threw a puzzled look my way.

'Do what?' I jammed on my brakes and squinted at him through the rearview mirror, sensing something terrible was about to go wrong in front of God, the news media and everybody, with me at center stage. After all, I was still chewing on this 'overembalming', and the cracked vault business.

'Well,' he calmly explained, in that rather cold, matter-of-fact way morticians have about them, 'someone offered me $25,000 dollars for Oswald's trigger finger back in '63 when I was preparing the body.'

'What!' I damn near lunged into the backseat for his throat.

'I was offered $25,000 for Oswald's trigger finger,' he repeated slowly, not certain that he should have said anything at all.

Everyone had worked for years to get every logistical 'i' dotted and 't' crossed so that Oswald's body could be exhumed, and this guy . . .

'Mr Dear,' he interjected, 'let me tell you . . . '

'Don't tell me . . . ' I stuttered. 'Don't tell me anything else about it.'

'Well, it's all very simple . . . '

'I said, I don't want to hear anything about who offered what for which finger. Just tell me Oswald's finger is still on his hand,' I snapped. I knew everything involving the body had to be as it was supposed to be or there would definitely be a problem. And now this guy was talking about missing fingers. My God!

We sat there on the side of the road in the dark for a moment while I regained my composure and caught my breath. I still wanted to strangle the little man for making my heart skip a beat. That's not healthy for a 43-year-old, no matter how much he works out. I often wondered if that's how the funeral director got some of his business. Still, what an unbelievable story. Imagine, someone was willing to pay $25,000 in 1963 value dollars for the trigger finger of Lee Harvey Oswald. What the hell were they going to do with it? Have it mounted and framed on the mantle beneath a prize set of deer antlers? Just the thought of it made me want to forget breakfast. Like I've said, I'm always amazed by people.

It was still dark as we arrived to a real party. The TV crews and what few spectators had shown up, I could do nothing about. Like the backhoe and lights, they somehow went with the territory. But as we drove into the cemetery, I saw high tents surrounding the grave site and yelled, 'What the hell are these for?'

At first the mortician and his assistant didn't want to tell me, but I demanded an explanation. 'These reporters,' I said, 'are feeding on anything that smacks of conspiracy and cover-up. Blocking the grave site from their view is only going to add fuel to an already out-of-control bonfire.'

Finally, the funeral director sighed and said, 'Look, let's understand something. We're in the funeral business. Vaults have a tendency to crack. Most people aren't aware of that and if the coffin is disturbed, we don't want the general public to know. It will hurt our reputation.'

I couldn't believe what he was telling me! Their reputation? I had suspected that was the reason for 'overembalming', and I was right. That coffin, and the vault in which it was encased, were supposed to be watertight! That was the only way we could be assured of a clean autopsy this many years after Oswald's death. Of course, they weren't saying it *would* be a problem; the vault and coffin might indeed have withstood time and nature. But in a quiet sort of way, one gentleman to another, whose professional reputation as an invesigator just happened to be on the line, the message was 'please don't say anything if you get down there and find the coffin disturbed.' Disturbed. A nice word for a contemptible situation.

To be honest, I was getting angry at the whole damned situation, but I knew my job was to make sure the event was secure. I would deal with the anger later. I pulled my car right up beside the grave and had the hearse park close in as well. Even in the dark, I could see there were a few people congregating, so I asked the police to set up a secure perimeter around the grave site and to keep everyone well back. I was getting very concerned that someone might take the opportunity to add a footnote to history by walking up and shooting the participants. I wanted to have the cars nearby to duck into if any shooting began.

Another thing bothered me. The ground looked as if it had been disturbed. I wasn't sure if it was just from the unusual traffic around the cemetery as well as the many people who had come to see the grave since 1963. But it still bothered me.

It seemed to take a lot longer than I had planned to get everything in place and it was getting humid as we got closer to sunrise. Even in October, Texas can still get warm, especially when you're nervous and busy helping direct an exhumation in a graveyard.

I looked around to see British author Michael Eddowes standing off to one side. He was financing the exhumation to prove his theory in his 1975 book about Oswald was correct. Essentially, Eddowes believed the grave contained the body of a Soviet spy, posing as Oswald and sent to America to kill the President. After the impostor was himself killed while trying to escape the scene of the assassination, the head of the real Oswald was put on the body of the spy, then reburied. Oswald had lived in the Soviet Union in the 1950s so it was feasible that he could have been killed there. After five years of legal maneuvering, Eddowes's wish for an exhumation was granted by the court. Still, I couldn't help but feel like a grave robber, even though we were doing everything exactly by the book, with the permission of the court and Oswald's widow Marina, though she and Eddowes were not on the best of terms.

Marina was waiting quietly in her simple, tasteful pinstriped dress, staring at the grave. I walked over to her and introduced myself. Somehow, through all of this, we had not had a chance to meet properly. After exchanging introductions and handshakes I said, 'Marina, is there anything I should look for once we've brought up the coffin, that will help readily identify that the remains are those of your late husband?'

'There is one thing,' she whispered, 'I placed two rings on one of his fingers. They should still be there. If they're not . . . then that's not Lee's body.' Her attention returned to the grave and I decided to leave the quiet lady in peace for the time being. But the trigger finger again nagged at my mind.

Just then I saw Eddowes walking my way. I hurried over to meet him. His tone was woody and appropriately dry for a British gentleman.

'I wish to stand there next to the grave with you.' He motioned toward the site with his cane. 'Since I'm paying for all this, I think I should be allowed to stand there and see what happens.'

'I don't think that's a good idea, Mr Eddowes.' I was polite, but firm. I sure as hell didn't need him in the way. 'I promise to keep you informed at every stage of the operation.' He looked at me coldly for a moment, without as much as a bat of an eyelid, then abruptly turned and left.

We had chosen the middle of the night to begin in hopes of not drawing much undue attention. A rather moot point when you've got a large backhoe tractor, several funeral home and forensic officials, tents, TV camera crews from around the world and lights everywhere. But somehow we felt getting started under the cover of night would keep the whole affair somewhat under wraps. It didn't.

There was something about digging up a grave in the purple hue of predawn morning that sent a shiver up my spine; even with a cast of, by now, hundreds on hand. Of course, maybe I'm strange. I mean, none of that seemed to stir the macabre notions of the curious who came to get a look at the grave. Yes, I had to be there, and yes, it was not just an assignment but a piece of history. But in a graveyard at night? I thought most folks would have, at least, some aversion to that whole thing.

With everything finally in place and anticipation running high, we managed to get underway about dawn, the diesel exhaust from the big tractor covering the area with thick dark smoke as it carefully lifted dirt from Oswald's resting place on to a growing pile next to the hole.

The police seemd to be conspiracy buffs. Most felt it would not be Oswald in the grave. 'Three to one says it ain't him,' I heard one say. 'Hell, I'll give ten to one it ain't the little bastard,' another told his buddy across the way. I'm not sure any money changed hands that day, but knowing policemen the way I do, I'd give twenty to one that some eagles flew from pockets that morning. I had great reservations, but deep down I felt it would be Oswald's body in the ground. I was concerned though whether all of the evidence would be intact.

The crowd was now into the thousands. I watched as the chain-link fence bowed out toward us with the force of humanity behind it. I worried that the fence might break and people would be trampled should they all begin running the fifty yards or so toward the grave. I told several of the officers to watch the crowd and make sure that none of the onlookers came over the fence. Actually, I wanted the mob of ghouls moved to the next county and out of my sight.

I was pacing around, waiting for the big shovel to hit the vault, when suddenly the wind picked up with the roar of aircraft engines as helicopters appeared overhead. Suddenly a figure stepped out of one of them. I yelled, 'Watch out! . . . He's falling . . . ' then I saw he was strapped to the helicopter getting video for one of the TV news outlets.

'Dammit!' I waved my arms over my head. 'Get the hell out of here!' Who was I kidding, they weren't leaving, even if they could hear me above the noise and wind. As I had warned the funeral director when I saw the tents in place, the TV news photographers were trying to get a shot of the digging. The workmen, on the funeral director's orders, tried to bring the tents around closer to the backhoe to keep the photographers from seeing down into the grave, but it didn't work. The peaceful cemetery had become the setting for a full-blown three-ring circus. The noise was so loud that at times I had trouble talking to the people next to me without yelling.

After about twenty minutes of digging, the backhoe hit a solid piece of concrete slab. We had them stop digging with the backhoe and asked the workers to get down in the grave and very carefully shovel out the remaining dirt covering the vault. Once again the tents came into play as they were moved over the top of the grave and within three feet of the surface. I moved in under the tents, eased myself down into the muddy hole and began inspecting the vault while the gravediggers finished digging around it to provide enough space to work.

Two of the best pathologists in the world, Doctor Linda Norton and Doctor Vincent DeMaio, headed up the forensic team on the project. Dr DeMaio immediately got down into the hole with me to inspect the vault and its contents. The vault was like the simple concrete crypt we had seen in Grapevine. A seam down the middle of the top of the box indicated where two lids, or doors, met like a pair of shutters encasing the coffin from the elements. The funeral director and the vault maker reiterated the importance of not letting anyone know should the vault or the casket be cracked. I acted like I didn't hear them.

By now, Dick Riddle had joined me down in the hole to help prepare the lid of the vault to be lifted out. The ground was wet and the clay dirt stuck to everything . . . my shoes, my clothes and my hands. Doctor DeMaio, clad in rubber boots, helped as we pulled the twin lids of the vault up and out and looked inside.

'There's moisture in there,' DeMaio said, 'this vault's cracked.'

'Damn!' I yelled back up out of the huge hole. 'The vault's cracked! There's water in it!' I was loud enough for every reporter and microphone there and a few back in Dallas to hear.

'Damn you, Dear! You sonofabitch,' the vault maker screamed, 'I'm gonna sue you!' He was furious! I really think had he had a gun he would have left me there in that muddy grave. But I'm not one to lie about important things. Besides, he had pissed me off in the first place, with his backslapping, smiling good ol' boy 'you can keep a secret, can't you' attitude. Despite his threat of lawsuit, everyone needed to know the condition of the coffin. Enough evidence had been lost or covered up and shipped away since that day in November 1963. It had to stop, *now*. Even if it was going to hurt the funeral industry's reputation.

The workers gingerly began lifting the vault lid from its foundation. The coffin, a wooden cabinet not the metal case I had been led to expect, was caved in. The remains of Oswald had been exposed to the muddy elements for eighteen years.

As we attempted to remove the vault lid and further inspect the wooden coffin, it fell apart in our hands. Oswald's body was badly decomposed. Some skin tissue remained stretched like leather over exposed bone, and much of the rotted clothing was still there, but for the most part it was a skeleton with some skin over it. It reminded me of one of the cheap zombie movies in which the main characters walk around with flesh falling off their rotting bodies. I've seen a number of dead bodies, and I've had bodies exhumed for investigation years after burial. They were in fairly good shape, but this one was plain grotesque.

What bothered me now, more than the condition of Oswald's

35

body, was the question of whether there had been a cover-up. For the first time in my life I really pondered the possibility. I knew our government was involved in things most people don't know about until something goes wrong. But would the government, or someone within it, go this far?

We tried lifting what remained of the coffin, but the foot of the casket fell apart and Oswald's body began sliding out. Dick had to grab the corpse's shoes and hold on to the remains while the rest of us worked to get a better grip on the whole mess.

I could tell the funeral director was uneasy, watching one of his wooden coffins disintegrate before him, especially given the fact that the vault was supposed to have been guaranteed for a century. I kept thinking he was just eighty-three years shy of being clear of the warranty. Another box, used for shipping bodies, was brought up as Dick and I and the rest of the exhumation team held on to the body and the rotten coffin. We slid the remains into the second box, trying not to disturb them any further. I suddenly remembered what Marina had whispered to me and quickly looked at the right hand. At this point, I was more interested in his trigger finger. There it was! At the same time I saw the two rings on Oswald's finger, just as she had said.

Oswald's eyelids were sunken where the eyeballs used to be and his hair, kept short while he was alive, was longer and had fallen down around his drawn, partially decomposed face. We wasted no time, once the remains were in the shipping crate. We lifted the body up from the hole and carefully placed it in the hearse.

By now, cameras were everywhere and the crowd of onlookers seemed to pour like desert sand across the cemetery as we moved the body. I was not so worried about the curious in the crowd as those who might be there to do harm. The fact that I had been hired meant someone thought there could be trouble. What if a group sworn to keep such a conspiracy under wraps was still about? Still active? What if a terrorist group wanted to seize the media moment to cause havoc? What if some publicity-seeking lunatic, as many had called Oswald, was lurking, trying to destroy the body or kill the investigators of one of the century's most famous unsolved mysteries?

I began to get worried. I realized we had so many in the crowd that watching them all, even with our trained team, the security personnel and uniformed police officers from both Dallas and Fort Worth, would be impossible. We couldn't guarantee anything. Once I saw the remains had been secured in the hearse, we moved fast.

'Let's get outta here!' I yelled, like a cavalry general sounding retreat.

The several cars in our small convoy moved out, through the cemetery and on to the street. Everyone's eyes were wide and searching as we crackled acknowledgments of 'all clear' on the two-way radios. The camera crews ran to get into their cars and sped ahead to be set up at Baylor Medical Center where the autopsy would be performed. I happened to look into my rearview mirror at that moment and saw the hordes rushing past the fence to the gravesite, picking up pieces of the broken coffin and rocks that came out of the hole. I couldn't believe there were so many ghouls running loose on a Sunday morning. The next day there would be a picture on the front page of the newspaper of a girl in shorts holding up rocks she had collected from the bottom of Oswald's grave.

I was feeling a lot more confident about the operation now that the cars were rolling and we were picking up speed. We had made it out of the neighborhood of East Fort Worth and had gotten on to the Old Turnpike, heading east for Dallas. We had traveled three or four miles when suddenly . . .

'What's that?' Dick saw a U-Haul truck parked on the side of the road.

'Keep an eye on it,' I instructed as I watched the road ahead. The truck looked unoccupied as we approached. Not a sign of life anywhere . . . until the back door rolled up exposing two men aiming right at us!

'It's a gun!' Dick yelled.

I reached for my Walther PPK under my seat, where I always kept it. It wasn't there! My gun was gone! I took evasive action, quickly steering my car to the left in hopes of blocking the other cars, and particularly the hearse, from the imminent gunfire. Dick and I started to drop below the dashboard. I knew we were going to get hit. I just knew it! Just as I started to duck, out of the corner of my eye I could see them.

Two video cameras.

It was not a pair of gunmen, but a damned TV news crew trying to get a close shot of the coffin in the back of the hearse and the main characters of this bizarre play behind us in the convoy.

I regained control of the car and sped by. For the second time that day, my heart had skipped a beat.

'Dick, I thought for sure we'd been had.' Dick didn't say a word, at least none that I heard. We radioed the hearse behind us, Marina Oswald's car behind the hearse, as well as our police escorts that everything was all right and I finally caught my breath. I felt like going back and kicking that TV crew's collective ass. Then I remembered my loss.

'Someone stole my gun!'

There I had been in charge of coordinating the most famous exhumation in modern times, worried about the condition of the grave, concerned about lunatics with ulterior motives, and someone had gotten into the car, parked right next to the whole operation, and stolen my gun. What really made me mad was the fact that it was one of my best guns, part of a matched set with sequential serial numbers. As the convoy sped on to Dallas and Baylor Medical Center, I began to wonder if it was going to be one of those days.

The forty-five minute drive to the medical center yielded few words between my associate and me. Dick and I usually talked quite a bit as we worked, but this time was definitely different. We had the remains of Oswald in tow and were extremely sensitive to everything around us. It seemed in my mind like every tree and highway overpass cloaked a sniper, waiting for his chance at us. I found myself searching every tree limb and concrete barrier like a foot soldier searching the jungles of Vietnam. We couldn't let paranoia take control. We had to think ahead, to the medical center, and what needed to be done. I went over the plan in my mind repeatedly, examining whether we had left any stone unturned, exposing the operation to a security threat. By the time we arrived I was, again, certain everything was in place.

Under extremely tight security, we pulled into Baylor medical Center, sealing the entrance behind us. Dick blocked the area with the entourage of police and security personnel as I helped take the remains from the hearse. We quickly wheeled the body from the hearse into the hospital and made a bee-line for the autopsy room. A path had been cleared by hospital security.

Once inside, the team led by Doctors DeMaio and Norton began examining the body. The first thing they had to determine was whether the head had been severed. As the clothes were slowly removed, the body was turned on its side. All of us looked to see if the head was attached to the body. I could see the head appeared to be attached to the spinal column, but I wasn't sure.

'Tell me,' I said to the doctors, 'is the head still attached?'

'Yes, it is,' DeMaio replied.

To me, this eliminated the theory that Oswald's head had been placed on someone else's body, thus making him the patsy.

Next, the forensic team decided to sever the head and inspect the intricate areas of the spinal cord at the base of the head. They would also use medical and military records to determine if the body was that of Oswald, rather than the new infamous phantom Soviet spy as Eddowes and others had speculated.

While this was going on, two of Marina Oswald's neighbors were in the room taking pictures. I had objected, thinking that they were not being supportive of Marina as they claimed to be, but were trying to get film to sell for the latest chapter in the story of the century.

Suddenly, in the middle of the autopsy, one of the neighbors bumped the table and Oswald's head fell off and went rolling across the floor! Had it not been so serious it would have been comical. A member of the forensic team retrieved the head almost as quickly as it had fallen. I don't know if her friends were quick enough to get a picture of that, but as I suspected, they did try to sell the film some years later. However, Marina brought a successful lawsuit against them and kept the film from being released. As the autopsy progressed I kept updating the news media on the events (though I omitted any reference to the head rolling off the table).

Once the autopsy was complete, Dr Norton told me they were certain that the body was that of Lee Harvey Oswald, and that no part of the body had been switched. They referred to Oswald's military and medical records, including his mastoid operation, as the basis for comparison.

Now that the autopsy was over, I went to the hospital's auditorium to talk formally with the media. After Doctors DeMaio and Norton began to speak on what they had found, I returned to the autopsy room where the mortician and his assistant were preparing the remains for reburial.

'I'm going to put a lot more of this on him,' the mortician said as he dusted the remains with an embalming powder to retard further decay. The team then placed the remains in a metal coffin provided by the funeral director and prepared to wheel it from the room. A motorcycle police officer walked up to me and asked, 'How do you want to take him back?'

I thought about it for a moment, then walked over to Dick and said, 'Let's end this chapter down the same road it began. I think we should take Oswald's body back along the same route Kennedy took when he was shot.'

'We'll take him down Elm Street,' I said to the officer, 'through Dealey Plaza and the triple underpass.'

'All right.' The stone-faced officer didn't offer much expression, but I could see he understood completely.

I walked to a phone and made calls to The Dallas Morning News and The Dallas Times Herald, telling them if they wanted to see a close to a chapter of history, to be at Dealey Plaza in a few minutes.

We left the autopsy room and took the body back through the halls, out to the hearse and left Baylor Medical Center just as fast as we had arrived. I don't know about everyone involved, but I was still tense. I was not going to relax until Oswald's body was back in the grave at Rose Hill Cemetery.

As we approached Dealey Plaza and began the descent into the area known as the 'triple underpass' I felt very strange. Here I was passing the very spot where President Kennedy had been killed, leading a hearse that carried the man alleged to have shot the President from that red-brick building to the right. Then it was called the Texas School Book Depository. Now it houses the offices and meeting rooms for the Dallas County Commissioner's Court, the head of Dallas County government. The sixth floor is a museum filled with Kennedy assassination memorabilia. As we passed, I could see the sixth floor and that distinctive square window, next to a row of arched windows, from where Oswald is said to have shot the President, and it gave me a sad feeling to remember that day. I hurt for everyone involved, including Marina Oswald riding in the convoy behind the hearse carrying her husband's body, and the Kennedy family which has endured so many tragedies.

I saw several photographers snapping shots as we slowly drove by. They were trying to get angles that would catch both Oswald's coffin and the window on the sixth story of the building (long since dubbed 'the crow's nest') now behind us. The angle was one the President might have seen had he looked back to see where his assailant was shooting from. Driving back to Fort Worth, I came to realize I truly felt Oswald was involved in the assassination. There was some doubt in my mind Lee Harvey Oswald pulled the trigger. I'm not sure he acted alone or if his bullet was the one that took the President's life. But after all of my research into the case and my involvement with the exhumation and autopsy, I'm convinced Oswald was a major factor in the assassination of President John F. Kennedy.

As we turned into Rose Hill Cemetery, to my amazement, hundreds of spectators were still waiting. They had been waiting for hours. What were they still doing here?

The vault had been replaced, while we were gone, with another one, 'watertight', and with another one-hundred year warranty. For what that was worth. I ordered the old coffin remnants not already stolen to be cleared away, gathered up and burned.

Then with Marina Oswald and her 'friends' nearby, along with several hundred spectators watching from a distance, my staff and

PRIVATE DETECTIVE

I took the coffin containing Oswald's body from the hearse. As I placed my hand on a handle of the coffin and joined the others in a slow, respectful walk to the grave, I remembered watching the President pass by me that November day on a street corner in Dallas, moments before someone shot him to death. Now, eighteen years later, I was a pallbearer for this man the Warren Commission called a presidential assassin.

BILL DEAR'S NOTEPAD: An Encounter with Robert DeNiro

I had just returned to my New York hotel room from taping a segment of 'Good Morning, America' with Joan Lunden concerning my latest book, *The Dungeon Master*, when I got a phone call.

'Mr Dear?'

'Yes.'

'I'm Jean DeNiro.'

'Yes.'

'My cousin is Robert DeNiro . . . the actor?'

Sure he is, I thought. 'Yeah, what can I do for you, Jean?'

'Robert likes *The Dungeon Master*,' she explained, 'and I'd like for you to meet with him about it. He might consider playing you in a movie version of the story.'

Uh huh, I thought, sure he would.

'Look,' she continued, 'at six o'clock, take a cab and pick me up outside of my hotel. I'll be waiting and we'll leave from there and go meet my cousin.'

I decided, what the hell, I'll bite. At six o'clock I pulled up to the hotel. Sure enough, there's an attractive young lady. She got into the cab, introduced herself and in the same breath said to the cab driver, 'We're late . . . hurry up.' She gave him the address of a restaurant. Man, she's not shy, I thought. But after that, she didn't say much.

The neighborhood we were getting into was starting to look pretty rough. It was the Bowery. And there I was with a suit and diamonds on, and no gun, in a part of New York I wouldn't want to be at in the first place, especially without a weapon.

'You missed it!' she suddenly yelled at the driver. 'Stop the cab! We'll walk.'

We got out, I paid the driver and we began walking. Now I was walking in the same area that minutes earlier I didn't even feel safe driving through. Just then, off in a nearby alley, I saw a guy beating a woman, right there in public! I started to run over and help but Jean grabbed me.

'It's not your concern,' she instructed, 'leave them alone.'

I was not believing this place. As we kept walking we came to the foot of maybe fifteen or twenty steps leading up to an old building. Well, I've come this far, I thought as we ascended the steps and opened the door to what appeared to be a dingy Italian restaurant right out of a Godfather movie. I was waiting for the man with a violin case to make an appearance.

Instead Jean said, 'Thank God, he's not here yet . . . Oh, I was wrong, there he is,' Jean murmured.

I looked across the smoked-filled room to see a man seated alone against a wall drinking beer. His long hair was pulled into a ponytail and secured with a ribbon; his face sported a full beard. A black gym bag in the booth to his left is what caught my eye. I was thinking I'd been set up. Maybe violin cases were out and gym bags were in. Of course no one would have seen a thing.

Instead Jean slowed her pace and then stopped as if she were about to address the Godfather.

'This is Bill Dear.'

He stood and stretched out his hand. 'I'm Bob DeNiro. Would you like a drink?'

'Yes,' I answered, 'whatever you're having.'

The voice confirmed it, he really was Robert DeNiro. As we sat down I immediately felt comfortable with him. His presence was dominating, yet he seemed to yield to the casual situation. Relaxed and confident, without being cocky, his sincerity laced what he had to say.

'My cousin gave me your book, *Dungeon Master*,' he said quietly, 'I liked it, but don't know if I'll have time to do the project. Right now I'm doing an off-Broadway play.'

We talked for about fifteen minutes back and forth before I finally said, 'Well, listen Mr DeNiro, I appreciate you talking with me.'

Just then Jean kicked me under the table. Soon we were all at the door and he turned back to me once we were outside.

'I appreciate you not taking a whole lot of time. I hope to see you again soon.'

'The same here,' I replied.

He turned and headed down the dark alley next to the building. I couldn't believe it. Even with Robert DeNiro, I don't think I would have walked down that alley alone. In the meantime his cousin was bitching.

'Why didn't you talk with him longer? Why did you cut the meeting short?'

'First of all,' I explained, 'we got our points across to each other. He's a busy man and I didn't want to wear out my welcome. And another thing, that damn kick hurt!'

She laughed for the first time since I had met her. 'Well, I wanted you to keep talking with him. I want Bob to buy the story, act in it, and I want to produce it.'

To this day, Jean DeNiro, who has become my friend, will call me and ask about producing *The Dungeon Master*. And every time I hang up the phone my shin hurts just a little.

CHAPTER 3
The Glen Courson Case

The telephone ran three times before I could get my door open, retrieve the key and get to the receiver. I had just gotten back into town after a few days away on a case. It was seven o'clock in the evening.

I knew the voice on the other end. It was Billy Courson; we had known each other for years. He had run for sheriff of Dallas County. His brother had been a well-respected motorcycle policeman for the Dallas Police Department for quite some time.

Billy had another brother named Glen. Glen Courson owned a profitable sporting goods store in the Dallas suburb of Irving, near the famous Texas Stadium, home of the Dallas Cowboys. Glen was instrumental in the organization of a real old-fashioned wagon train in celebration of the Texas Sesquicentennial (the 150th anniversary) in 1986. They had ambled from Texas to Washington, D.C., where Glen had met with Vice President Bush, another Texan, before returning to the Lone Star State. All of those happy memories shattered as Billy's voice softened over the phone.

'Bill,' he paused and I knew something terrible had happened. 'Bill, Glen's dead. They found him in the alley behind the store two days ago at three-thirty in the morning.'

'What happened, Billy?' I sank slowly into a chair as I listened.

'I don't know.' He exhaled emotionally. 'Glen was found with a shotgun blast to his stomach. The goddamned police department's already ruled it a suicide but I don't believe them.'

'I'll do anything you want me to do, Billy.'

There was another pause. 'We'd like to hire you to look into it. Do you think you could come over and take a look at everything?'

'Sure, Billy,' I said immediately, 'but it's too dark right now. We'll need to look over the scene first thing in the morning, when there's light.'

'Well, the problem is,' Billy explained, 'the funeral's in the morning at nine o'clock.'

'All right,' I said, 'meet me out there at the store at the crack of dawn, around six. That'll give us a few hours. If we feel there's something wrong at that point we can make some decisions. And make sure Glen's lawyer is there.'

After I hung up the phone, I couldn't help but think that Billy Courson was like the rest of the Courson boys. None of them would take anything off anyone. So, in the knowledge that Glen was not the type to commit suicide, Billy was not going to let the police and forensic officials rule such a finding without investigating it thoroughly.

Billy had told me that a shotgun had been used in the shooting. It struck me as odd that a man would come out of the comfort of his warm business office on a cold winter night and kill himself with a shotgun. He could have stayed inside and chosen any weapon in his store. A pistol is a more traditional suicide weapon, and much easier to handle. If his aim was to die, a pistol would have made him just as dead. Or he could have taken the shotgun out to one of his ranches and laid the gun across a barbed wire fence and pulled the trigger so it would look like an accident while he was hunting. Why in the hell would he have committed suicide in an alley at three-thirty in the morning?

Early the next morning, I met J. W. and Billy Courson, along with Clarence Maberry, at the shopping center location of Glen's Sporting Goods. Clarence Maberry was an employee of Glen's and had found his body behind the store. The family attorney was also there. It was just a few hours before Glen's funeral.

As we walked around to the back of the shopping center I still couldn't imagine why Glen would have killed himself like this. It was a chilly morning in February, and I tried to imagine that cold dark night, Glen standing alone with a shotgun behind his business; a business he built from scratch. It just didn't add up.

I had walked past the location where Glen's body had been found and was looking around the area when Billy called to me from the spot where his brother had died.

'Bill!' Billy yelled as he squatted over the spot, 'look at this!'

Naturally we all walked over to see what Billy had discovered.

'Shotgun pellets,' he said as he looked up at me.

'They didn't even pick up the pellets,' I said. It puzzled me that the crime scene investigator had not picked up hard evidence and bagged it. I started counting the pellets when I noticed chips in the brick on the wall next to where we were standing. The marks were fresh and it was very evident they were made by the pellets now laying on the ground amid sucker rods used in building construction.

Why had the investigator at the Irving Police Department not marked the red brick where the pellets had chipped the wall and fallen into the sucker rods? It would give the investigators the exact angle of the gunshot through Glen's body and determine the height where the shot came from.

'Billy, get me a can of spray paint.' I had decided to mark the chipped spots myself. Then I photographed the marks and the pellets laying in the sucker rods below. Finally, I picked up all of the pellets and put them in a plastic bag to be used as evidence; which is what the police investigator should have done to begin with.

I was quickly becoming more of a believer in the murder scenario the family held than the suicide scenario offered by police and forensic investigators. Just comparing the angle of the chip marks in the brick to where Glen had stood indicated that he must have been doing some sort of ballet tip-toe routine to get the shotgun high enough. In addition, there was the matter of where the shotgun was found.

Clarence told the police investigator and me that he saw the shotgun was about twenty-two feet from Glen's body. The police said the gun was thirteen feet away, a hell of a discrepancy. That's a long way, in fact, for a dead man to throw a heavy shotgun. As

I looked back across the alley to where the shotgun had been spotted by police, it was also clear it was in the wrong place for a suicide.

Glen had apparently been facing the rear wheel of the stakebed truck parked behind the shopping center. Had he held the shotgun up high, as the angle of the chip marks indicated, the recoil of the weapon would have sent it a few feet away from him in pretty much the same direction he was facing. Chances are the gun would have hit the truck bed and fallen down by the wheel . . . or maybe even high enough to land on the bed. But the gun was between thirteen and twenty-two feet to the right of Glen's body when it was found. Glen would have had to have shot himself, then hurled the gun to the right. Fairly difficult for a man who has just suffered a severed aorta from a point-blank shotgun blast.

These discrepancies really bothered me as I gazed over to the spot where the gun had been laying. There was too much evidence for me just to say, 'Yeah, it's a suicide all right.' Over and done with. I decided the body had to be re-examined. It would be weeks before the official autopsy pictures would be back, and besides, I was not feeling certain about the job the forensic team had done. Too much didn't fit for it to be such a quick and easy ruling. Glen's funeral was just hours away. We decided to ask his wife Marianne for permission to remove the body from the grave after the services. She quickly agreed just before the funeral and signed the paperwork with her attorney present.

Marianne Courson told me early on in the case that her husband did not kill himself. I could tell it was not just another widow wanting to believe the best about her dearly departed loved one, but a woman speaking about a soulmate.

'Glen was a fighter,' she told me once, 'I know he wouldn't have killed himself.'

I believed her for several reasons; she was his wife of many years, everyone I talked with about the Coursons told me how much they loved each other and depended on each other. You don't live with someone, sleep with someone, share your life and raise a family with someone without getting inside that person. Besides, the loss of Glen Courson was a financial blow to the family. Eventually, the surviving Coursons lost their home and the business Glen had built through many, many years of hard work. She could've taken a cash settlement at any time and left the death certificate marked 'suicide,' but Marianne Courson was as proud and determined and as much a fighter as her late husband. She wanted his murderer(s) caught and his case solved.

I knew from the beginning I couldn't turn my back on this case or this family as their daughter, Carrie, tearfully hugged me and begged, 'Mr Dear, please find the people who killed my daddy.' I was their last hope against a bureaucracy that had written off the Courson death the easiest way it knew how. With a death marked suicide, the case is marked CLOSED; there are no loose ends to tie up and no murderer to look for in an ongoing investigation. It's nice and tidy.

Glen Courson was not only loved by his family, he had a world of friends, and they all turned out that morning for the opportunity to pay their last respects to their friend and offer comforting support for his family. I remained outside the funeral home to take photos of everyone who attended the funeral. It was possible that if this was indeed a murder, the murderer might attend the funeral. It happens a lot more often than most people think.

After the funeral services, we all left for the interment. It was a cold, gray, rainy day. It seemed somehow fitting that the man everyone in town admired would be buried on such a winter's day. The graveside service was short, and typically somber. I hate funerals, especially when it's someone I know. I knew Glen and his brother well. It wasn't easy to be there, particularly while I mentally searched each person present for a clue as to who might have killed Glen.

Slowly, as the service ended, everyone began making their way back to their cars. Hugs and handshakes were exchanged among the friends and families. I could overhear people who hadn't seen each other for a long time planning casual get-togethers I knew somehow would never take place. I had arranged with Colonial Funeral Home to have the casket returned to the surface after the family had left. The funeral director and I, as well as a couple of cemetery employees, sauntered over to the grave when it appeared most everyone had gone. A worker hit the reverse on the lift and the casket slowly rose from the vault in the ground. We lifted it from the mount on which it sat and moved toward the hearse. Just then a lady, a cousin from across the country I think, saw us and began yelling, 'Hey, where are you going with Glen's body?'

What an awkward situation we suddenly found ourselves in! I wasn't about to tell the tearful woman we had to take Glen back to the funeral home and perform another autopsy.

'Just a minor problem with the concrete vault in the grave,' I gently replied with the sincerity of a mortician. 'As soon as it's been taken care of we'll place the coffin back in its final resting place.'

Fortunately, the cousin seemed to believe me and even looked somewhat reassured that we were taking such good care of Glen. I hate to lie, but if it eased a moment of anxiety for her, then so be it.

I had attempted to reach Dr Charles Hirsch of New York, one of the world's top medical examiners, but he was away at the time. So I made a call to Dr Marilyn Cebelin, who was the Assistant Medical Examiner of Broward County in Fort Lauderdale, Florida. I trusted her judgment far and away over that of Dr M. G. 'Margaret' Gilliland, who had performed the original autopsy. Ironically, Doctors Cebelin and Gilliland had interned together some years earlier, and there was no love lost between them.

Gilliland was a little stub of a woman, not popular at the Dallas County Medical Examiner's Office. She was verbose and domineering, despite her small stature. Though I had lost respect for her some years before, she still carried authority, and if she said 'suicide', it was suicide. The trouble was, in this case I was quickly beginning to think she was dead wrong.

Gilliland had investigated the brutal murders of two girls and a man down in Waco, Texas sometime earlier. During her autopsy of one of the female victims, she failed to note the teeth marks on the breast and the fact that one of the nipples had been bitten almost completely off. Something like that doesn't take a degree in pathology to notice. She finally amended her autopsy report as the case went to trial, when an orthodontist pointed out the teeth marks she had overlooked.

I later would learn that Gilliland had an answering machine on a private phone line to her office; she received calls for outside forensic work without her employers' knowledge, and her County case load was so backed up that she was at one point 4,000 cases behind. It wasn't long after that I was able to expose her freelance ventures and she was forced to resign.

On the way to the funeral home with Glen's body I was joined by one of my investigators, Richard Russell, and Dr Cebelin. All of us were to be involved in the part of the investigation I hated the most. Once at the funeral home, we pulled the hearse to the back entrance and removed the casket, placing it on a gurney, and wheeled it into the funeral home.

The room we were to use was very small and very cold. The pale blue walls offered only a clinical setting, no warmth at all. This was an attempt at discovering cold hard facts. I was having a difficult time because of my closeness to Glen and his family. We set up both video and still cameras to record the autopsy. I assisted as Dr Cebelin cut the stitches that formed a huge 'Y' across Glen Courson's body from the chest to the pelvis, and began removing the packing in the body cavity placed there as part of the embalming process. Sometimes Dr Cebelin would have to turn the body in a way that required me to hold it in a certain position. Most people can't stand the thought of even touching a dead body, but I had to do it. It was for Glen and his family. At some point, during the autopsy, the body became just that. A body. It wasn't Glen, or at least that's what my mind was telling me. Perhaps that's what made it easier to assist the doctor. It just appeared as a rigid mannequin with scars.

We soon saw the gunshot wound that killed Glen, but one of the first things we also noticed was a mark on the bridge of the nose and scrapes on the knees and elbows. None of those markings were reported by Dr Gilliland. I wanted to know if a struggle had occurred before the shooting; if Glen had perhaps grabbed the barrel of the gun in an attempt to get it away from his assailant as it went off. I just couldn't see this as a suicide with a shotgun.

Oh, they've occurred all right, but they're clumsy as hell and the victim usually has to place the barrel in his mouth or under his chin and stretch his arm way down the barrel to reach the trigger. In what few cases of shotgun suicides there are, the gun's weight causes the victim to lower the butt of the weapon and shoot up into his face. Courson's wounds indicated the shot came from slightly above chest level. Not normal. Not at all. The likelihood that Glen Courson had held that heavy shotgun out slightly higher than perpendicular to the ground and fired it while holding it against his chest was slim at best. In fact, a check back at the office, on the computer, yielded no such accounting for that kind of angle by any shotgun suicides I could find. 'Classic' case? I knew better than that, no matter what Dr Gilliland said.

But I also knew that bucking the system would cause problems, especially in Irving. I had worked for a brief time at a small suburban Dallas police department when I first moved to Texas in the early 1960s. I knew the routine. Grand Prairie was, in many ways, a photocopy of Irving's police force. To be honest, it was not much different to what I had encountered in Miami. There were those we arrested and those we didn't arrest. There were those we ticketed and those we didn't ticket. And if the powers that be said it was a suicide, it was a suicide, case closed. No need for a smartass upstart to come along and muddy up the water with a bunch of useless details, especially if those details showed a major police department screw-up and cover-up. And that's exactly what had happened in Irving. Someone had screwed up at the crime scene and asses had to be covered or heads would be rolling.

Cop shops are something of a fraternity. It's a brotherhood that protects its own. It's taught to you from the first day of the police academy, and for a very good reason.

As a policeman you rely on other police to back you up in dangerous situations. You know when you call for back-up, as bullets are flying and you're alone, that within minutes the cavalry will arrive to save your butt. But the other side of that coin is, if you don't back up a partner's story, or even a whole department's political structure, you may suddenly find yourself the victim of an intentionally slow arrival and it could cost you your life (as it nearly did in the movie *Serpico*). I saw that kind of attitude in the 1960s in Grand Prairie and left. I also saw that was happening in Irving with the Courson case, and the simple question, why, didn't take long to answer. But a more immediate question persisted, one that Dr Cebelin was working to answer.

After a thorough examination of the body, now deceased three and a half days, Dr Cebelin finally turned to me and said, 'As far as I'm concerned Dr Gilliland messed up. This was not a suicide, this was a homicide. There is no doubt in my mind that Glen Courson was murdered, Bill. Just like you say, this is not a suicide.' She turned the body over to the funeral director to be restitched and placed back inside the casket for burial. I walked out the door of the Colonial Funeral Home and was certain what I had to do.

The next morning, I followed the hearse from the funeral home, back out to the cemetery. I helped carry the casket from the hearse to the grave, where Glen would be laid to his final rest. As I watched the funeral director again press the button that lowered Glen Courson's body into the ground, I knew I had to get to the bottom of his murder, no matter what happened. I kept the findings of the autopsy confidential.

Captain Charles Caperton of the Irving Police Department was not happy to see me, and when I asked, he assured me that the gun was field-tested.

'Do you have pictures?'

'Yes,' he replied, 'indicating that when the gun was test fired, it recoiled twenty-two feet on its own.'

I looked deep into his eyes and could tell he was lying. There is no way a shotgun will travel twenty-two feet on its own and land forty-five degrees to the right of its projected landing spot. Caperton was covering up for his department.

'Look, Dear,' Caperton went on, 'Courson was in debt. He needed to make it look like a robbery or a murder to let his family collect the insurance money and pay off his debt. It was all just too much for him to handle.'

What Caperton didn't realize, as I stared at him, was that I knew

Glen and his family. He had been in debt and out of debt as often as any businessman. He had a temper like most people, perhaps a little worse sometimes, and he occasionally drank. But Glen Courson was not the type to kill himself over debt. It just was not in his makeup.

'Besides,' Caperton went on, 'we found damage to the stock of the shotgun where it had landed on the pavement. It means just exactly this, Dear: Courson fired the gun and slung it. As a result of the gun striking the pavement the stock cracked.'

'So, you're telling me that Glen Courson put this whole scenario together, walked into the alley behind his business, after first telling a story about two people trying to steal something off the back of his truck, and killed himself so his wife and family could collect the insurance. What about the suspects?'

'He made up the suspects part,' Caperton interjected.

'But Caperton' – I pointed straight at the Captain – 'your own report indicates Glen mentioned seeing two suspects around the premises while talking on the phone to Jim Harris of Winchester Firearms.'

'He just made them up. Wouldn't be the first time.'

'So you're putting a whole lot of emphasis,' I said, 'on a theory that the gun traveled all that way because Glen threw it there, and that the stock was cracked because it hit the pavement and that he made up a story about the two suspects.'

'Yes, I am.'

'Do you have any other facts to back this up?' I asked.

'No, don't need any more.'

I could see I was getting nowhere, but I let Caperton keep talking until I got bored with his obvious attempts at an impromptu cover-up, so I decided to leave. But as I walked out of the office, I turned and looked at Caperton with a puzzled expression on my face, as if I didn't really understand what I was about to say.

'You know, Caperton, I wonder why a man who wanted to kill himself over insurance money wouldn't just go to one of his ranches and make it look like a hunting accident. Glen could have easily done that. Maybe laid the shotgun across a barbed wire fence and pulled the trigger so that it looked like an accident. It would have been double the money from the insurance company, plus he probably had some of those "free" accidental policies through a bank or credit union or a bank card. Hell, all of his debt probably could have been paid before any of his primary insurance money would have been needed.'

Caperton now had the puzzled look I had faked and I wore the smile he had donned early in the meeting, which was now over.

I walked out the door, knowing I would be on my own, with no help from the police. So, the next thing to do was to talk with Clarence Maberry. If anyone knew Glen as a businessman, it was Clarence. He had been with Glen for seventeen years. In fact, as far as Clarence was concerned, Glen was like a father to him. Glen sometimes treated Clarence unsympathetically, but Clarence was always there for him.

I went over to the sporting goods store. It was a painfully quiet place that day. The people there were mostly employees, but it was like they had shown up because force of habit didn't let them go anywhere else, and now their leader was gone. Many just sat there in the store, not knowing what to do but sit. Clarence, a stocky country boy, came out and met me cordially, like an old friend. I put my arm around his shoulder.

'Things are going to be all right, bud. Why don't we go talk.'

As we went back into his office, I saw the tears well up in his eyes, though his conversation was totally detached from his emotions. He was acting like he wasn't about to cry, but the big man was broken. We talked for a few minutes about how he was doing. He really blamed himself for Glen's death, because he was supposed to have moved the truck that night, which in his mind meant the burglars wouldn't have shown up and Glen wouldn't have encountered them.

'Now, Clarence,' I said, 'just tell me exactly what happened.'

'Well, we moved the stakebed truck back into the alley that evening before a meeting in the vacant part of the shopping center. We needed power for lights so Glen could show a group of investors the space and work on another deal. The truck had a generator on the back that provided electricity.

'I pulled the truck back there and set up the saw horses . . . twenty feet or so from the truck on either side to block the alley from traffic during the meeting. We hooked up the cables and set up the power. During the meeting we had a couple of drinks, watched the meeting and it went real well. I was supposed to go back and move the truck, but me and Scott Philyaw decided the meeting was going so well we left and went for a few drinks and finally decided to go down to Harry Hines Boulevard and hit a few titty bars before returning. Hell, everybody was feeling good, Bill, 'cause the meeting was going well and Glen looked like he was on the verge of another big business deal. Me and Scott figured we'd go back later and I'd move the truck like Glen wanted. He'd probably already be at home in bed and wouldn't know if we moved it right after the meeting or early in the morning.

'About one thirty in the morning we decided to stop off and get something to eat 'cause we had been drinkin' a good bit and could probably do with some solid food in our stomachs. Finally, about three thirty maybe, we left and drove back to the store. It was damned cold, Bill.'

I could see he was twitching a bit as he relived the moments that led up to him finding Glen.

'When we got back to the store, I told Scott, I said, "Listen you go on home and get some sleep. I'll take care of the truck. Glen'll never know we didn't move it 'til early in the morning. It won't matter." So Scott said, "Okay."

'So I got in my own truck, warmed up the engine and the heater for a minute and tried to get warm myself. After a minute or so I pulled around to the alley from the east and pulled up right square with the sawhorse blocking the way.'

He broke. 'I'm sorry, Bill . . . give me a minute.' Tears rolled down the weathered face of Glen's grieving friend. After a few sobs, Clarence regained his composure.

'I got out of the truck . . . I . . . I saw something in my headlights . . . it was someone lying there next to the stakebed truck. I went around the sawhorse and . . . God, Bill it was . . . it was Glen! It was Glen!'

The big man cried as he tried to tell what he had come upon. 'I said, "Glen, Glen! Please God, NO!" I pulled open his shirt . . . there was blood all over and on the pavement where he was laying . . . and the big gunshot hole in his stomach . . . his guts were pouring out . . . ' Clarence was fighting to tell his tale.

'I looked around for help, but there was no one there . . . but over by the other sawhorse was a shotgun . . . there was a shotgun laying there, Bill.

'I thought, "Got to get some help." So I ran around to the front of the building to the shoe cobbler's store and yelled, "Jimmy, it's Glen, we need help, please!" I saw his light was on but he wouldn't open the door. He said, "It's too early, Clarence, I'm not opening this door." "Glen's been shot." I screamed, "I need help!" . . . I looked and saw the 7–11 store and I ran all the way.

'I saw the night manager, Barbara Barclay, working there, and I yelled, "Glen's been shot . . . get the police." I didn't even think, I ran back to the alley and stood by Glen's body. I didn't want anyone to touch him. I didn't know what had happened, Bill! Hell, I felt it was my fault for not moving the truck and maybe Glen had tried to stop somebody from stealing the truck. You know how he was, he didn't take shit from nobody.

'A few minutes later I saw headlights coming from way down the other end of the alley and I raised my arms to wave 'em down. The cops got out and ran over and asked what happened. I said, "Glen's been shot! Somebody's killed Glen!" Just then, Bill, the other officer goes over and picks up the gun and ejects the shells from it. Bill, he picked up the gun! I swear to God, Bill, I watched him . . . I watched him! He picked up the shotgun and ejected the shells . . . then he laid it down a lot closer than where he had picked it up and then he put the shells down beside it. I know I was upset . . . but I saw it . . . I saw what he did! But all I could think was, it was my fault, I kept telling them that . . . "It's my fault." I guess they probably thought I had done it.

'And as I watched the officer lay the shells beside the gun, the other officer said, " Clarence, why don't you go down to my car and wait for me." Then they started talking, Bill, now I don't know what they were saying. But then you tell me later that the shells were still in the gun? Bill, I saw this cop take them out and set them down beside the shotgun after he had moved it!

'Then a couple of fire department trucks arrived and some fire department people were walking around in the alley. But that's when they took me to the police department and interrogated me for four hours, Bill. They wouldn't even let me use the bathroom. They tested my hands for gunpowder. But I told them, I never fired that weapon. I hadn't even seen that shotgun since Glen and I went to his ranch to find some turkeys for a turkey shoot he was putting together.

'Hell, there's no way Glen could . . . he just wouldn't . . . I mean, sure, he was having some financial problems but he wouldn't . . . '

I could see it was hard for the big man, but he was at least able to tell his story to someone who would finally believe him.

'Bill, you say the medical examiner said the shells were in the gun?'

'That's what the report indicates, Clarence.'

'Let me tell you something, Bill,' Clarence went on, 'when they brought me back from the police department to the store, some of the employees were standing at the front door. I got out of the police car, walked over and unlocked the door. When I did I noticed that the rod-iron door, which is always locked, was unlocked. And I'll tell you something else, the alarm was always set when Glen leaves to go home, but it wasn't set as I walked in. That told me that Glen planned on coming back into the store fairly soon.

'Anyway, I got the employees in the store and told them what happened. Then me and a couple of the others started walking from the front of the store around back toward the alley. As we got up to the alley, Sergeant Burson hollered, "You two other guys get outta here . . . Clarence, you can go ahead and get your truck." I walked over to my truck and started to open it from the passenger side. Just as I did I looked in and saw that goddamned shotgun in my truck! It was barrel down, stock up, laying against the driver's seat!

'I wasn't going to get in my truck! I would have had to move the shotgun. I yelled over to Burson, I said, "Hey, listen, the gun's in my truck!" He walked over and said, "Well, get in and let's talk about it. Is this the shotgun?" I said, "Yeah." He got in on the passenger side and I opened the door to get in on the driver side. Then he said, "Well, show me how you found it." I said, "Burson, I'm not touching this gun . . . this gun killed Glen. He was like my father. I'm not touching this gun." So then he calls over a uniformed officer, reaches down and picks up the gun and hands it to the officer to be put in a police car. Now I don't understand this, Bill, why would they put the shotgun in my truck?'

As I listened to Clarence, I realized that this was a royally botched-up job on the part of Irving Police. Now they were in the process of covering their collective ass. The police had taken it for granted that Clarence had shot Glen when the first officers arrived on the scene. They just figured they had the suspect, so the shells were ejected to make the gun safe around the suspect and then, better still, you move the gun to keep it away from the suspect altogether. Perhaps the officer who had picked up the weapon and ejected the shells was a rookie and didn't think. So his older officer, once he realized what had happened, had to develop a cover for him, which would be the reason for sending Clarence to the police car and talking quietly between themselves. It was cover-up time. But I believed I could determine exactly what happened if I could just get my hands on those 'on scene' photos and check just one little detail.

But Clarence wasn't the only one who witnessed the gun being moved at the scene. It turned out later that an Irving firefighter named Jerry Nichols also saw it. The handling of this weapon was becoming a major factor in my mind, so I visited the Dallas Medical Examiner's investigator who was first on the scene.

Cindy Galamba told me that she felt the crime scene had been altered before she got there; the shotgun was thirteen feet two inches from the body and the shells were still in the gun when she arrived. Galamba also told me something I found unbelievable. When she later checked to see what kind of fingerprints they got off the shotgun, she was told by the Irving Police Department there were no fingerprints on it *anywhere*! It had a smudge mark instead, as if it had been wiped clean. Of course, as it turns out, the weapon had been handled by more people than a Harry Hines streetwalker.

Now I had to contend with the fact that there were no fingerprints on the weapon, whatsoever. And I knew what they were trying to do. They were trying to get Clarence Maberry to put his hands on the shotgun before they took it to be tested. Once they tested it, it would be Clarence Maberry's fingerprints on it, not the officer who botched the investigation, not the officers who were now involved in the cover-up. Clarence Maberry could've been spending the next thirty years in prison for murder . . . except for the fact that he didn't touch the gun.

Because of all the pressure from my investigation and all its coverage by the media, Police Chief Benny Newman made a statement to reporters, saying, 'The officer at the scene wiped the gun because there was "dew" on it and we didn't want it to rust.'

One reporter asked, 'If that's the case, and you were trying to protect the evidence, why did you put it in the suspect's vehicle?'

'To keep it out of the rain.'

I checked with the National Weather Service in Fort Worth. There was no rain that night. Newman was trying to cover some butts. Why take a gun at the scene of a murder and wipe it clean, unless you were protecting someone? Why would you put it in the suspect's vehicle, when you've got seven police cars at the scene? Besides, the gun was not going to rust before it got to a lab. It takes a little more than some dew over a couple of hours on a well-oiled gun to create rust. If everyone was so concerned about the condition of the weapon, why hadn't they placed the shotgun in a plastic bag, sealed it and taken it on in to the crime lab?

The hope was that Maberry, once told he could get his truck and leave, would get in with one of the investigators to talk, and without thinking move the weapon, thus placing his fingerprints on the gun. They would be the only set of prints and he would be the murderer. But Maberry didn't pick up the gun and the Irving Police were left with no prints and no suspect.

As for the dismissal by Caperton of Courson's story of the suspicious individuals, I talked with Barbara Barclay at the 7–11 store.

'Yeah, Glen had been in a couple of times that night,' Barbara said. 'I had seen the guys he was talking about. In fact, they came in here and I thought they were going to rob me. After I told him about them, Glen said he would come in from time to time during the evening and check on me. And a couple of times he did. So help me God, Bill, these two people do exist. I can describe them perfectly, the same way Glen did.'

I made a number of trips to the Medical Examiner's Office, but the pictures still weren't ready! That wasn't unusual for that office. They should've taken them to Fox Photo One Hour Service. But I did get the shotgun released to me, along with Glen's clothing.

It was now apparent I would have to approach this thing from the beginning. Which meant re-enacting events to find if my theories concerning the death of Glen Courson were right. Richard Russell and I bought camera equipment and returned to the crime scene. We moved the same stake-bed truck into place in the alley, exactly where it had been. Then, using the actual shotgun from the shooting, one of my staff acted as the murderer.

Courson had been on the phone with Jim Harris from Winchester Firearms.

'Goddammit,' he said to Harris, 'there are those same two guys I chased off from the alley earlier, when they were loosening the bolts on the generator on my truck. They're trying to get that generator.'

'Glen,' Harris asked, 'you okay?'

'Yeah, I'm okay.'

'You got a gun?'

'Yeah,' Courson replied, 'I gotta shotgun, don't worry. I'll talk to you later.'

'You want me to come over?'

'No, thanks,' Courson said, 'I'll take care of it.'

At that point, Harris said, Courson quickly hung up the phone. My theory was that Courson got into his pick-up and drove to the front of the strip shopping center, passing by the convenience

62

store where Barbara Barclay worked, then around to the back of the shopping center and down the alley. He had turned off his headlights and left only his parking lights on. Rolling his window down to try and hear anything as he approached, Glen then pulled up near the stake-bed truck and stopped. He got out with his shotgun and walked over to the truck.

Without thinking, Courson laid the shotgun on the bed of the truck, pulled a pack of cigarettes from in his left front pocket, put one in his mouth and placed the cigarettes back in his pocket, then retrieved a red cigarette lighter. He lit his cigarette and bent down on his right knee to look at the bolts holding the generator to the bed of the truck. He was checking to see if they had been loosened any further.

At that moment, he heard a noise, looked up and saw one of the suspects, who had been hiding behind the plywood cover of the generator. The suspect grabbed for the shotgun. As Courson started up from his kneeling position, the suspect pointed the gun at him. Courson then grabbed the barrel of the gun to get it away from the suspect. When he pulled it toward him, it fired, striking Courson in the chest. Courson fell back. The suspect jumped off the truck, realizing that Courson had been shot. It was no longer a burglary. Now it was murder.

The other suspect, who had remained hiding behind the plywood cover, came around and they both started to run, one with the shotgun. Knowing someone might see them coming from the alley, the trigger man dropped the gun by the sawhorse as they ran in panic. Therefore, the shotgun was about twenty feet from Courson when it was found.

Otherwise, Irving Police investigators would have everyone believe Courson fatally shot himself with a big gun, then before he died, threw it across the alley. It's about as far-fetched as the joke about the man with twelve stab wounds to the back and the police detective says, 'The worse case of suicide I've ever seen.' Except this was no joke. And once we re-enacted the whole thing, all of the incidental marks on Courson's body made sense. The bridge of his nose was cut because he likely bumped his head against the edge of the truck a split second before falling back against the pavement. The knee had debris from where he knelt to inspect the truck. It was all there, I just needed the photos from the crime scene to compare.

After several attempts, I finally got the on-scene photos from the M-E's office. I lost no time in blowing up the pictures. I found a lot of things Dr Gilliland failed to note. A cigarette lighter next to Glen's body, for one. Just as I thought, he probably laid the gun down on the bed of the truck and reached for a cigarette, when someone picked up the gun and aimed it at him.

But my theory on the gun was what I most needed to prove. When the enlargements came back, I studied the ones of the shotgun laying on the pavement. With a magnifying glass, I looked over the gun even closer. Right there, in living color, was the breechblock, closed and locked! Dead men don't close the breechblock on a shotgun, then hurl it several feet away. Someone else had closed it, just like that someone reloaded the shells. And that someone was wearing an Irving Police Department badge.

My next big break concerned the crack in the stock of the shotgun. I found the previous owner of the gun, a young man who had sold it to Courson, and brought along the shotgun for him to look at.

'Yeah,' he said, standing at the door of his home, 'this was my gun.'

'Is there anything,' I said, 'anything at all different about the gun than when you sold it to Glen Courson?'

'No,' he drawled as he took the weapon and looked it over, 'No, Mr Dear, hell it's the same gun. I even see here the stock is still cracked. Guess Mr Courson didn't get that fixed.'

'Was the stock cracked when you sold it to him?'

'Oh, yeah,' he chirped, 'that's why I didn't get as much for it. Hold on I'll show you.'

The young man handed me the gun and went back into his house. I heard him rummage around for a moment before he returned.

'See here.' He unfolded a piece of paper. It was the sales receipt from Glen's Sporting Goods. 'He even wrote it down, "cracked stock". Hell, Mr Dear, Mr Courson paid me a hundred less than the gun should of sold for because of the crack in the stock. 'Course, I guess that was only fair.'

There went Caperton's theory of the cracked gunstock.

Still, with all the evidence I was collecting, I couldn't rely on vague recollections of those involved as the investigation continued into weeks, months and years. So in an attempt to get a break in the case I decided to probe the mind of the closest thing we had to a witness, Clarence Maberry.

Naturally, Maberry had been a different person since the shooting. Things were bothering him that would bother any of us. On occasion I've used qualified hypnotists to bring up some deep dark secret lurking in the minds of witnesses. I thought something hidden from Maberry's conscious mind, buried deep in his subconscious, might be the key that would unlock the door I was working hard to get open. I took Maberry to one of the best psychologists in the country. Dr Harvey Davisson is a white-bearded, very professorial man with a slight Texas drawl. I knew Dr Davisson could retrieve something wedged in Maberry's subconscious and bring it out into the open. What I wasn't sure of was whether that something would be a sudden and surprising confession by Maberry that he had killed Courson.

'It's very possible,' I told Dr Davisson just prior to the session with Maberry, 'that Maberry and Courson could have met earlier in the evening and even had words out in back of the store about moving the truck with the equipment or an altercation over something else.' I grabbed Davisson's coat, imitating what I thought could have been Courson upset with Maberry, perhaps even slapping him. I knew Courson had slapped him before.

'If Courson had the gun there,' I speculated, 'Maberry could've grabbed it and the two struggled over it before it went off . . . and Maberry's mind won't let him remember. Maybe all he presently remembers is coming up on Courson's body around four o'clock that morning.'

'It could be,' Davisson replied.

'If he's actually the killer,' I added, 'like it or not, I'll have to take him in – and he knows that.'

Once Clarence Maberry was comfortable on Davisson's office

sofa, the doctor relaxed him into a lulled sense of well-being, and took him through the earlier hours of that cold night in 1987. Maberry had not seen Glen in back of the store prior to finding his body. There had been no harsh words between employee and employer. I felt somewhat relieved for Maberry's sake, he was a nice guy who had been hurt enough. I fully realized just how much when Davisson took him back to the moment he found Courson's body.

'It's 4:08 a.m.,' Maberry mumbled like he was talking with someone. It was Scott, the buddy he'd been having a beer with; the big man was calling it a night, but he explained that he wanted to go by the store and check on the equipment in the alley.

'. . . We'll see ya' in the morning, Scott . . . ' The speech was slurred as Maberry floated in some dark vacuum of the mind. It's a dreamlike state, but with very real and detailed dialogue.

'. . . Three hours . . . ' he mumbled, '. . . that's plenty.' It seemed to me Maberry had plans for getting up about seven o'clock, but I'm not sure if he thought the plan or was verbalizing it to his friend. It was sometimes hard to tell where he was in his recollection until his face changed expression dramatically.

'. . . What's that . . . whose truck is that . . . ' His body became noticeably more tense. '. . . What's . . . Oh, God. NO . . . OH GOD, NO! GLEN!' The big man broke down and cried. Davisson let him continue.

'. . . Please . . . please . . . OH! GOD! Got to call an ambulance . . . ' Maberry was still crying when Davisson pulled gently on his mind and let him drift away from the discovery and back to an earlier hour that night.

Maberry had last seen his boss alive at an investor's meeting much earlier that evening. They were at the store. Maberry looked out the window to the front.

'. . . Guys casing the place, Glen . . . ' he mumbled as he faded into the recollection, 'goin' to have to watch it close tonight.'

I motioned to Davisson not to bring Maberry out of the 'sleep' he was in. It dawned on me that he might be able to give a description of the men he saw. Could Davisson get him to examine his memory of the sighting like a football coach examines each frame of a critical play on film?

'Yeah,' he assured me as he slightly raised his steady voice to Maberry, 'Clarence, I want you to look at the men you're seeing, what do they look like?'

It took a moment of quiet for the big man to recall.

'. . . One's got a beard . . . long hair . . . the other's clean shaved . . . '

Maberry, his eyes closed most of the time, would rub his face like a sleeping man on the verge of waking up. The hypnotic state is very delicate, unlike what some nightclub magicians might want an audience to believe.

'What are they driving?' The words are soft, but their essence filled the office. We were walking through a man's mind with him, sharing thoughts he'd probably shared with no one, not even himself.

'. . . green truck,' Maberry almost moaned, 'Chevy pickup truck.' I was writing every word he uttered.

'A green Chevy pickup truck.'

'Damage?' I whispered to Davisson.

'Any damage or marks on the truck, Clarence?'

Maberry mumbled and then became quiet. I could almost see him looking into his memory.

'Just take your time, Clarence,' Davisson instructed, 'let the truck pass on by in slow motion just like a movie.'

Clarence took his time. I wanted to reach over and pull the answers out of his mouth, but like Davisson, I remained outwardly patient.

'. . . Right rear quarter panel . . . '

A break! I hurriedly jotted down the damage description and whispered in Davisson's ear again.

'Clarence,' Davisson asked, 'can you see a license tag?'

Both of us were on the edge of our chairs, literally, waiting for our witness to search his foggy memory. Maberry wiped his face.

'. . . Numbers,' he mumbled, '. . . numbers . . . I can't make out the number.'

I released a deflating sigh. Oh well, sometimes you can't bat a thousand, but this was at least a three-base hit with runners on. It verified what Barbara Barclay had said.

I looked at my scribbling on the legal pad. The staff would run down every green Chevy pickup truck we could find and try to get a make on the license number and an address of the owner. Meantime, Dick Riddle would hit the streets in Irving, looking for a green late-model Chevy with damage on the right rear quarter panel. It was like shooting in the dark, but I'm a hell of a marksman.

Cases don't get solved in an hour like they do on television. And I don't work on just one case at a time. A lot go on the back burner until something breaks. So it was with the Courson investigation. Dick had searched every green Chevy he could find, but nothing. The staff had crisscrossed every kind of computer reference available, but nothing. Then one day, a call. Someone, who wanted to remain anonymous, saw an article about the case in the newspaper and decided to call me. It seems they had a license plate number. We ran a check on the computer and bingo! There it was!

Dick and I wasted no time in staking out the very average-looking cookiecutter home in Irving with a green Chevy parked out front. It was only three blocks from Glen's Sporting Goods!

There was fender damage on the exact opposite corner from where Maberry described it, but he could have been mistaken. This was the best lead we had and I would not see it lost.

It took hours of waiting with both a still camera and a video camera in our surveillance van, but we finally caught two white males on film and tape. Both seemed to fit the description Maberry and Barclay had given us.

But the subsequent call to the Irving Police Department produced nothing. They really weren't that interested. In fact, they didn't even return my calls. Here I had two prime suspects and they didn't even want to check it out. I was giving them the suspects on a silver platter, pictures and all, and they were still worried about the cover-up.

It took a year and a half and a deposition before they finally brought the two suspects in for questioning, but decided to release them. But by this time I had already confirmed information on these two suspects through a friend of theirs. The information? The two had confessed to the killing of Glen Courson. But the Irving Police Department still did nothing.

Then sources of mine were telling me that Irving was putting out the word to other police departments not to have anything to do with me. Not only that, but I've since learned that the Irving Police are investigating *me*. I have to wonder how they are going to justify the money spent following me around, including trips to Canada, to try and dig something up. I'm glad I don't have to pay taxes in Irving.

As far as the Coursons, they've recently received a substantial out-of-court cash settlement with Glen Courson's life insurance company, based on my investigation. This letter from Marianne expressed the feelings no investigation fee could buy:

April 27, 1990

Dear Mr Dear,

I am writing this letter on behalf of the family of Glen D. Courson. We wish to express to you our heartfelt gratitude for your outstanding work on our case. It is because of your persistence and extensive knowledge of criminal investigation that we hope one day to vindicate Glen's death. We as a family felt such a loss at his death, but also such an added burden at the police's suicide ruling. A ruling that was totally unjustified in our opinion. But you were there from day one, assuring us that you would find the truth.

You have been true to your word in uncovering the facts and evidence not seen by the police. We appreciate your professionalism in backing your findings with experts, witnesses and opinions.

We realize the sacrifices your determination to find the 'real truth' has cost you professionally. We have read the articles trying to discredit you in order to add credibility to those whose toes have been stepped on. We want you to know the admiration we have for you because of this willingness not to back down and to take 'the heat' on our behalf.

We have the utmost respect for you and your professional abilities, and know that because of the superb job you have done, with time, the 'real truth' will come out, and Glen can then rest in peace.

With gratitude,
Mrs Marianne Courson

Glen Courson's killer(s) still roam the streets to this day, perhaps waiting for the opportunity to kill again. Or to kill me. But a lot of people have tried to kill me. Some have come damn close, but no one has succeeded yet.

I still hope to bring those who killed Courson, and those of the Irving Police Department who botched the investigation, to account.

BILL DEAR'S NOTEPAD: Island Governor

I once arrested the Governor of Hawaii while he was drunk on a jet plane at Miami International Airport. Actually, the perpetrator was a well known actor, but let's just call him David Nerman, even though that's not his real name. At the time, in the early 1960s, he was playing on a shortlived TV show about the U.S. Border Patrol, which was shot on location in Miami. It was later that he became famous as the man who played the Governor of the exotic island in *Hawaii Five-O*.

But on this particular day, long before the series, Nerman was flying into Miami on a major carrier with a problem. Him. We were told over the two-way that someone on board the aircraft had arrested two Russians, claiming they were spies.

A few other Dade County Deputies and I rushed to the gate and ran on to the aircraft. There stood a drunk David Nerman weaving and yelling, in the thick tongue of an intoxicated man, 'I'm U.S. Border Patrol, officers, and I've arrested these two men. They are Russian spies.'

Yes, the two men, looking quite perplexed I might add, were Russian. But they were not spies; didn't even have dark glasses or trenchcoats. Nope, they were just fine, which was more than I could say for Nerman.

'I said they're spies, Officers!' He was getting louder, though most of the other passengers were enjoying the free show.

I played along. 'Of course they are, Mr Nerman. Joe, watch those two. Mr Nerman, we need to get you to a safer place since you've executed this espionage arrest. And we'll need a report.' I played it to the hilt. In fact, it was kind of fun playacting with a well-known actor, even if he *was* drunk.

The other deputies apologized to the Russian travelers after another officer and I escorted Nerman from the plane. He was a super nice guy, and really thought he had saved the country from a communist takeover. A couple of weeks later, after the story got out, Nerman's Border Patrol show was canceled.

Every time I saw him on the TV after that I couldn't help but remember his 'arrest'.

CHAPTER 4
Dade County Lawman

About the time I graduated from Coral Gables High School someone, somehow, had heard me comment that I wanted to be a policeman. It had been a lifelong dream, but like most eighteen-year-olds, I was looking in so many different directions I didn't know exactly what I wanted to do. I wasn't sure whether I should attend the University of Miami, something I had considered for a number of years. But fate has a way of helping with these decisions.

A few days after graduating high school, there was a knock on the door of my parents' home. When I opened it, there stood a six-foot-tall, muscle-solid Florida State Trooper wearing a stetson hat to top off his starched and perfectly fitted uniform. He looked like one of those bodybuilder ads in the magazines, and probably could have doubled as the Highway Patrol recruitment poster model if they had one. He spoke with a deep clear voice.

'I'm Sergeant Bill Stevens and I understand you want to be in law enforcement.'

I said, 'Yes, sir.' I think my mouth was gaping.

'Well, we've done a little investigating and you come highly recommended. We've never hired anyone under twenty-one years of age in the history of the Patrol.

'However,' the Sergeant continued as he shifted his weight and looked straight at me, 'we've been considering a new program, by which we would hire someone right out of high school, who really cares about the profession, and train them in the office in the Communications Division. Eventually they could decide if they want to go on to be a State Trooper at the age of twenty-one.'

I couldn't believe my ears. I was just elated. Here I was eighteen years old and the proverbial opportunity had knocked.

'We would like for you to come down, if you're interested,' Sergeant Stevens added, 'and talk with our captain.'

I knew my decision to join the Highway Patrol under this new program would mean no college. I also knew that no college meant no career with the FBI and the Secret Service, two other law enforcement careers I had dreamed of since I was a kid. Looking back, I don't think I would have made the same choice again. College is extremely important. But when you're eighteen, right out of high school and a trooper offers your dream on a silver platter, you take it. I guess, in my young mind, I figured I could bypass college and eventually join the FBI or the Secret Service with the experience I gained from the Highway Patrol. At any rate, I chose my path and began the journey.

The first day after I was hired, I reported to the Headquarters of 'D' Troop of the Florida Highway Patrol, headed by Captain Lee Simmons.

I walked into his office, a cavernous room that seemed to be about the right size for the man. Simmons was at least six foot four inches and about 275 pounds of muscle. Quite intimidating to a 135-pound rail-skinny eighteen-year-old, still wet behind the ears. I was first greeted by a matronly lady named Doris Haggerman, the captain's secretary. She immediately commanded respect, in a very nice, motherly way, although she had the biggest set of boobs I'd ever seen. It didn't take a person long to see that in those parts she was the boss! With a smile, she introduced me to the captain.

He looked at me, nodded slightly and said, 'My number is "Nine." Any time you hear that on the radio, you'll know it's me, understand?'

'Yes, sir.' I thought my voice would crack, but fortunately it didn't.

'Good to have you on board,' he added, 'I hope you won't let us down.'

'I won't, sir,' I answered clearly and confidently, 'That's a promise.'

'Good.'

The next thing I knew, Sergeant Stevens was there and directing me into the storeroom to get a uniform. He took my measurements, stepped back and said, 'How the hell are we going to get you into a uniform as skinny as you are? I guess we'll have to fatten your ass up. That won't take long around here.'

I had a twenty-seven-inch waist and stood about six foot two. The sergeant handed me the smallest uniform he had and told me to go to a tailor and get it altered.

Next he took me into the communications room and introduced me to a guy named Clarence. Clarence was going to teach me how to operate the radios and stay in contact with the troopers.

'Do you know the area?' Clarence asked.

'No, not really,' I replied.

'What do you mean? You've lived here all your life and you don't know the area?'

I didn't know what to say. I knew my neighborhood and a few other places, like anyone would, but not the entire Miami area that 'D' Troop covered.

Clarence hit a switch at the radio console, 'Miami 77, report to the office.'

'Miami 77, 10–4,' came the acknowledgment, sounding like Broderick Crawford in *Highway Patrol*.

A few minutes later, I saw a patrol car pull up and another huge granite statue emerge. He walked into the communications room. He was Number 77, Howard Gracey. Clarence looked at him as he walked in, but pointed at me.

'This guy just joined and he doesn't know anything about the area. Take him out and show him where everything is.'

Gracey didn't say 'Hello . . . kiss my ass' or anything. We just left the room and got in the car. Without looking at me, the trooper said in a deep monotone voice that was used to talking over a radio or to a speeder, 'Now, I'm going to tell you once, and only once so you better listen up.'

'Yes, sir.' I had said, 'yes, sir,' more times that day than any other day in my life.

'But before we leave,' Gracey continued, 'get out of the car.'

He led me into another building with bunkbeds and shower stalls.

'Someday,' he said, 'you might sleep here, like the rest of the troopers. Someday, maybe. But until then, you're the radio operator and there are lives depending on you for help . . . Don't *ever* forget that!'

We left the building and got back into the car and drove away.

After a short while Gracey suddenly blurted, 'This is 27th Avenue . . . do you know what it is?'

'Yes, sir, it's 27th Avenue.'

'What is it?'

'Twenty-seventh Avenue.'

'Thank you.'

We drove on, 'This is 441.'

'Four forty-one.'

'This is U.S. 1.'

'U.S. 1, yes, sir.'

We did that all day long, one street or highway after another. We didn't stop to eat or anything. Just street after street after street. Gracey would return to certain streets and ask me what they were and what streets came off of them. I didn't know if I could keep it all straight.

By the time we got back, he had yelled at me so much and drilled me so hard I wanted to quit. It was just like being in the military. As we got out of the car he started up again, 'All right, repeat all the streets I told you about. Where's U.S. 1?'

I started rattling them off. I was just a tape recorder repeating what had been fed into me. I finally finished as Gracey walked over to me and put his arm around my shoulder.

'You'll do,' he said. 'You'll be all right. If you need anything. Just let me know.' From that point on, Howard Gracey became like a father to me.

I soon learned the radio, and got to the point where I would ride with the troopers every night. In fact, I soon began spending all my waking hours with the troopers. After a while, I became something of a mascot.

Doris became like a mother to me. She could be a tough old bird, someone you certainly didn't want to cross. If you did she could make your life miserable. But we were the best of friends until she died just a couple of years ago. She even had a picture of me on the table next to her hospital bed. The last thing she said was to a nurse. As Doris looked at the picture she said, 'This is my boy, Bill.' Most people aren't lucky enough to have two mothers.

The captain was a great guy, too. Eventually he invited me to his house for supper. He had a very pretty daughter and before long we began to go out. But I could see where it might not be the best thing for my career to date the captain's daughter, so I stopped. She was a very nice young lady, but I figured it was better that way. Lee Simmons and I remained friends, even after I left the patrol.

By the time I was twenty years old, I had met a judge in the constable's office next door to 'D' Troop Headquarters. Judge Francis J. Christie was the Justice of the Peace. Well, one day the constable, Robie Love, stopped me and asked, 'How would you like to be my deputy?'

'Well,' I said, 'I'd like that, but I'm only twenty.'

'That's all right,' Love replied, 'I can get the judge to waive that.'

I had been with the Highway Patrol for almost three years by then, and I was anxious to get out on the streets as an officer, and this was my chance. I knew the constable was responsible for a lot of arrests, and was even the only person who could arrest the Governor, if need be. When the police needed to make an arrest with a warrant, they went through the J.P.'s office to do it. A constable had to serve the warrant. So, I jumped at the chance. As a result, I made a number of arrests and within three months was made Chief Deputy Constable, all before I was twenty-one, and in the largest precinct in the United States. Now when I went to see my old buddies on the Highway Patrol I was toting a gun and a badge. My dream had come true.

Little did I know it, but the job could go nowhere. The Constable was an elected position. And if my boss was beaten in the election, I could lose my job because the new guy might want some of his buddies as deputy constables. Happens all the time. Politics!

The more I thought about it, and the more I looked at the calendar with the next election coming up, the more I considered a job with the Dade County Sheriff's Office. After a while, I decided that was the best place to be. But again, my size was a problem.

I went over to apply for the job, still a skinny kid by the standards of the office minimum weight policy. My friends in law enforcement began filling me up with bananas to help me gain weight. I felt like Barney Fife on *The Andy Griffith Show* when he had to meet the minimum weight standards of the state. Trouble was, I didn't have Aunt Bea to cook for me. So when the day came for me to weigh in for my application process, a high school friend of mine happened to be in line behind me for the weigh-in. As I stepped on the scales, he kind of laid his foot on the scales to help tip them over. I was about three pounds shy, bananas and all, until his big foot rested on the scales. I know the fellow weighing us was able to see my friend's foot, but he kept looking away like he didn't notice a thing.

'All right, Dear, you passed,' he bellowed as he wrote down my weight, then added as he looked up with a slight glimmer of a grin, 'just by the skin of your teeth!'

Well, I went on through the academy, the skinniest guy in the class. I wasn't in good physical shape, especially compared to most of these he-men I had known since high school. But somehow I passed everything. Except my swimming test.

You see, you had to swim the full length of the Olympic-size swimming pool at the academy, then on your way back, dive down and pull up a weighted generator from the bottom of the pool. It simulated rescuing a drowning person of average weight. Well, I could barely swim enough to keep *me* from drowning;

pulling up that damned generator was impossible. So, we came up with an idea to help me out.

On the day of the test, my buddies in the academy helped me load cotton-filled plastic bags into my swimming trunks, which were actually oversized boxer shorts. We figured if I got into real trouble I would at least pop to the surface and float. So we thought. When it came my time to swim, I dove head first into the water and began battling the pool toward the other side. When I got there I was exhausted, but I knew I still had to get the generator. So, I took a deep breath and dove straight down to the generator. My lungs felt like they were on fire as I pushed against the ballast of the cotton filled plastic bags. I could see the generator coming into focus as I got near, and I could feel myself sinking down much easier than before. I wondered for a moment if the cotton-filled plastic bags in my shorts were actually doing the job . . . because it was suddenly easier to swim down deeper into the pool. I cleared my head of thoughts and concentrated on the task before me.

I grabbed the handle on the generator, turned myself upright to the surface and began kicking my legs and paddling with my free arm. The generator wouldn't budge. I even looked down to see if they had nailed the damned thing to the floor of the pool. Looking back up I could see all my buddies waving their arms, encouraging me to surface with the sunken treasure that held the reward of my certification as a peace officer. My lungs were now in flames, screaming to my brain for air. I knew that any kind of movement by my lungs could buy precious seconds, so I let some escape. Still holding on to the generator I pulled with all my strength, the inertia forcing more air from my lungs. I could feel the weight give and start to rise, then quickly fall back. The burning in my lungs had spread to my head and with one more glance to my cheering comrades above, I let the weight go and shot to the surface.

Breaking through the surface like a submarine-launched missile I gasped for air. A couple of my friends jumped into the pool and pulled me to the side. I opened my eyes to see some concerned and smiling buddies and one stern-faced instructor looking at something in the pool. My eyes followed his line of vision . . . to several plastic bags of cotton, floating on the surface. No wonder it had gotten easier to submerge toward the end of the dive!

I tried and tried, but I couldn't pass the swimming test to save my life, much less someone else's. But the department decided I had done so well in the academy that I could graduate, as long as I practiced, returned within one year and passed the swimming class of the next academy. Here I was a uniformed deputy. I would drive up in a patrol car, go in, change clothes and swim with the young recruits, then take the test. I failed three times.

But it was one thing to fail in the swimming pool at the academy. What scared me was the prospect of not being able to save a life in the field.

One night, while on patrol, my fear was realized.

'Miami 637,' my radio crackled with the dispatcher's voice.

'637,' I answered, 'go ahead.'

'637, advised we have a car in the canal . . . with victims trapped inside.'

Oh, my God, I thought as I hit the lights and siren and peeled out toward the canal. I had no idea what I was going to do once I got there except somehow save the people. I also knew that it could kill me. I drove through Dade County like a bat out of hell, taking off my gunbelt and shoes as I drove. I figured, at least I could get them free of the submerged car and perhaps up to the surface, but if they were unconscious or even worse panicking, we would all die.

I pulled up to the location, threw the gear shift into park and started to open the door. Just then another deputy slid to a stop next to me. He knew my problem and jumped into the canal. I coordinated traffic and emergency vehicles and aided the victims once they had been pulled out of the water-filled car by my fellow officer. The feeling of how serious this all was made me shake, but we both did our jobs. The next day, I went to the pool, and with an instructor present and a class of new recruits cheering, I pulled the generator up. I've never been afraid of jumping in after a drowning victim again.

★

During those days everybody was into the numbers racket. People would bet a quarter or fifty cents or a dollar on what was called 'Bolita' at the supermarkets or drug stores or even little mom-and-pop stores. Trouble was, it was illegal. But many were making money at it, including policemen.

Once a police friend of mine said, 'Bill, I can show you a way to make an extra couple of hundred a week.'

I said, 'How?'

'Turn your back,' he answered.

'Turn my back? What do you mean?'

'Well, when you see these guys at the stores picking up these little bags with betting sheets and money in them,' he explained, 'just turn your back. They'll give you a cut if you do.'

I was enraged. He actually wanted me to take bribes from these 'bag men' as they were called, so they could run their numbers games. 'Get away from me!' I yelled. 'I came here to be an honest policeman.'

'Then you'll end up getting more trouble than you know,' he warned.

Sure enough, one day I arrested a couple of bag men for number running, I was quickly put into a punishment tour by patrolling the Miami International Airport. I was never told why I was being punished, just that I was to patrol the airport, on foot, until further notice. But I knew it was for disrupting some crime boss's Bolita take for the week.

So I decided to fight fire with fire. I had gotten in trouble for arresting people running the numbers, so I became a superior pain in the ass at the airport by doing it *by* the numbers. The legal, 'pain in the butt, what idiot made this a law' numbers. I wrote parking tickets to people, including mob figures, who were barely in violation of airport parking laws. I was a horse's ass to anyone doing anything marginally wrong.

'Step aside,' I would say to people barely standing where they weren't supposed to be standing. 'Let's move along,' I'd say to a group of tourists waiting in a congested area that was actually supposed to remain clear for traffic or something. I knew it would piss them off, without actually hurting anyone, so I'd do it. I was

81

a 'letter of the law' policeman. Finally, I had so many complaints against me to the sheriff, that they put me back on the streets. I mean, he couldn't get mad at me for doing my job. But he knew I was being a pain at the airport just so they would send me back. It happened to me twice, being sent to the airport for punishment. Or should I say, stepping on someone's toes. During my second tour, I met a lieutenant in the Sheriff's Office who approached me with an offer to get out of the airport. He told me I could be transferred to the Southern district of Dade County. After I got there I found out why.

It was a mostly black area where the crime rate was incredibly high, and no officer wanted to be sent there. I later heard through the grapevine that I was sent there in the hope I would get hurt, because I wouldn't fall into line with the numbers racket and some of the other illegal activities that went on. The problem was ever-present on the force, even in subtle ways that many police didn't really think were illegal or immoral.

Sometimes during the midnight shift, we'd get a call to the scene of a burglary. Often the sergeant would arrive and just look at one of us and quietly say, 'Help yourself.'

Some police would. They would take a few things, even with the owner watching. Usually the owner would tell them to take what they liked, the insurance would pay for it. So there would be police leaving with things in the trunk of their cars, and all under the approving eyes of a superior officer and/or owner, because they knew the insurance company would pay. Since I never took anything, I came under suspicion. As long as everyone took something, no one would say anything. Whenever someone refused to take something, they were a watched suspect.

I learned a lot about people during those years. And a lot about reality. Good and bad. The good came when, on a few occasions, I delivered a baby.

Once, a call came in to send a deputy to a woman in distress. She was in distress all right. As I pulled up to the front of her house, she was sitting on the steps of her porch yelling, '*I'm having a baby!*'

Just as she stood up, the baby fell out. I ran over and grabbed the bloody baby and shocked mother and carried them to my car. Placing them in the back seat, I realized I didn't have a knife to cut the umbilical cord. I finally put the cord to my mouth, bit it off, tied it in a knot and sped away to the hospital. They both survived.

We had a great many shootings in southern Dade County and once we got a call to a shooting out at a migrant camp. When I got to this farm and drove up to the house, I saw a man sitting on his porch. A stream of blood was shooting straight out a couple of feet from his forehead. He was just sitting there like nothing was wrong. He even spoke to me.

I thought, Oh my God, as I ran over to him. I bit the fingernail off my little finger, jammed it into the tiny hole in his head that had been made by a .22 caliber bullet and waited for help. Moments later, the ambulance arrived and that's how we rode to the hospital; with my finger in the head of this gunshot victim. Believe it or not, he lived. I'll never forget him.

Working down in that area could be scary at times. There was a lot of tension between the races and occasionally riots would breakout. We were always hearing, "Hey honky, gonna kill ya'" as we'd drive through certain neighborhoods. I couldn't really blame some of the blacks for being mad at police. Some of the police treated blacks like animals. I didn't go for that, but those were the times we lived in; blacks sat in the back of the bus and ate at their own restaurants. There was only so much one policeman or a few policemen on a force could do. We tried, and sometimes we succeeded, but most of the time we were almost as unpopular with the bigots on the force as the blacks were.

Once a few fellow deputies took me off to the side and told me that I shouldn't be eating at those 'nigger' cafés and diners. I told them in no uncertain terms that they wouldn't tell me where to eat, just like they didn't tell me how to dress or what to do in my spare time. They took me seriously and I never heard another word. Truth be known, I ate at the black diners because it was cheaper and police aren't the best-paid people in the world. Not only that, the white restaurants had me eat at the back door to get my meal at a price I could afford, while the blacks allowed me to eat in the main room with everyone else. Besides the food at those diners was damned good. Taste buds don't know color.

But there was crime, and sometimes it got scary. Like the time, around one o'clock in the morning, when I heard gunshots as I drove south on U.S. 1, the main highway. I sped over toward the shots and found two cars, the windows blown out. Just then, BLAM! BLAM! And someone screamed, 'No, don't shoot!'

I ran toward the sound, drew my weapon and eased around the edge of a nearby building from where the shots came. Rounding the corner as carefully as a nervous cat, I was surprised when suddenly a man stood a few feet from me, obviously very scared, his gun level with my face!

I lowered my gun and said, 'I'm a police officer.'

'I know what you are.' He shook as he spoke. 'I've already killed two people. One more won't matter.'

'You don't know that they're dead,' I said calmly, although I was screaming with fear on the inside as I stared down the barrel of that gun. 'Besides, it'll only be worse if you kill a policeman.'

It had only been a few nerve-twisting minutes, but it felt like days before my backup arrived and quietly circled around behind the gunman. I started to walk slowly toward him.

'You take another step,' he screamed, almost begging to be helped out of this situation, 'and I'll kill you where you stand! I swear I will!'

'Let me tell you what's about to happen,' I explained methodically, 'I'm going to raise my gun and fire on the count of three. I don't want to have to kill you but I will. Now, you're gonna have to decide if you're gonna kill me because one or both of us is going to die when I get to three.' He shook even more as I started to count, 'One . . . Two . . . '

'I caught this guy screwing my wife!'

'That's justification,' I lied, interrupting the count I didn't want to make, 'I'd probably do the same thing if I were in your shoes. But you're gonna have to put the gun down before I count three or I'll kill you.'

With his gun barrel still shaking, I could see he was about to cry.

'One . . . I'm not kidding,' I warned, slowly raising my

weapon, 'two . . . you'll die right here . . . ' WHAM!

My backup clubbed him on the head with his nightstick. I sank against the wall, all energy zapped from my body.

It was pressure like that which made police bend the rules in some areas of law enforcement. I don't think it occurs as much anymore, but it used to be that everyone carried a 'drop knife' or 'drop gun'. If you shot a person at the scene and were unable to find the weapon he had tried to use on you, you simply dropped your 'spare' next to the body or wrapped his fingers around it before anyone arrived. It was virtually standard procedure. To be honest, a lot of police probably killed people thinking they saw a weapon aimed at them. In some cases, there really had been a weapon used, but during a chase or a scuffle, it was lost and the policeman was trying to protect himself. It was illegal, but it happened. Then there were other tricks police used; sometimes to expedite justice.

Once, while I was riding with a particular patrolman, we were after a man we knew had shot two people and gotten away. We knew where he worked and drove over to get him. It was nighttime, and the suspect worked at a fruit and vegetable packing plant on the night shift. His boss verified he had not been there during the time of the shootings, so we handcuffed him and took him away.

After we put him in the car, my partner walked around the patrol unit with me and said, 'If we don't get a confession, the charges will never stick. There's no hard evidence. So, we're goin' to take him out to the woods.'

'What are you going to do?' I asked.

'Don't worry,' he replied, 'just follow my lead.'

After we got way out in the woods, my partner pulled the car over, got out, opened the back door where the suspect sat, took out a handkerchief and blindfolded him.

'Get out! The policeman pulled him from the car and led him to the front of the vehicle. 'Stand there!'

'What are you gonna do . . . you gonna kill me?' The suspect was becoming scared. 'I didn't do anything, I told you.'

My partner went to the back of the car and opened the trunk, then took out a burlap sack. The prisoner was still yelling, 'You better not kill me . . . you better not!'

'Shut up!' he bellowed back in a deep voice.

I saw that he had a big rubber snake with rattles on the tail. He looked at me and winked, then loud enough for the suspect to hear said, 'Hey Bill, help me catch a rattlesnake, there's plenty out here.'

'You better not kill me.' The suspect was becoming *very* nervous now. 'I didn't do anything!'

The policeman went over to the suspect and pulled his blindfold down. 'We're gonna just let a snake bite you and then leave you out here in the woods to yell yourself to death.'

'I didn't do anything.' He was becoming frantic. My partner pulled the blindfold back up over the suspect's eyes, then walked off into the woods. A few minutes later he made some scuffling noises. 'Goddammit, Bill I got one.'

He fumbled with the sack.

'Looks like a big one,' I lied.

'I didn't do it,' the suspect was whimpering, 'I didn't . . . I didn't!'

'Yeah,' the patrolman sighed as he returned, fighting the sack filled with the rubber snake, and more importantly, the rattles. 'yeah, this'll do just fine.'

He walked up to the scared suspect, holding the sack gingerly and fighting it like the big snake was about to come out and bite everything within reach. He slipped the rattles clear of the bag.

'I didn't do it!!' The prisoner screamed.

'You better talk to me you lyin' sonofabitch,' the officer warned, 'or I'm gonna open this sack and let this bastard loose on ya.' He fought with the sack, making the rattles shake for emphasis. Hell, it scared me and I knew the snake was rubber. Just then, with the rattles shaking inches from his face, the prisoner broke.

'All right! All right! I did it . . . I shot 'em.' He screamed and cried for mercy, wincing away as the sack drew in closer. 'Please don't let that snake bite me . . . I shot 'em . . . I did it!'

'Where's the gun,' my partner pressed.

'I'll take you there! Please don't let it bite me!'

The officer put the prisoner back in the car and I'll be damned if he didn't take us right to where he had stashed the gun. We had the weapon and the confession, though by actions which would probably not hold up in court today. Not to mention we would more than likely both still be in prison for violations of a suspect's civil rights.

Of course, these were older guys I was riding with who had been around for years. And times were much different than today. It was nothing for one of these guys to drive up to a group of black men and say, 'Hey, get that hat off.' If they didn't, these guys would get out of their car, walk over and knock the hell out of them and say, 'Next time, nigger, if I say "get the hat off" you get the hat off.' And the next time we came upon them, their hats would come off.

I didn't like riding with them. It wasn't my idea of law enforcement. Then the police wondered why they had riots on their hands from the black community.

The first time I ever sat in a limousine was, ironically, while I was being punished by working at Miami International Airport. I noticed one day a big beautiful 'stretch', driven by an older black man, was circling the drop-off and pick-up area near the entrance of the airport. He was being very cooperative, not blocking traffic or trying to park in the no-parking zone. Each time he passed I looked at the beautiful car, thinking how fine it must be on the inside and figuring I'd never know . . . not on a policeman's salary. Finally, during one of the car's orbits around the parking area, I stopped the driver.

'Is there a problem, Officer?'

'No, no problem,' I answered. 'I just thought since you've been good about not blocking traffic and keeping the car moving, I'd let you park here and wait a few minutes for the people you're picking up, as long as no traffic backs up behind you . . . and, you let me sit in the back seat for a minute.'

He smiled genuinely. 'Of course, Officer,' he said as he emerged from the car and opened the back door for me.

It was better than I had imagined. Keep in mind this was about

1959, so a TV and a wet bar in the car, not to mention a telephone, was just out of this world to me. I soaked it all in; the plush interior, the gadgets, the aroma of prestige. After a few moments and having seen everything, I got out, shook hands with the gentleman and thanked him.

'My pleasure, Officer,' he replied in a most well-mannered and sophisticated way. I could tell this man was a professional. Years later, when I eventually owned five limousines of my own, I made sure my driver was a man of similar character. He eventually became a good friend as well as my personal bodyguard.

Returning to my post at the entrance area of Miami International, I noticed a distinguished-looking gray-haired man walking to the limousine with a woman wearing a lot of jewelry. Before getting in the limousine, they began talking with the driver. A few moments later the gray-haired gentleman began walking my way. I thought, Oh, hell, I've done it now. But I decided to meet him halfway. As we approached I said, 'Can I help you?'

'Yes, are you the officer who let my driver park here?'

'Yes, I am.'

He smiled, 'Thank you, we appreciate it.'

I returned the smile. 'You're welcome.'

'I've not seen you here before,' he observed.

'Oh, I'm being punished,' I replied, 'So, I'm here at the airport.'

'Well, we're in and out of here a lot,' he said. 'We live in the southern part of the county.'

'Oh, well, that's where my station is located,' I said, 'when I'm not being punished.'

We shared a chuckle and he gave me his card. 'Come by sometime.'

About a week later, the limousine pulled up and the driver got out and waved me over. After our greeting, he handed me an envelope.

It was a written invitation to dinner at the gentleman's home. The driver spoke up.

'I'm supposed to pick you up,' he said with a smile. 'My boss sent me to deliver the invitation and find out where you live so I can be there to pick you up tomorrow night.'

'I'm sorry,' I replied as I shook my head, 'I can't go.'

'Why not,' he asked quietly, 'a person doesn't get an invitation like this very often.'

'I know,' I said, 'but I'd better not, besides I don't have anything real nice to wear.'

'That doesn't matter.'

'Well, maybe not,' I sighed, 'but you'd better tell your boss I can't make it.'

The next day the man himself came to see me and asked me personally. I finally accepted his invitation . . . minus the limo ride.

The dinner party was on a Sunday. I bought a cheap suit, though it was expensive on my salary of a few hundred dollars a month. Driving in awe down the road lined with beautiful estates, toward the palatial home of my rich friend, I became rather self-conscious of my old beat-up car, so I parked down the street and walked. When I got to the house, I went to the back door and met the driver and his wife, who happened to be the maid.

'Why are you coming to the back door?' he asked.

'I guess I'm used to it,' I answered, 'since I eat at the back door of the diners on my beat . . . you know, out by the trash cans.'

'Well here, Mr Dear, you'll go to the front,' he fussed like a mother hen. 'Besides, if I let you in here, the boss will get mad at me.'

So, to the front I went and rang the doorbell. Lo and behold, the driver greeted me warmly, as the butler. I guess you have to play by the rules of etiquette sometimes. He escorted me to the main room where the other guests were talking, and announced my arrival.

The dinner party was wonderful, and my host invited me back to his home. On many occasions, I would stop by in my patrol car. I found that he was a businessman from Chicago and he and his wife had no children. Soon he was teaching me to play tennis and we three were becoming great friends.

One day, I got a call to report to the office. When I arrived at the substation, there was a detective and lieutenant there along with my captain, who said, 'I understand you've been frequenting the home of a particular Chicago businessman here in the area.'

I said, Yes, sir.'

'Well,' he said in a tone denoting a direct order, 'you can't go over there any more.'

'Why?'

The captain hesitated, then said, 'He's a mob figure.'

'Well, all I know is he's never asked me to do anything wrong and I wouldn't if he did.'

'Hell, Bill,' the captain sputtered, 'I know you wouldn't, but you can't go by any more.'

'But I've been invited to a dinner party.'

'Then you need to decide, the party or your job.'

The rest of the day, and most of the next morning, I thought about my choice. It didn't seem fair that I had to make such a choice, in the first place. Sometimes the ways of this world are so screwed up, its no wonder we all can't seem to get along. My friend and his lovely wife were nice people. They had always been nice to me; even treated me like family. I couldn't see the need to hurt them this way. It just wasn't fair. I knew what I had to do.

I went by the house, stopped my patrol car once I cleared the security gate, and sat there for a moment. Dammit, I really get tired of this crap, I thought. After a few moments, I got out of my car and walked into the mansion to tell the man that I couldn't come by any more. He seemed genuinely saddened.

'Bill, I don't have any children and I always wanted a son. I would've liked to have had you as my son. In fact, I was going to ask you if you wanted to work for me, first running papers for me back and forth. Then I would teach you my business.'

'I appreciate that,' I said, 'I really do. But I can't.'

Then he told me something I'll never forget. He said, 'Bill, I'm glad you're a policeman. I'm glad there are some honest police out there like you. But you will never get anywhere being a policeman. If you're a policeman today, you're going to be a security guard when you retire, because while you're a policeman, everybody likes you. But when you're through and can't do anything for anyone, you're nothing.'

He put his arm around me and I told him how much I appreciated his wife and him being so nice to me. Then I left. A year later, someone put a bomb in his car.

I used to get prowler calls late at night, arrive at the home of a distraught woman whose husband was gone and then be shown to the bedroom where they would say they saw the prowler. The next thing I knew they'd have their hands between my legs. I found that approximately 75 per cent of all prowler calls, when the husband was gone, were fake, so the lady could have sex with a policeman. It happened all the time. There was something about the uniform. If an officer resigned or quit the force, he usually couldn't get a woman to speak to him; if he was in uniform, some women couldn't keep their hands off him. A lot of police took them up on their offers. And yes, on occasion, so did I.

Many a night, I left the substation where I worked after a shift and would go to a party or go see some girl who had left a note on the windshield of my car. The next morning I'd get up and leave, probably never knowing their real name. I hung my gunbelt on the bedpost of more than a few women during those days, but, for the most part it was the badge and the uniform that did it. Maybe my old mob friend was right after all.

BILL DEAR'S NOTEPAD: They Stiffed Me!

One night, not long after I started with the Dade County Sheriff's Office, my older partner and I had to take a shooting victim to the hospital. Even though he was a prisoner, we weren't allowed in the emergency room while the doctors worked on him. 'Let's get a cup of coffee,' my partner suggested.

'I don't drink coffee,' I said as we walked down the hall from the emergency room toward the waiting area. 'But I'll take a soft drink or some milk.'

There was an intern standing nearby. 'Any cold drinks around here?' my partner asked him.

'Sure,' he answered. 'Just go down the hall to that third door on the right,' he told me, pointing down the corridor. 'Go down the steps, then to the left and all the way back in the corner. It'll be dark, but there's a pull cord when you get to the corner. It's right over the cold drink cooler. Just help yourself.'

'I'll be right back,' I told my partner. He raised his cup of coffee in acknowledgment.

When I opened the door the intern had directed me to, I could barely see the steps leading down into a rather cold storage room. At the bottom was a wooden walkway that actually kept the pedestrian about six inches above the concrete floor. I felt like I was walking across a fishing dock. The door at the top of the stairs closed automatically, the booming slam reverberating around the frigid cavern for a few seconds. I had to strain my eyes to make out the dark path as I stared down at the floor. Each step was an uncertain one. I held out my hands to try and keep my head from being the first to encounter an obstacle. I could see things stacked on either side of me, but I was only paying attention to the faint outline of the wooden walkway below. My eyes had started to adjust to the pitch-black room, and there against the back wall sat what looked to be my goal, the soft drink cooler.

The cooler seemed to keep moving further and further away.

Each step echoed against the stacks and stacks of dark outlines in the shadows on either side of me. I don't know why, perhaps instinct, but I noticed my right hand resting on the stock of my gun, nestled firmly in its holster, while the other hand still groped ahead of me. Finally I reached the cooler. I fumbled for the string above it; the light came on, and the room was filled with a bone-chilling revelation.

I screamed, and almost fainted. The stacks all around me were freshly autopsied bodies. There must have been fifty of them in there in huge stainless steel trays with name tags on their toes. This was the morgue where they were kept until the funeral homes came for them. There were men, women and even children of every description. Every scary movie about mad scientists and zombies rising up to claim their unsuspecting victims came to mind at once. The incisions on the bodies, made by the examiners, were laced together like baseball stitches, with large sutures. I didn't notice if I was standing before a soft drink cooler, though somehow I doubted it. I broke and ran like hell up the steps and into the laughing faces of a half dozen people in on the joke, including my partner.

'You sonofabitch!' I yelled, but this only made him laugh harder. Apparently it was the same trick they pulled on every new guy in the Sheriff's Office. Suddenly it wasn't a soft drink I wanted . . .

CHAPTER 5
The Gas Station Murders

For about three months my area of Miami was plagued by a number of murders of gas station attendants. The suspect, described by those who had survived his reign of terror, was a young white male. That's all we had to go on. But we began to notice the man would hit about every other weekend, during the very early morning hours at all-night service stations.

At that time, all of us at the Perrine Substation of the Dade County Sheriff's Department would gas up the police cars ourselves after each shift. We used a Shell station not far away and we all knew Jack, the attendant. He was a hard-working family man. He didn't own the service station, but he worked like he did. It was always a pleasure to visit with Jack while I filled my car. He was not only a friend, he was a pretty good set of eyes. He would let us know if things didn't look just right around the neighborhood; the kind of community assistance every police officer needs.

One night, about eleven thirty, as I began my 11–7 shift, I stopped by the Shell station to talk with Jack. He seemed worried about this murderer running loose. But of all the service stations in the area, this was the one that had police cars in and out all night.

'Listen, Jack,' I said reassuringly, 'I'll be around, checking on you while this is going on.'

'I appreciate it, Bill,' he replied, 'I really do.'

As we chatted, I got a call over my radio.

'Miami, 637 A.' 'A' indicated I was riding alone that night, as I did most nights.

'Go ahead, Miami.'

'Need you over in the vicinity of Tropical Park Racetrack tonight,' the dispatcher ordered. It happened to be the area of Miami where I grew up and threw newspapers as a kid.

I told Jack I wouldn't be around that night after all, but that somebody else would be checking in often.

'No problem Bill.' He waved and smiled as I set off for my assignment. Actually it was disappointing. I enjoyed dropping in on occasion during the shift to see Jack . . . maybe have a soft drink.

We knew the murderer was hitting all-night sevice stations and there were some prime choices in the part of town where I was heading. Thinking about it, I noticed my feeling of impending doom. Somehow it made sense that these half dozen stations in the old neighborhood would be visited by the murderer, but leaving my usual area, and Jack; well, something gnawed at me. I tried to put it out of my mind. Besides, all of the sheriff's deputies went to that station; it was almost like a substation of our substation.

The next few hours were fairly routine, in fact boring. Approximately 1:45 a.m., however, a call came. Nothing major, but it did break the monotony. Seems like it was a loud party, disturbing the peace sort of thing. It was something to do on a quiet night. *Too* quiet. I opened my door to get into my car.

'All units! All units! Shooting!'

The radio dispatcher cut the silence of the night, repeating his breaking new, 'All units, repeat, shooting . . . shooting at the Perrine Shell Station.'

'*Oh no*!' I screamed at no one, firing up my unit and burning most of the tread from the tires.

I was not the first on the scene. There were police cars scattered everywhere as lights of red bounced off every conceivable object; reflecting, flashing and bouncing again. It was lit up like the Las Vegas strip. Several officers stood at the side of the building, their faces long in sorrow, jaws locked in anger. The murderer had taken Jack into the restroom, made him kneel down next to the toilet, then shot him five times in the back of the head, neck and shoulders.

He had the money. Jack had assured me he would never try to fight someone over a few dollars for the Shell Oil Company, nor would the company want him to fight. But it wasn't enough to rob the place, the suspect *wanted* to kill. At that moment, so did I!

The next day, I selected four stations that could be likely targets for the murderer. They were in my old neighborhood, near the racetrack, and I knew all of the attendants well. If the murderer was going to strike, he would strike one of these. So, for the next few nights I staked them out; parking my car in the shadows and watching. Bob, the attendant at the Shell Station on Bird Road, told me his concerns. I worried about Bob. He worked the all-night shift by himself, just like Jack. He was a prime target. I would sit in the dark recesses during the wee hours of the morning and watch Bob's station when I had no other calls.

Sitting quietly in my patrol car during those early morning hours was an interesting study in human nature. It's a peculiar time of the day. For someone forced to roll out of a comfortable bed and make a living at that hour, it's the lonely start of another hard day. For someone wrapping up an evening of parties, clubs and booze, it's still the wild night before. After a while, even in Miami, most of the rebel rousers make it to their beds and pass out. The hard-working stiffs get on with their business. What's left are the weirdos that come crawling out through the darkest hours like roaches in a kitchen. My experience has been that someone out at that time of the early morning, cruising the streets at a snail's pace or walking aimlessly, is trouble waiting to happen.

After a few nights of watching, most of the time staked out at the Shell station, a feeling welled up inside of me that another friend of mine who pumped gas to make ends meet was about to die. But I seemed helpless to stop it. All I could do was patrol the area and watch my stations and pray.

I had told Bob not to worry since I would be across the street much of the time. With the exception of a few urgent calls, I found myself across the street from that Shell station more and more, watching the occasional overnight traffic that came through.

I had been assigned an unmarked car, one without the police logo or even a county emblem, to use for what had developed into a serious stakeout to find this killer. My sergeant had given me free reign to watch the stations closely, as long as I was available for the more serious calls that really needed me for back-up. The smaller, more routine calls would usually be sent to a marked unit, keeping me out of the normal flow of nightly police business and concentrating on my case.

One night as I sat silently in my car, eyes fixed on the lamb waiting for a wolf, my radio crackled with a call.

'Miami, 637 A'

'637 A, Miami,' I replied.

'Suspicious persons cruising the Sinclair service station on Tamiami Trail,' came the order.

'Advised Miami,' I said, 'I'm on stakeout here at the Shell Station on Bird Road. Are there any other units available for Tamiami Trail?'

'Negative 637 A,' the dispatcher droned, 'and caller advises the suspects, two white males in a car, have been cruising the station several times in the past hour. I think one of these may be your guy, 637 A.'

'10–4.' I hit the lights and siren and waved at Bob as I sped away. He returned the wave and knew I'd be back as soon as possible, as on the other occasional calls that had taken me away from his location during the previous nights of my stakeout.

Heading down 72nd Avenue to Coral Way, I kept wondering about the Shell station. This Sinclair station had two attendants. The murderer hit stations with only one overnight attendant. But who knows, maybe one of the two suspects was the murderer and he brought someone with him this time. I turned onto Tamiami Trail and shut off the lights and siren. I still couldn't shake that feeling, the same feeling I had the night Jack was killed. I approached the Sinclair station with no headlights, so as not to startle the suspects. I was really praying we had our murderer. These guys were white males and young; the same description we had on the murderer. My heart was pounding the walls of my chest with anxious anticipation. Would one of the guys really be the murderer? Would there be a violent confrontation? Would I have to kill someone here tonight? There were two of them; would I be gunned down by one as I shot the other?

I tried to shut off the questions and concentrate on procedure as I saw the Sinclair station ahead, its large Dinosaur logo illuminating the night, but the nagging feeling that I should be back at the Shell station would not go away. In fact, it grew stronger.

Bill, I told myself you've got to forget it for a few minutes. Besides, this could be it right here and you don't want to risk blowing it because of a lack of concentration. Just as I pulled into the station and up behind the suspect's car, my back-up arrived from the other direction running 'silent' as well. The guys never saw us coming until we flanked their vehicle, leaving them no room to run. It scared the hell out of them. My back-up got out of his car and began talking with them. It didn't take long for me to realize that these weren't the guys.

They had probably been casing the service station for a robbery, but they didn't have a weapon. A lot of robbers can bluff their way through a robbery without a weapon; hands in coat pockets as if holding a gun they don't want a passer-by to see, a lot of noise and quick orders from someone who comes in like a police raid, making the victim turn around so they can't tell whether there is really a weapon, scaring the victim to death with uncertainty since they can't see what's going on behind them; all common tactics. But the target the two were deciding on wouldn't be tested that night. Still, I had hoped they would have been the people we were after.

Just then the dispatcher came blasting through my radio, '637 A . . . CODE THREE! CODE THREE! SHOOTING AT THE SHELL STATION . . . BIRD ROAD! 637 A . . . CODE THREE!'

My back-up had also heard the frantic dispatcher and looked across the suspects' car at me with the same 'Oh, my God!' expression that was on my face.

I wheeled around, leaving smoke and burning rubber all over the parking lot as my patrol unit screamed out of the station and through the dark streets of Miami. I raced through intersections with lights and siren exploding with color and roaring a warning to anyone within six blocks of me to get the hell out of my way. I clipped curbs on turns and took wrong lanes to get by traffic that would stop upon my approach and let me maneuver through. I had to catch this murdering bastard before he killed again. These were my friends he was ruthlessly knocking off with the cold-blooded detatchment of a Nazi.

I hit Bird Road doing 95 miles an hour. The turn was so fast my car was up on two wheels. The Shell station was coming up, but no one was out front, no car, no nothing. Where was Bob?

I rolled up into the Shell parking area and slid to a stop. Jumping out, I drew my gun from its holster. God! How I hoped the bastard would jump from behind a doorway with a weapon. I was ready for him; I wanted to kill him right then and there! Inside, the cash register was open, but no Bob, only a streak of blood from the cash register to the service bay. I could hear a groan as I ran to the bay. Bob was leaning against the wall by a pay phone, covered in blood.

'Bob!' I ran to grab my friend as he began to slide down the wall, leaving a bloody smear.

'Bill,' he coughed and wheezed, 'Bill, you just missed him.'

'Hang on, Bob,' I pleaded, clutching him in my arms and easing him to the cold concrete floor. Blood poured from the five gunshot wounds in the back of his head, neck and shoulders. Just like Jack.

He coughed and told me exactly what the murderer looked like. Fear racked his face as he recalled what he had just gone through and as he realized what he was about to face. His body shook, convulsing hard with each cough. He shook even harder and gasped for a few short breaths. Within a few minutes Bob was gone.

The ambulance and other police arrived moments later and the service station became the latest crime scene of the most brutal string of murders I had ever heard of in my young life. I was covered in Bob's blood, but somewhere, out in that humid city, was the man with Bob's blood on his hands.

As soon as the back-ups arrived, I was in my car, bloody uniform and all, looking for the murderer, heading in the direction

Bob told me he thought the man might have gone. We all searched for the murderer, but he had vanished into the night. No doubt we eventually would find him. But I'd better not find him first or there wouldn't be anything left for the executioner. Three days later, the Palm Beach Police Department caught up with the suspect and brought him back to Miami. That night, after starting my overnight shift, I went down to the jail to see him. The killer was named Dennis Whitney. He was eighteen years old.

We had taken everything off of the floor of the cell that he could possibly use to commit suicide, so he had to sleep on the cold, hard concrete. That didn't bother me at all; he was still getting a break since he was allowed to draw breath. The jailer opened the cell and I walked in. As I stood over him, his face held a defiant smirk. Raising my foot over his head and neck, I wanted to kill him; to squash him like the roach he was. He had killed seven people. Two were friends of mine.

'When I hit that Shell station,' he suddenly said, 'I was afraid someone would be layin' for me. I thought I was gonna get caught right then.'

My feeling had been right; I shouldn't have left the parking lot. During the trial he said he would watch the police patrol patterns to know when to hit a place. At the Shell station where we filled up our cars in Perrine, he would watch us and see when we filled up or came by to talk with Jack. That night, after the last deputy had filled up, he hit it and killed him. When asked why he killed seven people he said he was imitating Dennis Starkweather, a notorious mass murderer from a few years earlier, who had traveled the country with his girlfriend and killed eleven people.

'I wanted to be better than Starkweather,' Whitney said in his twisted way.

When questioned in front of the jury about the murder of Jack he said, 'I shot him once in the back of the head then grabbed him by the collar and drug him to the bathroom. The guy begged me, he said, 'Please don't kill me, please, don't kill me,' but I just threw him in the bathroom and shot him again. Then I shot him again . . . and again.' There was no remorse on the animal's face. Whitney was a cold-blooded killer and that's all there was to it.

The jury wasted little time in convicting Whitney. But, despite the fact he killed seven people during robberies and made Jack beg for his life, he did not get the death penalty. Whitney was sent to prison for the rest of his life, with no parole.

True Detective magazine did an article after the case was over. The story centered around my narrowing down the targets of the killer and missing him by, as police records indicated, only about three minutes. I still can't help but think that Bob would be alive but for those three lousy minutes.

It wasn't long after the Whitney murders I began to seriously consider my options. I wanted to be a detective, but it would take perhaps seven or eight years to reach that level in Dade County, and then there was no guarantee I would end up in Homicide. On top of that, it was insulting to think I had to wait my turn, when bozos in rumpled suits were calling themselves detectives, always taking over the scene from the patrol officer and never letting him forget he was patrol.

We would rope off the area of a crime scene, gather the witnesses, and then these sloppy, usually overweight detectives would come ambling up and say something like, 'Okay officer, you can go now.' If that much.

I wanted to follow through on the process of piecing together the puzzle and finding the killer. It was intriguing to me. But in a large city like Miami, I wouldn't get to investigate murder cases until I was an old man.

Over time, I began to resent the obstacle in the middle of my career path. Many times, I would pull over and stop my patrol unit on some quiet, almost abandoned stretch of road in Dade County, and think about the options that lay before me. More and more I could see the options in a city like Miami were few for me. You could have gone through the ranks of patrol forever, but that wasn't what I wanted to do. I wanted to investigate murder cases. I could be a very good detective. But it wasn't going to be; not in Miami.

The mental tug of war raged for six months; I liked my job. I hated the feeling of entrapment. I enjoyed police work. I wasn't getting any closer to being a detective. I grew up in Miami, but I felt myself slipping away somehow. Being honest with myself, I knew I would leave. But one doesn't uproot on a whim. A stepping stone was needed. My parents had moved to Texas and they liked it. But they're such good people they could make hell bearable. Still, Texas started getting my attention. From the days of the Alamo to the era of oil barons, Texas has meant a fresh start for hard-working people with a dream. I had a dream of spreading my wings and being the best. A temporary job with a small-town police department would offer a better opportunity for advancement and would allow me eventually to establish myself as a private investigator.

You see, the other thing about being on a police force, even as a detective, was the fact that you could starve to death. Oh sure, a lot of people make a fairly good living at it, but most are doing just that . . . making a living. Many have to depend on the income of a spouse to help make ends meet. I wanted something different. I was tired of sitting in the service entrance of restaurants for my meals while on patrol because sitting in the dining room was too expensive. I was tired of never having a nice suit of clothes other than my uniform, which I kept cleaned and pressed at all times. There was plenty out there for anyone willing to work for it. But what did the trick, was sitting in the back seat of that limousine. I had decided then and there that *this* skinny kid from Miami was going to be somebody. And somebody with a lot of money. With money, you can make a difference. With money, you can help people. With money, and your own private investigation agency, you can do whatever is necessary to solve a case, return a kidnapped child, or find a missing loved one, without being shackled by the bean counter at city hall or the county courthouse. You can also help the needy, like orphan children. I knew how they felt, I was adopted. But none of this would come together until I started my own firm. Moving to Texas would be step one of the plan.

So in 1961 I went to work for the Police Department in Grand Prairie, a suburb of Dallas. It didn't take long before the department heads knew they had a good police officer. I had been well trained in Miami, with big-city, tough crime experience that most of the young guys in Grand Prairie didn't have yet, despite the good training available in Texas. What I didn't have was experience with small-town politics.

About a week after joining the force, I was riding with Officer Bill Key. A big man, Bill weighed in at about 280 pounds of muscle on a six-foot-three frame. We came upon an accident in town in which a big beautiful Cadillac had run into the back of an older car driven by a black man. As we got out and went up to the accident, the driver of the Cadillac got out and ambled over to me. As soon as he was within a few feet of me I could smell alcohol. I had smelled it on drunken drivers a thousand times before.

I said, 'Sir, I'm placing you under arrest for driving while intoxicated.'

'Do you know who I am?' He squinted up at me, moving very slowly from side to side.

'I don't care who you are, I'm placing you under arrest for DWI.' I had no sooner said that, than the man took a drunken swing at me. Grabbing his fist as it came around, I whipped his arm behind him. 'Cuff him,' I told my partner.

His driver's license said his name was Chris Hykel*. I had only been there a week but I knew he was the owner of a major steel fabrication company based in Grand Prairie. But I didn't really care. We put Hykel in the car and called for ambulance assistance for the other driver, who had suffered a few minor cuts. I told the dispatcher, 'Be advised, I'm enroute with a DWI, VIP.' Which, of course, meant a Very Important Person. Then I told the dispatcher who it was.

When we arrived at the police station, there were a lot of cars parked out front. We drove around back to the police entrance and brought Hykel in, cursing and yelling at the top of his lungs. As I pushed him into a holding cell, two sergeants were standing there. One asked, 'Do you know who you've arrested?'

'No, who?'

'The most important man in Grand Prairie, that's who.'

'So what?'

'Well,' he warned, 'your shit's fixin' to happen. They're waitin' for ya'.'

I walked on into the station. There stood the relatively new Police Chief, Fred Conover; a one-armed man I soon learned was State Senator George Parkhouse; and Harold Graff, who owned the Graff Chevrolet dealership in Grand Prairie. They immediately began.

'You can't arrest him!'

'Don't you know who he is?'

'What do you mean arresting a fine, upstanding . . . !'

It went on and on for several minutes until finally Senator Parkhouse said, 'Release him, now!'

I turned, looked the Senator in the eye and said, 'I'm not releasing him. He was drunk and driving a motor vehicle and he caused an accident that injured a man. I'm not releasing him!'

'I'll have your job, you no good son of a . . . !'

'No, you won't,' I replied calmly, then turned to my captain, who had joined the little conference. 'He was drunk *and* he took a swing at me. I'm not dropping any charges or releasing him.'

My partner walked in and said, 'That's exactly what happened, Captain.'

Finally, Harold Graff spoke up. 'Look, can't we work this out?'

'I'm not working out anything,' I replied, 'I'm not into politics. I'm here to enforce the law, and that's what I'm doing.'

I had been on the night shift, was getting very tired, and so I left. As I walked through the door to the outer office, I encountered a small group of people, including the president of the bank, waiting to see what was going to happen. I didn't care, I was going home.

Getting out of the car, I was greeted by my sweet little landlady.

'Bill,' she smiled, 'hear you're in a little trouble.'

I returned her smile. 'Boy, news sure travels fast in a small town.'

We both gave a little chuckle and I went upstairs, showered and went to bed. I had barely settled into my pillow when the phone rang. It was Chief Conover.

'Bill, I've got someone here who wants to talk with you.' I

heard a muffled voice as the Chief handed over to one of the attorneys from the Grand Prairie City Attorney's office.

'We'd like to have lunch with you,' the legal eagle said pleasantly.

'Sir,' I replied, 'I haven't had any sleep.'

'Well, go ahead, get a few hours sleep and meet us at the country club for lunch.' His manner was cheerful, which led me to believe my ass was being greased. Later that day, after a few hours of sleep, I met with Chief Conover before heading out with the country club set. The Chief was very straightforward with me.

'I've only been the Chief a few months,' he said, 'and I've worked hard to get here. Now, you do what you have to do, but I want you to know it's going to cost me my job.'

The Chief wasn't playing the heavy, we were friends, and still are to this day. But he was being honest and he was right. If I didn't work out something, he was going to lose his job. That's politics.

At the country club, amid surroundings I hadn't seen since my wealthy friend in Miami, the city attorney talked.

'Bill,' he sighed as I turned down a drink, 'can't we work out something?'

'I'm not working anything out. I told you that this morning!'

'Well, just think about it overnight. I'm not filing the charges today, I'll wait until tomorrow. And you think about it. For everyone's sake.'

The message could hardly be clearer.

By the next morning I was getting pressure from all sides. One sergeant came up to me and said, 'If you don't drop those charges you'll be on my shit list.' Then another sergeant came up to me and said, 'If you *do* drop those charges, you're on my permanent shit list, you hear?'

Here I had been on the force a week and I was on everyone's shit list. Well, enough's enough. Hykel's attorney was called to the station and I met him in the Chief's office.

'Okay,' I said, 'here's what I'm going to do. Tomorrow morning at eight o'clock, you have Hykel in the Chief's office and I'm going to give him a piece of my mind. Then I'll reduce the charges to Drunk in Car and he can pay a fine with the court.'

'He'll be here,' the attorney promised.

The ironic thing here is the fact that thirty years later the attorney who represented Hykel is now my personal lawyer. The next day, after I finished the night shift, I went home, cleaned up, then returned to the station. Hykel's attorney showed up to pay the fine.

'Wait a minute!' I yelled. 'Where is Hykel?'

'Well, Mr Hykel has to fly to a very important meeting this morning,' the Chief explained.

'Wrong!' I said. 'If he's on his private plane out at Grand Prairie Airport, then he can be called back and driven here. And if he's not here in thirty minutes, I leave and the charges stand.'

Sure enough, they sent a car and within thirty minutes he was delivered to the Chief's office like a fresh hot pizza. With extra anchovies in the form of Senator Parkhouse, Graff and the banker. Hell, I began to wonder if Hykel even went to the bathroom without these guys hanging around. Of course, he was mad when he sat down. But so was I.

'Let me tell you something, Hykel,' I began, 'I may be just a police officer, but you're no better than me or anyone else in this town. We all put our pants on one leg at a time. I didn't know when I started here that this town was so political. I didn't know it was operated by the bank and the car dealership and the steel company. That doesn't make any difference to me. But I'm gonna do it. I'm gonna reduce the charges. However, before I do, let me just tell you one thing. I don't think anything of you and I don't care what you think of me. But if I ever see you drinking and driving or if I ever get the chance to arrest you again, for anything, I will. And I'll prosecute you to the fullest extent of the law next time. Do you understand that, Hykel?'

'Yessir.'

I won the battle, but could see the war was never going to be over. Word of my little tiff with one of Grand Prairie's upstanding citizens got around and offers came from all over the state to work in a variety of police departments. The Pasedena Police Department even flew me there for an interview after they completed an investigation of me. But I told them that I was getting tired of police work. And I was.

One night, while patrolling on the edge, and I mean on the edge of Grand Prairie, next to the Dallas City Limits, I came across another Grand Prairie Police Officer who had found a man passed out in a car. We got out and determined the man was all right, just passed out. My partner then asked, 'Wanna help me move this car a few feet into the Dallas City Limits?'

'Why?'

'So we don't get stuck with the paperwork.'

I said, 'No, but I'll block traffic.'

So, my fellow officer moved the car and advised Dallas of a drunk in a car. That did it. I was through with police work. The Retail Credit Company needed a private investigator and I was their man. I haven't put on a badge since.

BILL DEAR'S NOTEPAD: He Wasn't a Tough Guy, See?

For two days, Edward G. Robinson's son, Ed Jr., was handcuffed to me in Miami, Florida. The son of the famous 'tough guy' was a regular in the court system in Dade County. It was sad in a way. The tall, quiet kid had everything he wanted, and could've really been something, yet he was nothing more than a convicted armed robber, occasionally mixed up in drugs. A real embarrassment to his famous father.

In fact, that's what he told me himself, during those two days I escorted the young man around the court system, while I was Dade County Constable. I recall, on this particular occasion, the young man, already having served jail time, was back before a bench and involved in an armed robbery case. I didn't pay much attention to the particulars of the case, except that I was to bring him to court whenever they called for him. And I was responsible for his custody as well as his personal safety.

His father, the well-known gangster of the silver screen, never showed up for his son's arraignment or any other court appearances. He always sent someone. I wondered, as I walked around with the infamous son, if the roles his father played had some strange effect on him. To me he was a nice, sometimes quiet young man. But other times it was like his way of living up to his father's screen image. He was no big criminal figure, that's for sure. He was almost a petty criminal, hardly worth the trouble. And I noticed that whenever he got into trouble, it never seemed to show up in the newspapers.

Still, a lot of people knew about it. Especially his father.

'You know,' I said sarcastically after a day of escorting him from jail cells and holding areas to courtrooms during a case, 'you're really a helluva reflection on your father.'

'Yeah,' he quietly replied with a sincere air of remorse, 'I'm actually quite an embarrassment to him, Constable.'

I never heard what happened in his case during those two particular days, but even now I can't help thinking of the poor little rich kid whenever I see his father on the screen, and feeling just a little bit sorry for him.

CHAPTER 6
A Brush With Politics

I had decided I could make a difference to society, however small, by becoming a Dallas County Justice of the Peace. I had seen the system work, and I didn't like it. I had also been on the streets of Miami and Grand Prairie and I knew something had to be done. Crime was only half the problem; making the judicial system more efficient was the other half.

So, in 1964, at the urging of a large number of people, I went down to the Republican Party Headquarters on Ross Avenue in Dallas to file as a candidate for Justice of the Peace in the Republican Primary. Now, even though Texas was, and for the most part still is, a politically conservative state, being a Republican in those days was like being a black activist at a Ku Klux Klan rally. And as our Governor of Texas likes to say, 'That ol' dog won't hunt.'

In fact, they use to call Texas a yellow dog Democrat state; or as native Texans say it, 'a yeller dawg Demicrat' state. The saying came from the pen of a magazine writer in the early part of the century. He was travelling Texas to get a sense of the political climate.

Ever since Reconstruction Texas, like most southern states, had had a bad taste for Republicans. Republicans had been nothing more than trouble-making 'carpetbaggers', so called because they moved in with their cloth satchel luggage after the Civil War and took over, making life hard on the former southern rebels. When the Republicans were finally run off, no one wanted to vote Republican again, though the state was very conservative and most candidates were actually home-grown Republicans in Democratic clothing.

When the writer asked a Texan just how loyal Texans were to their Democrats, he is said to have replied, 'Son, they could take and run that yeller dawg layin' out there in the road as a Democrat, and he'd beat any Republican on the ballot.' The phrase stuck.

The problem with the system is that once the Democratic leadership selects a candidate, the race is over. So, I went to file with the Republicans, only to find it was the same procedure. I guess I figured, hard-pressed as the Republicans were, they would be happy to get a qualified candidate. They weren't. They wouldn't even accept my filing fee of an astronomical $2,750. That is until I told my story to the papers and returned with reporters. Suddenly, they saw where they could process my application and filing fee with no trouble.

But a matter of days later, I was called by a party official and told there were seven other candidates for the primary election, and the leadership had already selected the Republican candidate for the General Election in November.

'You've got to be kidding,' I exclaimed. 'You can't do that!' They seemed to be forgetting that the Primary Election was supposed to allow voters to decide who would run on the Republican ticket in November. After an argument, they gave in and invited me to their next meeting.

When I arrived, I waited in a hallway of the party headquarters until someone came and ushered me into a giant room. I was seated in a straight-backed chair in the middle of the room, before a semicircle of twenty men and women. All they needed was a bright light in my eyes.

They began drilling me with questions:

'Why do you want to be a Justice of the Peace?'

'What makes you think you're qualified?'

'Do you really expect to get any backing?'

'Do you have any idea who your opponents could be?'

'Who's behind your decision to run?'

'What's your position on . . . '

'What's your feeling about . . . '

It was obvious that they were trying to discourage me from running. But, after what seemed like hours of interrogation, I was more determined than ever to win this damn thing. And I started out immediately.

I went out and got an old trailer and a 1949 Ford Convertible. I hitched the trailer to the car and put the Ford's top down. I had huge signs made and placed on the trailer with a three-piece band. Then I walked alongside and shook everybody's hand, and I mean everybody!

President Kennedy had done the same type of thing during the 1960 race. But, while his car drove across the country with Frank Sinatra singing, 'Oooops, Here Goes Another Kennedy Fan' on a record, I had to settle for whatever the little band could play.

Still, I worked and campaigned and worked and campaigned until the night of the Primary. I had given it everything I had. I was totally committed. I had put in more hours and worked harder for my election than anything I had ever done in my life, and it paid off. I won the Primary over more than half a dozen candidates, and without a run-off; something very rare in a race with a large field of candidates. But I did it, I got 51 per cent of the vote!

Now, I was the Republican party nominee for the General Election. But more than that, I was suddenly the party's fair-haired boy, the candidate for the future; 'our man' for bigger and better offices. And just as quickly, I was making the circuit with the biggies. The late John Tower, former ranking Senator from Texas, was stumping for the Grand Old Party ticket that included Senator Barry Goldwater, running for President of the United States; and George Bush, seeking the congressional office that would launch his political career and ultimately place him in the White House in 1988.

There were many times, in 1964, when I was on the stage with the major-league players that I hoped their clout would rub off on me. The down-ballot candidates, the ones listed below the party candidates for President or Governor or Congressman and so forth, can be carried in or out of office on the 'coattails' of the major candidates. Barry Goldwater was the coattail I was riding when the General Election in 1964 was held; though I almost didn't need a coattail at one point in the race.

Just before the election, my Democratic incumbent opponent Charlie Davis called me and said he was holding a news conference to resign from the office of Justice of the Peace and give up the race to me.

'I have strong reason to believe,' Charlie told me, 'that you're goin' to win. Hell, you've been campaigning like you're runnin' for the United States Senate.'

Not a bad idea, I thought, maybe I will someday.

'I'm gonna call the reporters and tell 'em,' he said, 'I'm gonna tell 'em you're the new JP.'

I was as happy as a clam. The trouble was, his wife wasn't. She was a ranking member of the Dallas County Democratic Party. She liked her husband being the Justice of the Peace, and didn't like the idea of giving up the race, and her place in the party. So, Charlie didn't quit. He later apologized to me for going back on his word. Imagine that, a politician who was truly sorry for going back on his word.

So I had to do all I could on my own, and of course, hope for the best from Barry Goldwater. Unfortunately, Goldwater couldn't keep his mouth shut, and he kept alienating people. That, coupled with the fact that he was running against Texas's number one Democrat and Vice-President Lyndon Johnson, made my political foray short-lived. Or so I thought.

The next day, after the election, while streamers and balloons still floated aimlessly in the headquarters of my campaign, I got a call from Janice Swanson*, head of the Republican Women's Organization. Within a few days, I was meeting with Janice and some of her friends; all ladies, all rich and all very powerful in the party.

'You, sir, are a box of Wheaties,' one of the ladies proclaimed. 'You are a *plain* box of Wheaties! But we will market you! We will get you elected!'

I was somewhat shocked! At the same time, I was intrigued.

113

'Men don't get you elected! *Women* get you elected! We'll teach you what to say, how to say it, and when to say it! And Mr Dear, you *will* go far in this party.'

When I thought about it, I knew they were right. The women of America had elected Kennedy.

For the next six months, these women took me to the parties I needed to go to, the homes I needed to visit, and introduced me to the people I needed to know. Some of these Dallas mansions were unbelievable. And the parties were out of this world. I couldn't believe the money behind all of this. I had new suits bought for me by the women who knew what a groomed candidate should look like. I attended women's lunches and spoke to the ladies who controlled the hearts, minds and genitalia of the most powerful men in Texas. Then I began to notice something I had not experienced since I took off the badge and uniform. Seduction.

Women who were grooming me and showing me off as the next candidate for the state legislature would come up to me and whisper, 'Come here a minute. I want to talk to you.' We'd go into a bedroom and their hands would suddenly be all over me.

Once, during a party of local political supporters, the woman of the house followed me into the bathroom. At first I chuckled politely when I thought she had walked in by mistake. But when she locked the door, I stopped chuckling. She brushed her body against mine as she unzipped my pants and slowly fell to her knees. I knew what was happening. This was going on with her husband not fifty feet beyond the door, entertaining their guests at the party. For some of these rich bitches, that's how they got their thrills; watching as a Congressman or State Senator debated a bill on the floor of the legislature or in the House of Representatives, knowing he had been theirs for a night. I began to feel like a whore.

Finally, one day at a function, a fifty-year-old woman came up to me, a kid in his twenties, and whispered, 'I want you to come over to the house tonight. I have some things I want to talk with you about. And just plan on staying the weekend.'

I knew her husband and I knew he was going to be out of town.

All day long her invitation, delivered up close and reeking of gin, repulsed me. There's nothing worse than an old drunk woman trying to seduce you. I figured I would go over, talk about what political issues she had on her mind, if any, then leave.

I drove to her north Dallas estate, stopped the car and sat there for a moment. It reminded me of the time in Miami when I had to decide between my job or my friendship with the gray-haired old man they called a mobster and his sweet wife. I had always felt a sense of not being true to myself because I chose my job under the pressure of my captain. As I sat in the driveway of that stately Dallas mansion, I wondered about being true to my own convictions. I thought about Washington. I knew it was inevitable. If I just played the game, I could eventually become a United States Senator. I had no doubt! As long as I played the game. Finally, I turned the key in the ignition, drove home, called her and politely offered my regrets and thanked for her invitation for the weekend. The next day, I left the Republican Party and politics for ever.

BILL DEAR'S NOTEPAD: Hotel Dick

There was a sick feeling in the pit of my stomach as I looked around my hotel room to discover I had been burgled. The emotion quickly turned to rage. Forget the loss of valuable equipment. Knowing that some bastard had the gall to violate my privacy made me want to catch him and beat the hell out of him.

I was staying at the Holiday Inn Cascade Center in Akron, Ohio, working on the murder of Dean Milo. A uniformed police officer was hanging about the place, which seemed odd given the fact it was an upscale hotel. Not five-star, but the Cascade Center was a nice enough hotel that one felt one could leave valuables without worry. I quickly learned the police had been hired as a deterrent, because of a rash of burglaries. I told Lieutenant Larry Momchilov that a lot of equipment had been left behind. Perhaps the burglar took what he could in one trip and didn't want to chance any more time and getting caught.

'I think that means he'll be back, Larry,' I speculated. 'Just as soon as I leave in the morning.' I was convinced of it.

The next morning, after breakfast, I met Larry in the lobby and got in his police car as if to leave. But instead of leaving, I went to the back and up to my room through a rear entrance. Once inside, I laid my gun on the bedside table, sat down in a chair and propped my feet up to wait for a burglar. After an hour and a half I began to think maybe I was barking up the wrong tree and the thief wasn't coming back. Finally, I decided to leave and get back to work on the Milo case. But suddenly, I heard the noise. It was a knock on a door several rooms down the hall.

'Bellman!' The voice waited a moment, then I could hear jingling as one key entered the lock to open the door. A few minutes later, I heard the same thing, except a little closer. A few gentle raps on the door.

'Bellman!'

The key was sliding into the lock and the door was opening. A few minutes later the same thing, again, moving ever closer to my room. Finally, after several doors, the voice was outside mine.

(Knock, knock, knock) 'Bellman!'

Not making a sound, I reached over, grabbed my Walther PPK and quietly stepped against the wall behind the door. A moment later the key slid into the lock and the door opened. In walked a young black man in a bellman's uniform, carrying a clipboard. As he cleared the doorway, I leveled the gun at his head.

'No!' he screamed, turning to see the weapon.

'What are you doing?' I demanded.

'I'm checking the rooms to make sure they've been cleaned,' he answered as he stared down the barrel of the gun.

'Well, I don't recognize you,' I replied, 'and I've been here for quite a while.'

'Your name is Dear?' He checked his clipboard.

'Yes.'

He had a number of names on a computer printout on the clipboard, 'I'm really just checking to make sure the room is clean, sir.'

I relaxed and lowered the weapon, 'All right, it's just I was burglarized yesterday.'

'I understand, sir,' he said, 'but I knocked on the door.'

'I know, I heard you.' I was disappointed it wasn't who I was waiting for. Walking over, I laid the gun down on the table as he excused himself and left.

Dammit, I've been here long enough to know everyone at this hotel. Something's just not right. Hey, wait a minute, I thought, bellmen don't check on housekeeping. That's a completely different department of the staff. I grabbed my gun and ran outside. He was running for the elevator.

I ran after him and got to the elevator just as the doors were closing. I jammed my hands between the closing doors with my gun in one of them, trying to force the doors back open. There was only three inches of space between the closing doors. The sonofabitch was inside, pressed against the back wall. I screamed,

'I'm gonna get you, you bastard! I'm gonna get you!' The whole time my gun was pointing right at him.

I couldn't hold the doors and they snapped to as I pulled my hands out of the way. I ran to the stairwell and down the stairs to the lobby. A uniformed police officer was flirting with the front desk clerk.

'Hey you!' I screamed as the thief left the elevator and ran out the door, 'There he goes, I just got hit again!'

The cop took off with me after the bastard. The thief had dropped his clipboard and was in full gallop. We couldn't keep up and he got away, but only for a while.

A few days later, the Akron police caught him. He had people inside several of the hotels helping him. That's how he got the uniforms and walked freely in and out of rooms, casing them until he picked the ones he wanted to hit. I had to hand it to him. It was a great cover. When he came walking in on me it looked legit.

By the next day the story was in the Akron newspaper, PRIVATE EYE GETS BURGLARIZED, complete with a little comic strip. Thank you. Now everyone knew. At least he was caught. Of course, that wasn't the only time I was burglarized.

I once checked in with a lady to a hotel in New Orleans. We left our jewelry, watches and the like in the room while we went to the pool. Just moments after having left the room, I decided to return, only to find all of our jewelry was gone. We had just left! I yelled for security and within moments they arrived.

'They haven't had time to get out of this hotel,' I said. 'They've got to still be here; and it's got to be a bellman or porter or maid.'

We searched the hotel as security kept an eye on the entrances for any hotel staff that might be leaving. It wasn't long before, in a laundry chute on the second floor, we found a towel tied in a knot and hanging just inside the opening where no one would have seen it. I reached down, pulled it out, opened it up and there was all of our jewelry. We never caught who did it.

These days I'm very careful to protect my valuables when I stay in a hotel. Now, I just get mugged at the front desk when I check out.

CHAPTER 7
Howard Hughes Had Nothing on Pete Coffield

One day in 1976, I got a call from an attorney in Rockdale, located east of Austin in the hill country of central Texas.

'Mr Dear,' he began, 'My name is Jerry Forrester*. You've been referred to me by a Dallas lawyer we both know. He says you're honest and do good work, and I have a client that needs some investigative work done. Could you take care of it?'

'Sure,' I answered. 'What do you need?'

'My client would like for you to investigate a young lady by the name of Kay Salisbury*. She owns Kay's Florist in Dallas, just off of Forest Lane near Marsh.'

'Well, what is it that you want to know?' I asked.

'Everything about her. In two weeks. Can you do it?'

'Sure,' I said. 'No problem at all.' It seemed like a fairly normal case.

Over the course of a few days I learned everything there was to know about Ms Salisbury, a very attractive lady in her late thirties with blonde hair and a fairly successful little florist business. It seemed pretty routine, nothing out of the ordinary. That in itself made me wonder why someone wanted her investigated. But mine was not to reason why, mine was just to pay the rent. The rundown on Ms Salisbury was pretty standard, but I was thorough, even though it seemed a little boring.

Once I had compiled all of my information, I called Mr Forrester back and told him I had everything he asked for.

'Fine,' he said. 'Meet me tomorrow morning at eight thirty in the lobby of Cooper Aeromotive at Dallas Love Field. And bring your report so we can go somewhere and review it.'

The next morning I was at Cooper Aeromotive at eight thirty on the dot, watching the dozens of private planes landing and taking off and taxiing to the terminal for service. My attention was caught by the arrival of a Baron twin-prop, a nice-looking plane. Within seconds, the side door flew open and a huge black guy, probably six foot four or five and weighing close to three hundred pounds, stepped out of the aircraft and looked around. Two other guys exited the plane and stood next to the steps. Finally, an older, little guy, standing maybe five foot seven, wearing a fedora like the one Dallas Cowboys Coach Tom Landry always wore, stepped out of the plane, and the group headed for the terminal, slowing down to allow the little guy, who must have been in his late seventies, to keep up.

Once inside, one of the business suits introduced himself as Jerry Forrester.

We shook hands cordially, and soon the others, including the pilot, had introduced themselves, all except the little guy. He didn't say a word to me. 'Do you have the report?' Jerry asked.

'Yes, sir.'

'Great. Let's just go to a motel and look at it.'

Within a few minutes we were checked into a room at a Ramada Inn near the airport, spreading out copies of my report on the table. There were dates and times and certificates and pictures all over the place. I had done a thorough investigation on Ms Salisbury, which included the fact that she was married with children.

The old guy, who still hadn't said a word, sat on the edge of the bed, staring at my report.

'Here's the information on her bank account and home and marriage certificate.'

'Take me to all these places,' he suddenly said. 'Show me her business and home and so forth.'

As we got up to leave, Jerry pulled me aside and said, 'Mr Dear, how much do we owe you for the report?'

Bill Dear: the public image

Rookie Cop: the young dispatcher, Florida Highway Patrol

Shaking hands with Richard Nixon

The Glen Courson case: police scene-of-crime photograph

The murder weapon, with the cracked stock clearly visible

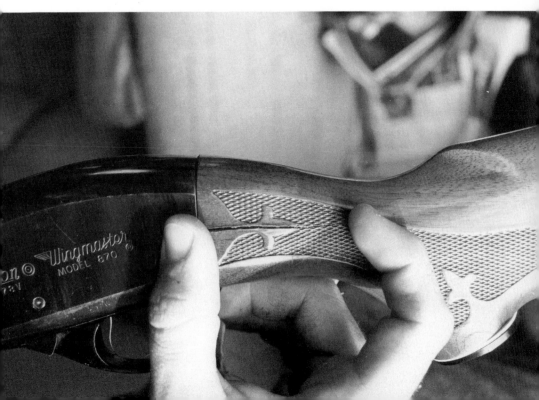

The Courson case: testing out hypotheses in the alley

With the Medical Examiner, testing the trajectory of the shotgun pellets

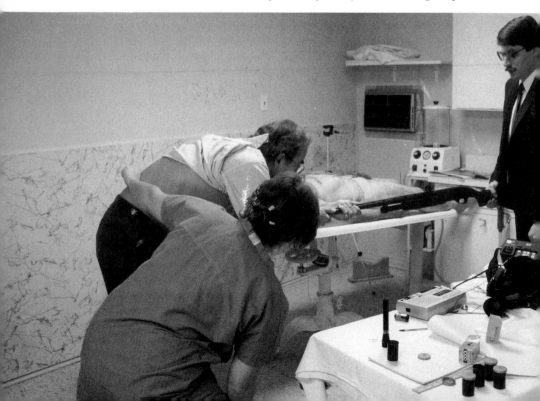

Cherie Ann Kennedy comes home: at left, her parents Andy and Penny

Standing godfather to Cherie Ann

Safe at last: arriving at Dallas/Fort Worth airport with Guinevere

The successful private investigator at home

Bill Dear: the private image

HOWARD HUGHES HAD NOTHING ON PETE COFFIELD

'Five thousand dollars.'

In a second, the briefcase one of the men was carrying was on the bed and open, exposing what must have been a hundred thousand dollars in cash.

'Sign this receipt, please.'

I signed, the money was peeled off, the briefcase was slammed shut and the keeper of the briefcase snapped his charge back into his protective grasp.

Then we all left and took a little tour of some of the sights of Dallas that centered around the life of one Kay Salisbury. After a couple of hours and a lot of driving through some beautiful Dallas neighborhoods the old guy spoke up. 'Take me back to the airport.'

So, I wheeled around and started making my way back to Love Field. On the way, the old guy began to talk.

'How long have you been in business?'

'About ten years,' I answered.

'I hope what you've told me here is the truth.'

I said, 'You can count on that, sir. I'll only tell you one thing and that'll be the truth.' I never asked him why he wanted to know all about Kay Salisbury, but I was sure curious.

After we arrived back at the airport, Jerry asked me to wait for them while they went to the upper level of the terminal at Cooper. So with nothing better to do I began talking with the black guy, named Whitey, and the pilot.

'Who is this guy?' I asked.

'He's one of the wealthiest men in the world,' Whitey answered.

'He's very powerful in politics, used to be the Secretary of the Democratic Party,' added the pilot.

'Used to tell Lyndon Johnson when to kiss his ass,' Whitey went on. 'He's on the Board of Directors of Prisons and Parole, got ranches all over the place, homes everywhere, hunting facilities like you wouldn't believe and he lives in Rockdale.'

Suddenly, as we were talking, a car pulled up to a screeching halt and out jumped that same damned lady I had been investigating – Kay Salisbury herself! She ran upstairs where the men were meeting and walked right in.

'Boy,' the pilot moaned, 'am I glad I'm not you.'

'Why?' I asked.

'Oh, hell, that's the boss's girlfriend.'

'What!'

'That's the boss's girlfriend,' he repeated.

'Oh, shit!' I exclaimed as I looked back up to the second level of the terminal. 'And I was the one who told him she was married.'

We could hear a lot of commotion coming from the second level, people yelling and a woman's voice yelling right back. Within a few minutes, the door opened and out stepped Jerry.

'Mr Dear,' he called downstairs, 'would you come up here?'

I didn't know what to expect as I walked into the room. But there sat the old man and the young woman at a table, with his associates standing nearby. The expressions on everyone's faces coincided with the hellacious argument we could hear all the way downstairs. Obviously, a temporary ceasefire had been called long enough to bring me into battle.

'Mr Dear,' Jerry asked formally, staring at Ms Salisbury, 'would you please tell us what you've found in your investigation?'

'Yeah, you sonofabitch!' Ms Salisbury's first words to me indicated her beauty was maybe only skin deep. 'What did you tell them about me?' She turned on the old guy, 'And you, you fuckin' little bastard! What do you mean having me investigated?'

Damn, I thought, this woman seemed to be so nice; selling flowers and all. I watched for a moment, somewhat entertained, as she ranted and raved, not getting much of a stir from anyone. Except me.

'Hold on lady!' I leaned over the table, resting on my hands, 'I've heard about all the shit I'm going to hear from you! I don't know what's going on here, but I'm gonna tell you right now, you're hollering at this man for something you did.' Her face went pale and her mouth dropped open like no one had ever talked to her like this before; and maybe they hadn't, but I didn't give a damn.

'Number one,' I said, 'You're married. Number two, you've obviously told this man that you're not. And number three, you won't talk to me that way. I don't give a damn who you are!'

I could tell that the old man's associates were about to have a heart attack. Yet the old man hadn't flinched. Not a word. So I continued.

'You know, Ms Salisbury, if you had told the truth I wouldn't have ended up investigating you. And if I had investigated you and you'd told the truth, then the truth is all that would've come out. Apparently you've been lying to this man all along, so don't be putting on this dog and pony routine up here for us because I ain't impressed, lady! You are what you are!'

She was furious! Her face was so flushed I thought she would explode all over us. Finally, after the room had stopped reverberating from my yelling, she stood up, grabbed her purse and stormed out. Jerry said, 'Mr Dear, why don't you wait downstairs.'

Perhaps Whitey and the pilot were professional enough not to ask, at least until things cooled down, or perhaps they were just too scared to ask what happened. But it was obvious to them the bomb had been dropped. I think they were smart enough to mind their own business. We didn't say much for several minutes, just exchanged a little small talk about planes and the day. Actually, I think they were finally working around to asking about the loud meeting when the door on the upper level opened again, and Jerry stepped out and called me back up.

This time the old man did the talking.

'How would you like to work for me?'

'Beg pardon?' I asked.

'How would you like to work for me?'

For some reason, my mind's video player punched up the scene from *It's a Wonderful Life,* when Old Man Potter asked George Bailey to go to work for him. But this was definitely different. This old guy had a heart.

I asked what he wanted me to do.

'Just handle all of my investigation work and be available to me when I call you.'

'Well, sir, I'm sorry,' I answered, 'but I'm not in the habit of taking things off people and I don't think I could work for you and take anything off you either.'

'You won't take anything off me,' he corrected. 'Hell, son, I could tell you don't take crap, so it probably wouldn't do me any good to try and make you. Besides, I like your style. But, no, you won't be taking anything off me. Just do my investigation work.'

I thought Jerry and the other guy, who turned out to be John McCready*, his business manager, were going to have a coronary right there.

I told the old man what I would charge and he agreed to the rather expensive fee without batting an eye. I figured he could afford it. But even more important, given what I had just witnessed, I figured I would be earning my money. Every cent. Besides, if he wasn't serious, he could say the fee was too high, back out and no one would have any hard feelings.

'Just be available whenever I call,' he said.

Then I *knew* my fee was justified.

That was the beginning of one of the most interesting relationships I ever had. For almost four years I was H. H. 'Pete' Coffield's confidential aide. He would ask my advice, listen to my opinion and generally treat me like his own son.

Pete Coffield was an interesting old guy; a salvage collector that many people called an industrialist. Some people called him a fanatic. He didn't just collect old junk, he collected everything: art, coins, antiques, everything. And that stuff was spread all over warehouses across the state of Texas. He had property everywhere, it seemed. All of it was usually surrounded by glistening chainlink fences.

Coffield got his start selling old army surplus items in small towns all over Texas during the twenties and thirties. He would go into a town on a Saturday and start selling until he got arrested for some weak charge like peddling without a license. The truth of the matter was that he was taking business away from local merchants, right under their noses in a city square or small merchant center of the town. After the arrest and the fine, Coffield would leave, only to return the next weekend, always selling his army surplus goods and building a vast fortune.

Most of his early money was invested in real estate all over Texas. Land values were going up and his investments were sure to grow in value. But they weren't just ordinary plots of land. Many times, they were in very good locations for the future. Coffield had a knack for determining where the best land for future development was located. He sold some of his land to the Alcoa Aluminium Company for a tidy sum and even made a deal on land that would eventually become the site for the Glen Rose Nuclear Power Plant south of Fort Worth.

As his fortune grew, so did his clout. He became a very powerful leader behind the scenes in the Democratic Party, financing some of the state's most famous candidates for office. He bankrolled Lyndon B. Johnson all the way to the White House and dragged a string of other politicos along to boot. He certainly had the means to do it. It's believed he was worth over $900 million when he died in 1979. He was the epitome of the Texas millionaire. I had never been around such power. I knew as I left Cooper Aeromotive that this would be no ordinary job.

The next morning I received a call from Coffield, telling me to meet him at Cooper Aeromotive that morning. I drove him to Chez Ames*, one of the city's most exclusive restaurants, catering to the most influential business people and politicians in the state. The Antonelli*family, which owned the posh restaurant, had two sons who served time for armed bank robbery, and were widely suspected of having Mafia connections. People of questionable reputation from New York, Chicago and Detroit were in the restaurant about as often as the locals, although celebrities like sportscaster Howard Cosell and actress Dyan Cannon could frequently be seen dining there as well.

The first day I drove him to Chez Ames, he sat at a special table in the corner, I sat at a nearby table and my staff waited outside to watch for any trouble. As a member of the Board of Parole in Texas, he was as dangerous to sit next to as he was powerful. I quickly learned why he had Whitey with him. He had two Bloody Marys before lunch, a filet of sole for the entrée and another two or three Bloody Marys. As it turned out, that's what he had for lunch every *day*. Soon he insisted I sit with him at his table. It was a long way from eating at the back door.

Coffield soon told me he had decided to take the Salisbury

woman back. She was a soft spot in this ruthless businessman's life, something of a weakness I'd seen in a lot of rich and powerful men. They can rule worlds, yet a woman like Salisbury can control them by the groin. It wasn't any of my business whether he took her back. And he had assured me that I wouldn't have to listen to any of her crap. But how this old man kept up with her I'll never know. Vitamins, I guess.

It would be the same routine every day. After lunch I would take Coffield to a Ramada Inn near the airport and park in back. Sometimes his age, or more specifically his gout, would overcome him and he would ask me to pick him up and lay him in the bed in the reserved room where they would have sex. Then I would wait outside until they were finished.

Salisbury was given gifts of furs and diamonds worth thousands upon thousands of dollars; I know, because I signed the checks for Coffield. She was also given a lot of cash. On countless occasions I held briefcases full of money; thousands of dollars in cold hard cash. Much of it came from companies he did business with, payoff money for his many multibillion dollar deals.

The man would walk around with huge sums in his pockets. Every once in a while I would be standing next to him when he pulled out a wad of money for something and drop a large, and I mean large, bill on the floor. I could easily have pocketed it. But I couldn't steal from this nice old fellow. He would smile appreciatively, thank me and wad the money back in his pocket. When I think about it now, I wonder if, perhaps, the old guy wasn't as absent-minded or nearsighted as I thought. Maybe that's how he found out just who was honest with him and who wasn't; for him, a very inexpensive way of finding out.

It wasn't long at all before Pete Coffield and I became close friends. I could see I was stepping on the toes of his inner circle, particularly Jerry Forrester and John McCready. It didn't seem to take long before I was getting the cold shoulder.

Coffield had two ranches where he would take his friends and business associates and to go hunting. One ranch was spread over 100,000 acres in East Texas. It had a runway and control tower for his airplane and featured about forty deerblinds on the ranch, each with its own jeep. The main house was, as one might expect, a big, beautiful affair with all the comforts. There were also comfortable bunkhouses on the ranch, designed for guests.

I would often fly to the ranch with Coffield and greet his many guests with him as they flew into the small private airport. There were senators, judges and captains of industry from all over the world, invited for these spectacular hunts. The first time I was invited to a hunt by Coffield, I was on board the plane with Dan Eddy, who at the time was the public relations executive for the Salvation Army. Later, Eddy would become a Justice of the Peace in Oak Cliff, an old district in South Dallas. During the flight, Eddy looked over to me and asked, 'Who are you?'

'I'm nobody,' I answered, hoping to ride incognito until I knew more about this man in the seat beside me.

'Well,' he said dryly, as he turned back in his seat, 'if you stay in the house you're somebody.'

Sure enough, when I arrived Coffield asked me to stay in the house with his closest friends. Dan Eddy, it turned out, was assigned to one of the bunkhouses. It wasn't that they were uncomfortable; they were the nicest bunkhouses I had ever seen on a ranch. But they were a place of somewhat lesser status, where the associates and sidekicks of the people Coffield was really entertaining would stay.

Later, during the hunt, I ran into Eddy. He smiled and said, 'Looks to me like you *are* somebody. I've even heard you're Pete Coffield's son.'

That was said to me often.

Once, an ex-girlfriend of Coffield's planned to have him kidnapped. It was my job to keep my eyes open for anything that could be trouble. I found out about the ex-girlfriend's plan, so I checked her out. She was living in an apartment down in Houston.

One night I went to her apartment complex. She was very surprised when she opened the door and I said, 'I'm telling you now, you won't do it. I take care of Mr Coffield,' I added in a low intimidating voice, staring her down, 'and I know all about your plan. This is the last time you'll see me and the last time I expect to see you or hear of any plans of yours to hurt Coffield.'

She swallowed hard. 'You're Pete Coffield's son,' she whispered, 'I've heard about you.'

I didn't answer. I just turned and walked away. We never heard from her again.

Despite his years, Coffield had a string of ex-girlfriends. Most just took it for what it was worth, a good time and some wonderful gifts. Some took it differently. One girl left a note expressing her sorrow at falling in love with Coffield, put a gun barrel in her mouth and pulled the trigger.

Coffield loved to be in the thick of things. Once there was an uprising at the Texas State Prison. A group of Hispanic inmates had taken several prisoners hostage and were using them as human shields. The Texas Rangers were called in. So was Coffield. As a member of the Commission on Prison and Paroles, he knew the Rangers could handle the situation. These guys had a long history of 'tough'.

Once a Texas Ranger armed himself with a couple of shotguns and a service revolver on the docks of Galveston and faced an angry mob of striking longshoremen, one of the most daring standoffs in Texas history. He told the mob that they could all certainly kill him, but that he was armed with enough firepower to take out a bunch of them before he died. It was just up to them. After a few minutes, the mob dispersed. Cooler heads prevailed and the strike was negotiated to a settlement.

The Galveston Police Chief asked the Ranger why he didn't wait for other Rangers to back him up. The big Ranger turned to the chief with very little emotion in his deep voice and simply said, 'One riot. One Ranger.' Then left. There's a monument to that particular Ranger in the lobby of Dallas Airport.

So, once the Rangers arrived, it was just a matter of time before the prison uprising was resolved. But not before the stupid inmates tried to take on the law. The hostages were saved, the inmates died. One day while on a hunt with Coffield and a group of his famous friends, he pointed to a big fellow with a shotgun slung across his arm and said, 'Remember that prison uprising?'

'Yes sir,' I replied.

'Remember the Ranger that took out the ringleader and brought the trouble to a halt?'

'Yes sir,' I answered again.

Coffield, still holding his crooked old finger out in the direction of the guest hunter, turned his head to me and said, 'That's the Ranger.'

The man had cold steely eyes. Deadman Eyes someone called them.

One day at lunch Coffield turned to me and said, 'Kay wants to go to Vegas.' So naturally, I rounded up all the staff and off we went. He had purchased a larger airplane, an MU-2. So the flight to Vegas was quite comfortable.

Once we got there, everyone except Coffield and me sat at a table and gambled. We hadn't been there two hours before Coffield turned to me and said, 'Let's go.' He was like that. Again I rounded up the staff and we were on our way again, back to Dallas. No happy campers this time.

The problem with Coffield I soon learned, was that he was on heavy medication. He was being given shots of morphine in his arms and legs, sometimes as many as six or eight times a day. He was addicted to the stuff, but it kept him going.

Coffield was a man who slept only a few hours a day and worked seven days a week. Which meant I worked seven days a week. He didn't believe in holidays; not even Christmas. So there was no vacation time, just work. And if you didn't like it, you didn't work for Pete Coffield.

I would eat lunch with him everyday in Dallas, Monday through Saturday and have brunch with him on Sunday. Whether Salisbury was with him or not, I was. Eventually, he and I became so close, we would talk about his private business. We discussed problems with his staff in great detail. Coffield felt Forrester and McCready were stealing from him. Not only that . . . .Once he said that if anything ever happened to him by accident, like falling down the stairs, he wanted me to investigate the matter because he figured it would be no accident.

On several occasions he sent the plane for me and we would

meet somewhere privately. Other times, we would meet with his entire entourage along, and I could feel the mental knives they were throwing at me.

Once I flew to a private airport near Houston and met his plane coming in from Rockdale. His entourage of Whitey, Forrester, McCready* and Davis*, the pilot, were with him. We had several cars waiting to take us to a luncheon in Houston. As we started to pile into the cars, he told Forrester and McCready to ride in another car, he and I were riding alone. When we arrived at the luncheon he was led to the head table as the guest of honor. Forrester and McCready followed us, but Coffield stopped them.

'Bill's gonna sit at my right at the head table,' he said without much concern for etiquette. 'Ya'll find another table to sit at.'

Coffield had lost his son to suicide some years before and his wife, who was an invalid, had recently died. Perhaps I was a substitute for the family he couldn't have. Maybe it was because I didn't always stand with my hand out. Maybe it was because he knew he could trust me. Anyhow, Coffield later told me he wanted his fortune to go to me because he knew I would continue to make his fortune grow. We were a lot alike. We both started with nothing and climbed our way to the top.

Despite the fact he was a ruthless man, Coffield had a heart, even though he was very frugal. One day he called me and told me he was coming to my place to visit. I made him breakfast while he played with my son Michael, who was about ten at the time. While he and Coffield talked, Coffield pulled out a ten-dollar bill and gave it to Michael. Michael put it on the table and looked at me.

'Dad,' he whispered, 'what do I do?'

'Just wait a minute, son.'

About half an hour later, as Coffield was getting ready to leave, thinking no one was looking, he reached down and picked up the ten-dollar bill, put it back in his pocket and replaced it with a dollar.

At one point, Whitey, Davis and I were going to get together and take Coffield down to one of his ranches, place guards in the towers and seal off the area, in the hope of getting Coffield off the morphine and out from under the influence of some in his organization. Howard Hughes and his organization had nothing on Coffield. Whitey was really interested in helping me because he loved Coffield like a father, despite the way Coffield treated him. But someone squealed on us and the plan didn't come together.

A few weeks later, Coffield told me to get a lawyer to draw up the papers making me the heir to his fortune. I contacted Al Ellis, a Dallas attorney, and told him what Coffield wanted. As the papers were being drawn up, I received a call at one or two o'clock in the morning. It was Coffield.

'Bill, they woke me up to sign some papers.'

'What kind of papers, Pete?'

'I don't know what kind, Bill.'

Several hours later, after sunrise, Jerry Forrester called to tell me that Coffield had signed some papers giving Forrester, McCready and Coffield's private secretary, Miss Bogner*, Power of Attorney. He said 'Now we have control, and we'll do things our way if you want to ever see him again.'

I felt if I didn't go along with them, there was nothing they wouldn't do. My vulnerability was my young son. Before I gave up I negotiated some agreements. For one thing, they were to cut out the injections. It was agreed. Coffield was then allowed to come back and visit with me, never knowing I would not be the heir or even the executor of his estate.

One day Coffield came to visit me and his hand was badly infected. I took him to a specialist at the Irving Hospital who examined the hand, then x-rayed it and finally filled out some paperwork for Coffield to take back to his own doctor. After Coffield got back to Rockdale, I received a call from Forrester and McCready, chewing my ass out for taking Coffield to another physician. They threatened not to let him come back, but I calmed them down by agreeing not to interfere in his medical care again.

It wasn't long though, before Coffield deteriorated and had to be hospitalized. The last few times I visited him, he was so incoherent he made no sense at all. Drugs again?

He had long since begun to have difficulty remembering. For

131

about a year before he died, I would watch as people came toward him at the Chez Ames, governors, senators and the like. I would stand up, politely hold up my hand for them to stop some distance from the table, then I would whisper in his ear, 'Pete, this is Governor so and so' or 'This is Senator whomever' so Coffield wouldn't embarrass himself by not knowing someone he had placed in a powerful position or done business with in the past. As I look back, I think his condition was due totally to the drugs. During our last few meetings in his hospital room, my mind went back to all those times in the restaurant, then to earlier times when he was sharp, witty and took nothing off no one.

Within a few months of our last meeting in his hospital room, Coffield died, allegedly of pneumonia. But I firmly believe he died of drug abuse.

During his life, Coffield gave money to charities like nobody's business – except his own. The problem is several years after his death, three charities each still have documents indicating Coffield meant for each of them to have his entire estate.

His estate's holdings were managed by Forrester and McCready, including hunting leases Coffield is alleged to have left for his friends and lawyers to use for twenty years after his death. And the documentation for those agreements is signed with an 'X' in the spot where Coffield was to have signed. Forrester swears it's Coffield's mark, claiming he witnessed the old man signing agreements and that he used an 'X' because his ability to write was severely hampered by disease. I wasn't the only one that was suspicious of the whole matter of Coffield's signatures. Family members challenged the various documents, especially the ones with 'X' marks for signatures, saying that Coffield was on so much medication at the time, he didn't know what he was signing. But one by one each of their claims were dropped when out-of-court cash settlements were offered. Coffield's own money may have kept the truth buried with him.

In the meantime, Jerry Forrester has a big beautiful home, Davis has a new plane to fly and Whitey still works for the estate. Recently, during some of the questioning surrounding Coffield's death and will, I wrote a letter to then Texas Attorney-General

Jim Mattox indicating I could shed light on the matter from a perspective no one has; that he was worth a lot more than most believed. I believed Coffield's cause of death should be investigated as a possible murder. If his body was exhumed and an autopsy performed, I knew the results would open some interesting avenues to be explored. The Attorney-General never answered and has since been voted out of office. One of the Assistant Attorney-Generals was a close friend of Jerry Forrester.

Despite the controversy surrounding Coffield's death, despite the people who crowded his life and, in the end, made it miserable, and despite the questions that may never be answered about Pete Coffield, I know just one thing. Howard Hughes had nothing on H. H. 'Pete' Coffield.

BILL DEAR'S NOTEPAD: The Big Hose

It was a pretty South Florida day in 1960. My partner and I were sitting in a squad car near the city limits of Miami, talking of his training as a new, young deputy with the Dade County Sheriff's Office. As a police officer, you're somewhat surprised when you look up and see a car scream by doing ninety to nothing, with total disregard for the speed limit or your presence. But it happens! And every time it does you and your partner look at each other with unspoken expressions of mild shock as you step on the accelerator and hit the lights and siren. You'd think most people would have better sense than to fly past a police car like they were trying to break the land speed record.

As we gained on the vehicle, we could tell there was a woman driving. Though she had obviously not seen us before, when she finally looked in the mirror she wasted no time in pulling over. My partner got out of the driver's side and I got out to watch the passenger side, in case another individual, hidden in the car, came rolling out with a gun. This is standard procedure every two-man team employs to this day. The lady was fidgeting with her blouse and skirt as my young trainee approached her.

'Where's the fire, lady?' he barked as he pulled his citation book and pen from his pocket.

'In between my legs, Officer,' she replied without missing a beat, 'got a hose big enough to put it out?'

His jaw dropped. Her blouse was unbuttoned and her skirt was hiked up so far there was nothing left for the imagination. I had seen the routine a dozen times or more, as had most veteran police officers. Some women would do anything to avoid a ticket.

My partner looked at me across the car as I covered my face to laugh. Our female perpetrator was still gazing into his young face with a Marilyn Monroe look.

'Don't look at me,' I laughed (and I never laughed at a police

134

officer in front of a citizen, but I couldn't help myself), 'you got yourself into this, you can get yourself out of it.'

By now the lady knew she was getting off scot-free, and was enjoying the repartee. My young trainee's face was growing so red I thought he would explode. He went through the motions of looking at her license and registration. Then he took a deep breath and returned them saying, 'Ma'am, you've made my day. Please drive carefully.'

She winked as she leaned into the steering wheel and turned the ignition. The rookie cleared his throat, composed himself, returned his citation book and pen to his pocket, and marched back to the car. I spent the next half hour chuckling under my breath every time I looked at his young embarrassed face.

Finally, confident that I would not crack up, I looked at him seriously and said, 'Now, what have you learned today about addressing a citizen in the proper manner, Deputy?'

'I don't know, sir,' he replied.

Struggling not to laugh, I said, 'Never leave the car without your big hose, sir.'

CHAPTER 8
The Woman Who Kidnapped Herself

I awoke to the sound of the phone ringing on my bedside table. It was about sunrise on Sunday April 27, 1980. Though I was sound asleep, the ringing brought me around as suddenly and as wide awake as if I'd been up for several hours. The voice on the other end of the line told me that the head flight nurse for Alpha Aviation, one Jean Reynolds*, was missing and foul play was suspected; perhaps a kidnapping. Though the Dallas Police Department had been alerted, Alpha Aviation was extremely worried that Jean had been snatched because of her access to narcotics. I could well understand their concern.

Soon I was driving out of my estate, past the tennis courts I had planned on using that day. It was a typically beautiful spring day in North Texas, but I wouldn't enjoy much of it; I would be working. My destination was 2518 North Garrett in Dallas, right on the city's eastern edge. I was to meet the officials of Alpha Aviation.

A thirty-five-year-old divorcee with no children, Jean was studying for her Master's Degree in nursing from Texas Women's University in Denton, north of Dallas. It took me about forty minutes to get to the Garrett Street address.

I reviewed what little information I had so far. Alpha operated emergency helicopter ambulances. Jean had been with Alpha for quite a while, so the company knew her well. She had an adrenal gland disorder that required regular medication and the company

136

had already expressed concern for her medical condition. They feared her abductor might not be aware of or even concerned for her health once he got what he needed, be it money or drugs. So far no ransom note had been received by anyone, but that wasn't unusual. It had only been twenty-four hours since Jean had been reported missing; most ransom notes come only after the loved ones have had time to go out of their minds with fear and uncertainty and are ready to do anything for the safe return of the victim. Kidnapping is a crime rooted in mental terrorism as much as anything else.

I arrived at the Garrett Street address, an area of town that used to be quite fashionable, but had long since declined. The predominantly homosexual neighborhood was made up of one-storey framed residences, accented with a few old apartment complexes. Bill Block, the head of Alpha, was to meet me along with his assistant. I stood for a moment in front of Jean's home, mulling over a few other things I had learned during my brief phone call earlier.

A co-worker of Jean's, Ron Wood, had come by when Jean didn't show up for work. He saw the Saturday newspapers spread out across the couch as if someone had been reading them, then left for just a moment. A pot of coffee still simmered on the kitchen stove. Sunday's newspaper still lay untouched on the lawn. Huh, I used to always hit the porch when I threw newspapers. Sloppy. Jean's car, a Toyota, was still parked in the garage.

I was still waiting for Bill to arrive, so I decided to check with neighbors about anything they might have seen. Many of them, quietly going about their Sunday morning routines, getting ready for church, jogging or walking the dog, said they had noticed dogs barking on Saturday morning. A few thought they saw a vehicle backing out of Jean's driveway, but couldn't recall a clear description or license plate number.

I walked back to Jean's house just as Bill and his assistant arrived with Ron Wood in tow. Bill decided we should see if we could get inside Jean's house. Naturally, we tried the front door, as if it would just be left unlocked. It was. Strange. But Ron said that was just how he found it.

The house was in disarray, more so than if a family had been living in the house. It was just plain messy. It wasn't that things were dirty, just scattered about. It was hard to tell if a struggle had occurred because of the disorder. The coffee pot was still on the stove, though the heat had been cut off when Ron first came by the day before and discovered Jean missing. Paper was still in her typewriter holding a partially written paragraph. Her school books were open to the pages she had been studying; one was lying on her bed, which was unmade.

According to Ron, Jean suffered from a surgically induced case of Addison's disease which required a daily dose of cortisone. A check of her refrigerator indicated her medicine was still there. Ron and Bill became very concerned. I decided it was time to talk with the police investigators and asked them to meet me there.

The two officers said they searched the place from top to bottom and couldn't find anything. As we walked through the house, my second tour, we came to an attic door in the ceiling. I pulled the cord down and revealed a collapsing ladder leading into the dark cavern above that reeked of mildew. They said they had searched the attic, but I climbed the staircase anyway and shone my flashlight beam around its contents. I thought of searching it more thoroughly, but the men assured me that several officers, including detectives, had searched the attic completely and found nothing. So I climbed back down and lifted the spring loaded door up to close the entrance.

Perhaps it's my own experience as a patrol officer, but I feel that the uniformed men first called out to the scene of a crime are the closest to the actual evidence. Then I pick the brains of the detectives. I want to know who anyone, patrol or plainclothes detectives, talked with. Then I talk with those people as well. The system is good because it double-checks and picks up the small fragmented pieces of evidence that often fall through the bureaucratic cracks, evidence that can make or break a case. I've also found that people will talk with me rather than with the police.

I proceeded to canvass that old neighborhood, looking for anything. In the meantime, still no ransom note or communication from Jean or the kidnapper. It was as if Jean Reynolds had just vanished from the face of the earth.

On Thursday, I returned to Jean's house. Her doctor had told me if she hadn't taken her medication after several days, she could have easily died. I walked into her home, opened the refrigerator door and saw the medication untouched. Was she dead? I slammed the door and stood there in the absolute quiet of that house. The silence was overwhelming. I couldn't shake this funny, eerie feeling I had had since the first time I walked into the house, as if she was alive, though not really.

I noticed something very strange. Her dog never seemed to be upset that I or anyone else came in. I couldn't put my finger on it, but something didn't add up. Suddenly the silence was shattered by the shrill ringing of the phone. Without a second thought, I picked up the receiver.

'Hello.'

Nothing. No breathing. No background noise. Nothing. Then the phone clicked and my ear was filled with the dial tone.

I walked into her bedroom and sat down in a chair next to the bed. I glanced through some of her textbooks and found the material complex and mindboggling. I'm sure she understood the technical nature of the medical books, but I could tell, just from some of her notes and doodles, that even she was having difficulty. Jean appeared to be a dedicated professional. She was smart and always striving to know more. I learned she had many friends and they liked her a great deal. She didn't date anyone in particular. She was divorced, but on good terms with her ex-husband. She was close to her family and seemed to be a caring person. I checked her bank account and found that no money was missing nor was she involved in anything that led me to believe she was selling drugs or laundering drug money. She seemed normal in every way but one. She seemed to spend an inordinate amount of time alone. Something about that bothered me.

People who work with severely injured patients, such as burn victims from a disaster site, as Jean did, have a tremendous amount of pressure on them. They suffer with their patients. They know the reason they were called was to save a life the only way possible, and that patients are depending entirely on them. It's a big responsibility. Jean was charged with drug and equipment purchasing and remained on call twenty-four hours a day. To say it's a stressful job would be an understatement. That stress was not good for her precarious health.

Like the police and the officials of Alpha, I thought it possible that she was abducted to gain access to drugs. I also thought someone might have become infatuated with this nice-looking woman and kidnapped her. But why no ransom note? And why, if someone was infatuated with her, would they not consider her medical condition and let her get her medication from her home? As I thought of her health, I watched the clock in her bedroom tick away the moments. Each second we didn't find Jean pushed her closer to death, one way or another. Tick. Tick. Tick.

The thought suddenly occurred to me that someone who had a loved one die while on a chopper with Jean's team might be seeking revenge by kidnapping, and maybe even killing Jean. It wouldn't be the first time something like that has happened. For a few moments, the ticking clock held me in a trance as it seemed to grow louder and louder with each tick. I finally came back to myself. I looked down at the unmade bed and decided to collect the sheets into a bundle and have them searched for evidence of human hair or secretions that did not match Jean's in case someone may have tried to sexually assault her. I walked out of the room, the sheets in a bundle and the clock still ticking away.

I became fixated with finding her. Each time I glanced at my watch, no matter where I was or what I was doing, the second hand seemed to tick as loud as her bedroom clock. It told me I was running out of time. I talked to neighbors again. I interviewed friends and acquaintances over and over during the few days. I repeatedly went back to her house and sat in the chair beside her bed looking at her room, noticing how hectic her life was, always on call, always in a hurry. I played with her dog, and still couldn't figure out why the pooch didn't seem to mind me being there. I went over every piece of evidence I could find, even the physical evidence from the bedsheets. Nothing indicated that anyone else had been in her bed. Each time I sat in the room, the clock ticked so loud in my head I thought I would go crazy. I had to find Jean, I *had* to find her. And still, no ransom note. What did they want?

I began having dreams, though they were vague. She just made brief, almost cameo appearances as my subconcious tried to put some order to the evidence. Then, as it had when the case began, my phone rang at 5 a.m. on Saturday, May 3rd, one week after Jean disappeared. She had been found. They had dumped her over the fence at the back of her property, but she was back and alive.

I jumped out of bed, dressed, raced to the Garrett Street address and met Jean Reynolds for the first time. She understood who I was and we talked. Though very tired, she told me exactly what had happened. She said she had gone to the grocery store Saturday afternoon and was abducted on the way home. She told me her abductors had knocked her out, and when she awoke she was in a bare room in what she believed was an out-of-the-way area of Dallas. She said that for a week the only sounds she heard were from distant automobile traffic and a helicopter that flew by. The heat, she claimed, was exhausting in that little room. The only nourishment she received was a few packages of cheese and peanut butter crackers, a few packages of peanuts, a small box of raisins, a roll of Lifesavers and a candy bar. Her water was rationed. But she could not describe her kidnappers; the junk food was always just left for her.

Her return was just as strange.

'I woke up in the trunk of a car,' she said in a quiet voice, 'wrapped in a blanket. The fumes from the exhaust made me pass out. But a while later I felt them lift me out and throw me over the fence. I didn't know where I was at first, then I heard my dog barking. I could tell it was Teddy barking and I knew I was home.'

I felt great! We had her back. I no longer heard the ticking of the clock.

A little worse for wear; her hair was matted, and her clothes were rumpled and smelly. But she was back! We had her taken to Parkland Hospital and checked. She had a few minor scrapes and bruises, but she was okay, and so was I. For a while.

Something was bothering me about this whole thing. I didn't

want to admit it at first, because I was just happy she was back and alive. But something else replaced the ticking. Something did not add up.

Jean was brought back to her house from the hospital around nine thirty in the morning. A news conference had been called for noon. The press had been closely following the story of the missing nurse. I went out back where she said she had been thrown over the fence and looked around. The uncut grass still appeared pressed down where her body would have laid. Police investigators arrived to talk with Jean before the media got there. She told them the same story she told me. And later when the media arrived she relayed the story a third time as she lay in her bed sipping orange juice for nourishment. The news conference was the typical three-ring circus of jostling stupid questions. I sat in the back, out of limelight, and watched Jean. The story sounded good. It didn't change at all. But something just wasn't right.

Later, as the media packed up and left, I walked outside and talked with a few of the detectives. It was another beautiful spring day in Dallas and I was looking forward to wrapping this case up and perhaps salvaging some of the day with a game of tennis. I walked a few feet from the house and looked up at the clear blue sky. I glanced over to the roof line of the old frame house and, for some reason, noticed the slats just under the eaves in the gable of the roof line that allowed ventilation to the attic area. I had seen them before when we began the investigation and had looked over the house for clues of entry or evidence of disturbance. But for some reason, they didn't appear as they had before. The slats seemed to be turned differently, as if they had been opened further to allow more air into the attic. At first I just blew off the observation; after all Jean was back now, what the hell difference did it make how a set of slats in an attic were turned. Then I remembered. I hadn't gone into the attic, but had taken the word of the police officer that the attic had been checked. Just as soon as I remembered that, I recalled the scrapes and bruises on Jean's arms, legs and around her neck that had been treated at Parkland.

I didn't pursue my hunch at the time. Bill Block asked me to prepare my bill and send it to him. I had the bill made out, but I hand-delivered it to him and told him I wasn't sure about some things concerning the case and I wanted to check them out further. Though he seemed to think it was fine, I knew that I was on my own and not getting paid from that point on. I had considered maybe that so much attention to the case from me and the media had persuaded the kidnappers to return Jean. But that still didn't quite add up.

I contacted Jean's parents when she was returned and they were naturally elated. They had decided to come to Dallas from Iowa to be with their daughter. I knew she was in good hands with her family and friends around her. But within a few hours of their arrival at Jean's house, her parents received a number of phone calls like the one I had received that day standing in her house. The phone would ring and no one would be on the line. They became disturbed and decided to take Jean back to Iowa.

I wanted to talk to Jean alone. Even though her story sounded fine, and all of her friends, family and even the media bought it, I didn't. A few days after Jean and her folks were back home I arranged with her parents to meet at the Eppley Field Airport Inn in Omaha, Nebraska. They agreed to drive in from Woodvine, Iowa with Jean.

When I arrived, her ex-husband, an attorney by profession, told me he didn't think I should talk with Jean. I told him I had reason to believe she had fabricated the kidnapping and if the Dallas police found out, she could be charged with a crime. I told him I could help her, because I thought maybe she had suffered some sort of nervous breakdown which might stem the charges. The family allowed me to talk with Jean. I was gentle, but firm. I knew she had probably suffered a great deal and I felt for her, but I had to get to the truth. We talked for about an hour and a half.

The first hour, she stuck to her story. I had to hand it to her, she had it down cold. But when I talked about my discovery of the slats and my belief that she had faked the kidnapping, she broke down and cried. She admitted to me that she had, indeed, suffered a nervous breakdown and the whole affair was a hoax.

She was nervous about her exams at school, she had not been feeling well and she was beginning to think she was mentally sick as well. One thing led to another in her mind and she grew fearful of a brain operation; of having her head shaved. She knew she was slipping into a deep depression.

She had been hiding in the attic in a large cardboard box. She had taken some juice and water with her, along with some medication and a container in which she urinated. She had been huddled inside the box during the police search, and heard them walk right by her. I wondered how in the hell they could have missed the smell of urine if nothing else.

She told me she would come out of the box and sit by the slats at night and watch whatever went on by moonlight. Then, when daylight came, she would crawl back into her cardboard box. That's where she came up with the story of the kidnapping. Finally, around four thirty on Saturday morning, she came out of the attic and called Ron Wood and told him the story of the kidnappers. She even went out before dawn and laid in the grass next to the fence to make it look like she had landed on the ground after being thrown over the fence.

I assured Jean and her family I would go back to Dallas and talk with the police about what she had admitted. I couldn't give any guarantees, but maybe the police would not press charges if Jean promised to get psychiatric help.

As soon as I landed in Dallas, I drove to Jean's house on Garrett Street. The neighborhood was peaceful again, bare of cameras and lights and reporters trampling the flowers. The house was dead silent. Slowly, I ascended the little wooden folding stairway into the stale-smelling, dark attic. I took the small flashlight I brought from my car and cleared a path of junk by the faint light. There, in the darkness, was the large cardboard box, with a coffee can next to it. The smell of human urine filled the air. Jean's refuge was a shipping box for toilet paper, several feet square. I could see how she could sit down in it and hide from the world like a scared little child.

I rather believe the Dallas police felt the whole affair was an interesting educational experience for those detectives involved, because it was such a unique and intriguing study of human nature. They agreed not to press charges, once I had assured them that Jean would get help. I hoped she could make a fresh start, perhaps even get back together with her husband. They certainly seemed to care for each other.

I placed my report and Jean's statement in the police files. And rather unceremoniously, the case was marked '*Closed.*'

BILL DEAR'S NOTEPAD: Too Domestic for Me

Most private investigators hate domestic work. It's the bread and butter of a lot of agencies, but not mine. You can get killed doing domestic surveillance, either by the husband or the wife, or your own clumsiness.

Take the time a man hired me to spy on his wife, whom he suspected of having a lover. We followed her for three days. We couldn't find her meeting with any one but her girlfriend from the bank, so I made up my mind to hide in her attic – her husband had given me a key to their house. On my first day up in the attic I realized that the phone was in their bedroom, of which I had a good view through an attic fan. It was the time of year that few people used attic fans, and I was praying that the wife wouldn't use hers.

I heard the front door open as she came home for lunch, and I turned the attic fan blades so I could lean up against the opening. It wasn't a place I wanted to be, but being fairly new in the private-eye business, I had to prove to myself I could get the job done.

As the wife walked into the living room the phone rang. She ran to her bedroom, not knowing I was lurking just four feet above her. We didn't have the electronic devices then that we do now. We did it the hard way.

I heard her say, 'He doesn't suspect a thing. He's taking Melissa to a school play tonight. I'll have no trouble meeting you at eight.'

Bingo! Just what I needed. I lay there nearly two hours watching her preparing for her evening of bliss. I felt like a Peeping Tom, but from where I was she sure looked good and it helped the hours pass.

My eyes suddenly widened as I saw her walk over to the wall where the attic fan switch was. At the same time I saw that four-foot blade from the corner of my eye. What a way to begin and end a career! 'Mrs Dear, we're sorry to inform you, your son was found wrapped around an attic fan.' My heart stopped as she turned the light switch on instead. I took a deep breath. Thank God! Now if she would only leave so I could get down from this damn attic.

She made no attempt to leave. I heard the phone ring again and she rushed back into the bedroom. Please don't hit the wrong switch, I thought as she turned on the light and picked up the phone. It was my client, her husband. She told him she was probably not going to be home from work until late as they had to get the end-of-month statements to balance. Sure, lady, I was thinking, he may buy your story but I knew better from where I was perched.

As she talked to her husband, I felt something on my pants leg. I slowly looked over my shoulder, thinking what else can happen? There was a small mouse walking up my leg toward me. Why, Lord, all I ever wanted was to be a P. I. I wanted to jump up and yell to both of them, 'Hey, you down there and you on the phone, take this case and *SHOVE IT!*' I was mad as hell when she finally left. On the other hand, I had remembered the address she had repeated to her caller.

I called my client's attorney and said, 'It's on for eight tonight.'

'I'd like to go with you,' he said. He was a young attorney and I think he wanted the thrill.

'Okay, meet Leon, Al and me, and you can ride with us.'

At seven thirty Leon, Al, the attorney and I were ready and waiting. Sure enough, at eight, I saw her car come down the street and pull into the driveway. Within seconds, the door opened. Even with binoculars, there was too much shadow for us to see who let her in.

By nine it was totally dark. I got out of my car carrying one of the two cameras we owned. Leon carried the other one with the attorney following right behind us. I slipped to the side of the house and saw a light on from a bedroom window with a window-type air conditioner going full blast. There was no one in the bedroom so I quietly crawled to the back porch, where I could see two figures lying on a divan. I was closely followed by the crew, eagerly anticipating the excitement of the evening.

As I crept up to where I could see, I slowly began to raise myself up. As I did, my face nearly fell to the ground. There on the divan was my client's wife, nude, on top of another nude body, deliriously indulging in one of the most compelling and torrid kisses I had ever seen. The problem: it wasn't a man she was kissing, it was a woman. It was the vice-president of the bank where she worked.

I fell to my knees and turned to the attorney. 'You won't believe this one!'

'Why?'

'Just look for yourself!' I said.

'Oh, my God! What am I going to tell the client?' the attorney whispered.

I'm just the investigator, and for once in my life I could finally say, 'You're the attorney.' I didn't envy him his job.

We inched our way back to the side of the house to discuss what we had seen. More than likely they would leave the porch and head to the bedroom to finish what they had started. It was just a matter of time. And the light would be better for pictures.

We made our way back to the bedroom window and I checked to see if the window was locked. Fantastic, I thought as I slowly raised the window. There was a sheer curtain covering the now open window. I was banking that between their passion and the air-conditioner they wouldn't notice the window was up.

It didn't take long. Within thirty minutes the door to the cool bedroom opened and two heated individuals entered. I had hoped they would leave the light on, making this better than an X-rated movie. Wrong. Off went the light.

I had to write a note to Al and Leon telling Al to go to the car and be ready for a hasty exit. On my signal Leon would rise up and pull back each side of the curtain. I would take the first shot in black and white, then shoot the second shot with the other camera in color. I was hoping the first shot would catch them in a compromising position, and the second would give me a good shot of both their faces.

I counted to three, the magic number. One . . . two . . . three! Up I came, camera and flashbulb in hand – Shot one! Grabbing for the second camera, hearing the two women scream, I took the second shot.

I turned to run, with the attorney and Leon right behind me. All of a sudden the lawyer stumbled and fell into the rosebushes, yelping as he became tangled in the thorns. I hollered back, 'You're on your own!'

I ran for the car where Al was waiting and jumped in. Leon and the attorney ran for the second car. I was more valuable. I had the film! We met within a few minutes and I couldn't help but laugh. For once I felt an attorney earned his money. There was blood all over his hands and face. I couldn't wait to get to the office and process the film.

In the first shot you could see two twisted bodies making mad, passionate love. As the second picture was coming into focus, the lawyer was breathing down my neck. Oh no, the banker was underneath, our client's wife on top. They were recognizable, however.

I wonder what story she would give to her husband. She surely couldn't say, 'Honey, I thought it was you I was making love to!' Not tonight anyway.

Was this case a success? You could say so; he forgave her and took her back.

CHAPTER 9
Amber Cries No More

The headline in the *Dallas Morning News*, Tuesday, January 17, 1984, read: MURDER CHARGES FILED IN AMBER CRUM DEATH. A picture of James Britt Monroe graced the article, in which Dallas Police Captain William Gentry credited me with providing much needed information that resulted in Monroe's arrest.

The first headlines I noticed in this case was in the December 29, 1983, edition of the *Dallas Times Herald:* POLICE STILL LACK SOLID LEADS IN SEARCH FOR 2-YEAR-OLD GIRL. The paper quoted the plea of Amber's mother, Stephanie Hughes, for the return of her baby. As I usually do when such a case pops up in the media, I clipped the articles and made a file. I thought that if the police and a few dozen family members, friends and volunteers couldn't find Amber, I might be called. It may sound a little presumptuous, but it does happen. And a week later, I was proved right, when I got a call from Lynn Hughes, Stephanie's sister.

'Mr Dear.' She controlled her emotions, but I could tell it took everything she had. 'Would you help us?'

A special bonding develops among people working together when a child is in need. Though I was talking only to Lynn, I knew that I was also communicating with the collective heart of a family in pain.

She explained that their parents had come down from Columbus, Indiana, at Christmas to be with the kids in Texas, and most of all to see their beautiful granddaughter, Amber. It was to be a joyous occasion, filled with laughter and love. But a day later, the world crashed down upon the Hughes family as Amber disappeared.

Lynn asked if I could come over, and perhaps shed some light as to how these cases go and what can be done. The family was looking for hope and the police had exhausted its supply. I knew how desperate they felt. I told Lynn I would be right over. I re-read the file and left my office for Lynn Hughes's apartment.

When I got there, Lynn, her parents and her aunt were waiting. They had gone through a great deal since the day after Christmas, including several police interviews. The police investigators are trained to be sensitive in cases such as this, but the whole business of being questioned by officers and investigators, again and again, can take its toll. It is not a pleasant experience for anyone involved, including the investigator, police or private. But we talked frankly about the events leading to Amber's disappearance.

Stephanie and James Monroe, her live-in boyfriend, were at Lynn's apartment on Christmas Day to take showers because the pipes under their mobile home had frozen. Lynn noticed some tension between Stephanie and James but didn't pay much attention. She said she also noticed that Amber wouldn't have anything to do with James. She wouldn't let him hold her or even touch her, while she would cuddle up with everyone else there.

They asked if I would take the case. I explained that I would work with the police and share any information I had, because we were all working toward the same goal. It had been more than a week since Amber had been seen. We were in the throes of the harshest winter in years in North Texas. We tried to be optimistic, but the brutal cold, the shattered Christmas and the time already passed gave little reason for hope as a New Year began.

I left the apartment and drove out to Stephanie and James's mobile home on Dowdy Ferry Road in southeast Dallas. It's a rural area with a lot of mobile homes scattered about. Stephanie was only nineteen and had been married once to a fellow by the name of Larry Crum. James was twenty-two and met Stephanie while working as a plumber for the apartment complex where Stephanie and her aunt lived. Just before the Christmas holidays

Stephanie moved into this fine palatial mobile home. It wasn't the lap of luxury and I got a bad feeling as I got out and gazed at a yard filled with welding equipment and oil drums. It would be easy to hide, then dispose of a body in those drums. It may sound morbid to think such things, but I have seen everything in my business and nothing surprises me any more.

Just then a rusty old car pulled up and out jumped James Monroe. He was hostile and I think the only reason he didn't challenge me was because of my height, and the fact he didn't know if I was an armed police officer or not. Stephanie slowly rose from the passenger side. She was a young lady racked with pain.

In the meantime Monroe was getting in my face, or as close as he could without provoking a real confrontation. He reminded me of a skinny little chihuahua, making a lot of noise, but keeping his distance.

'Cops think I cut her up and fed her to my Doberman dogs,' he blurted in an uneducated redneck accent. He stood there with his head cocked slightly and his mouth barely open, like some schoolyard punk trying to bully me.

I just smiled, and in a relaxed voice that made it clear I wasn't going to take any bullshit, I said, 'I was hired by the family to find Amber. No matter what it takes. I'll need your help and I'll need Stephanie's help, too. Now, let's all go inside and talk like adults, shall we?'

I do believe the kid knew I was serious. I don't think he had the mental capacity to understand that I now suspected him of having something to do with Amber's disappearance. The funny thing was, he brought the suspicion on himself with his attitude. But soon other factors would point his way.

Inside, Monroe calmed down considerably as we talked about events leading up to Amber's disappearance. He told me he had gotten up the morning after Christmas and had taken Amber for a walk. I asked if it had been too cold for a walk.

He said, 'No, I put her mittens and jacket on her before we went for the walk. We came back and got in my pick-up truck and drove down to the McDonald's grocery store.'

The store he spoke about was a small 'Mom and Pop' type of country grocery store, where he bought Amber some soft drinks, along with a few grocery items he knew they needed at home. He told me he left her in the truck, with the door locked, while he went inside. I was still concerned about the weather. It was not just cold by Texas standards that winter, it was damned cold. And I don't know any parent cruel enough to leave a child out in a cold truck with no heat going, much less take her for a walk in freezing temperatures when she could have been inside a nice warm store bringing smiles to customers' faces. I got the feeling Monroe didn't concern himself much about Amber's comfort, though I said nothing.

He walked out of the store, put the bag of groceries in the bed of the truck and opened the locked cab to find Amber missing. She wasn't anywhere. He ran back into the store, thinking she somehow got out and went inside, but she wasn't there, or anywhere in the area. Then he drove home to see if she was there, but there was still no sign of her. He woke Stephanie and they decided to call the police. Monroe said that when the police couldn't find Amber, they began to treat him as a suspect. 'Their only interest,' he said, 'was to prosecute me. They took me in for questioning and badgered me . . . and badgered me. They said they were convinced that I had kidnapped and killed Amber.'

As Monroe talked I began to see numerous discrepancies in his story.

Stephanie gave me her version of the story beginning with the night before, Christmas night. When they returned to the mobile home after spending Christmas with her family she gave Amber her bath and put her to bed. She checked on Amber several times that night before she went to bed herself and didn't wake up until about ten thirty the next morning. Monroe was shaking her awake, saying that Amber was missing.

Throughout the conversations I took very detailed notes. I got the impression I was not being told the truth and that perhaps the police were right in their assessment of what happened. But I wanted to keep an open mind. After we talked I looked in the wooded area behind the trailer park where they lived, then returned and asked Monroe if he would recreate his trip to the store the next morning. He said he couldn't do it the next morning, but he could about the middle of the week. We agreed on the middle of the week.

When I left, I drove to the little grocery store. There I found a young lady named Tammy, who had served Monroe the morning of Amber's disappearance. A man called Robert, who also happened to be at the store the morning of the disappearance, was there as I talked with Tammy. Tammy remembered another man, named Charlie, who was in the store at the same time as Monroe. She called him and he agreed to come up to the store and talk with me. Now I had all three of the witnesses to Monroe's visit to the store. I asked if they could be present later in the week while Monroe recreated his visit to the store. They all agreed to do so.

When the morning of the recreation arrived, I had arranged for Tammy to be behind the counter and for Charlie to be there with his vehicle parked in the same spot as before. I also placed Robert inside the store, just as he was that day, with his vehicle parked just as it was the day Amber disappeared. A bag boy named Wayne was also present, as he had been that morning. The scene was set. I had my van parked where Dick Riddle, inside with a camera, could see us drive down Queen's Way and pull into the parking lot of the store. I drove to Monroe's mobile home, then followed Monroe as he drove to the store as he had on that dreary winter morning. Monroe didn't know I was filming the whole thing.

As he said he had before, Monroe made a wide turn into the parking lot and stopped next to a pick-up, directly in front of the ice machine and in clear view of the large picture window of the store. He cut the engine, locked the door of the truck and walked inside.

He picked up toilet paper and bread and even recalled how he mentioned to the bag boy, Wayne, that he had to get a six pack of Dr Pepper, or his little girl, sitting out in the truck, would never forgive him. He played it exactly as he had told me during our conversation. What he didn't know was that Wayne was in the back, listening to the recreation to check if he was lying or not.

154

Once outside, Monroe went through the same routine. He placed the grocery bag in the back of the truck, then he walked in front, as he did when he realized Amber was missing, to see if she was anywhere near. Then we had him walk toward the road, then back into the store to ask the same people the same things about whether they had seen Amber. They all went outside and looked in the same areas they had before, even in the nearby garbage dumpster. Then Tammy offered to call the police, but Monroe said, no, he would search for her on the way back to the trailer house, in case she had gotten out of the truck and wandered in that direction.

Monroe then left, but I stayed behind and talked with the store witnesses. They each told me Monroe didn't park his truck in front of the store, but on the south side, near the dumpster, and he had left the passenger door open. Charlie said when he pulled up he could see no one in the truck. They also said that each of them advised Monroe to call the police immediately, from right there in the store, but he refused.

James Britt Monroe was our number one suspect. I was also getting a terrible feeling inside about Amber's fate.

I started checking into Monroe's background. I was able to locate his ex-wife, who told me that Monroe never wanted children. His mother slept with any man who had the price of a bottle, and Monroe had apparently witnessed her numerous sexual exploits. He also had a violent temper, which was partly why his ex-wife left him; she feared for her life after Monroe found out she was having an affair. I was beginning to piece together a profile of James Britt Monroe, and the inconsistencies in his story were piling up:

1. Monroe's vehicle was parked in a different place from where he claimed it was during the alleged kidnapping. This was verified by the witnesses at the store.

2. He had indicated to me that he was supposed to go to work the morning after Christmas, but went for an early morning walk with Amber instead.

3. He said he was buying Dr Pepper for Amber, when he should have known Amber only liked to drink Coca-Cola; it was

Stephanie who drank Dr Pepper. But Monroe wanted to stress that he was buying something for his little girl, a ploy to make everyone believe she was actually in the truck.

4. He said he had put Amber's mittens on her to go for a walk that freezing morning after Christmas. We found that Amber's mittens had been left at Lynn's apartment. Besides, no one in the neighborhood recalled seeing the two go for a walk that morning.

5. Monroe denied he used drugs, but we established that he was lying. In fact, we found that he used 'crystal' or speed, on Christmas Day, and he had a misdemeanour charge of drug possession pending against him.

6. The clothes Monroe claimed to have dressed Amber in that morning were found in the washing machine, clean.

7. Monroe said he only played with Amber on Christmas night, but the truth was he shook and spanked the child on numerous occasions.

8. On that particular morning, the portable telephone at Monroe's mobile home was on 'talk'. This would not allow any incoming calls; the caller would only get a busy signal, indicating that someone was on the phone, and the phone itself would not ring.

9. Monroe later said he left the truck unlocked while he was in the store, changing his original story.

10. Monroe said he never struck the child, but spanked her only once. But several people testified that Monroe had knocked her to the ground on more than one occasion. They recalled seeing bruises and abrasions on the child's legs, back, stomach and buttocks where she had been abused. Lynn had asked Stephanie about it more than once, but nothing came of the inquisition.

11. Those same witnesses said Monroe would make Amber stand in a corner for two or three hours as punishment for something.

12. Stephanie said she once caught Monroe holding Amber in a tub of icecold water to 'make her mind'.

13. More than one family member talked about Amber's refusal to allow Monroe even to hold her, let alone bathe and dress her, or go walking with her as he claimed to have done that morning.

14. Stephanie said the couple's sex life had become virtually non-existent, which indicated stress of some kind.

15. Monroe failed two polygraph tests, by altering his breathing patterns in an attempt to throw off the machine.

16. His preoccupation with the police's so-called claim that he had killed the child and fed her to his Doberman.

17. The stress of his mobile home about to be repossessed.

18. Monroe's relationship with his father became strained after the disappearance of Amber, to the point where they stopped speaking. This suggested that his father might be uncomfortable with inconsistencies in Monroe's story.

19. Monroe claimed the police had nothing on him, unless he and Stephanie separated, and she testified against him.

20. On December 31, five days after Amber disappeared, Stephanie's mother Vada said Monroe and a friend of his, Timmy Marcom*, left Monroe's house in a pretty good humor, with a pair of motorcycles in the back of a truck. But when they returned the attitude of the two was completely different. Marcom just said goodbye and Monroe went straight into his bedroom. Stephanie couldn't do anything with him, and told her mother he was crying; so Vada went in. She found Monroe sitting on the edge of the bed next to Amber's crib. He said he was feeling 'guilty' about Amber.

I thought back to a course I took on recognizing child abuse. Monroe was obviously an abused child, who had grown up to take his rage out on a defenseless little girl. I talked with two doctors about the evidence; though they didn't want to be involved directly with the case, they did tell me that Monroe appeared to be a classic example of an abused child turned abuser. He could continue to abuse children, particularly little girls. As I put these facts together I grew extremely angry at this man, and my dislike of Stephanie began to build.

It was Friday, January 13, when I contacted Lynn and told her we had to make a move. We had to get Stephanie away from Monroe and talk with her. She set it up for Saturday night. I could think of better ways to spend a Saturday night, but this had to be done. Lynn had Stephanie come to her place, then arranged for

157

the family to be there. I walked into the apartment and sat across the room from a quiet young woman, her head hanging down. I didn't want to play the tough guy, but I had no choice; a child's life lay in the balance.

I began by asking Stephanie all of the questions I had and backing them up with my evidence and concerns. We talked for an hour and a half. I was stern with her, yet I was trying to be considerate as well. I knew she knew the real story, but it was still her child that was missing. Finally, after a couple of hours, she broke down and cried.

'I'll tell you everything, Mr Dear.' The tears streaked her face.

I advised her of her right to remain silent until an attorney was present. But she wanted to talk. She admitted the problems she and Monroe were having. She admitted that he had struck the child on several occasions. At last she told me what actually happened.

On Sunday, Christmas Day, Stephanie and Monroe had an argument before leaving to go to the family Christmas celebration at her grandmother's home in Dallas. The pipes had frozen at the mobile home, so they stopped at Lynn's apartment to use the shower. They were late to the Christmas dinner, arriving at one instead of noon. But the tension between Stephanie and Monroe had not subsided. In fact, it erupted into another argument during which Monroe took out his wallet and threw it at Stephanie. While they were there, Stephanie received a phone call from Teresa, a drug dealer, asking that Stephanie and Monroe meet her. They left around four thirty en route for her aunt's apartment. Stephanie told Monroe that Teresa had called, saying she had 'some good stuff'. The 'stuff' was drugs; 'crystal' to be more exact. Monroe mentioned that it was about time, since the last stuff hadn't been very good.

When they arrived at her aunt's apartment, two of Stephanie's cousins, Betty and Earl, were there. Monroe left by himself to visit Teresa and her boyfriend, a dealer known as Taco Tom.

About an hour to an hour and a half later, when Monroe returned, Stephanie asked him about the crystal. He said he wasn't able to get much, but Stephanie thought he was lying. He had been tired when he left but more hyper when he returned, which made Stephanie think he had already taken some. In the meantime, Betty told Monroe about a broken water pipe at the apartment complex. Since Monroe was the apartment's plumber, he fixed the pipe. Then around seven thirty Christmas night Monroe, Stephanie and Amber left to go home. They stopped only once to buy Stephanie a Dr Pepper at a drive-in, before getting home around eight. Monroe went into the bathroom and returned with a hypodermic needle and a 'bump' of crystal. But Stephanie told me she wasn't interested in taking drugs then, though she admitted taking drugs in the past. She said she saw Monroe go back into the bathroom with the hypodermic needle and return without it. He went outside to check on the frozen pipes and get water into the mobile home. After a few minutes the water supply was restored and Stephanie decided to wash some clothes. Monroe said he would give Amber a bath while Stephanie did the laundry.

Stephanie didn't hear anything for some time as she went about her mundane task. Then she walked into the living room and sat down to watch TV while the clothes were washing. Suddenly, she heard Amber scream an unmistakable piercing wail that cut straight to her soul. In a panic she jumped up and ran to the bathroom. She threw open the door and saw Monroe holding Amber, pushing the toddler's head down into the toilet. 'What are you *doing*? What's going *on* here!' she yelled at him.

'Get outta here, Goddammit! I'll handle this! Get outta here – *now*!' Monroe screamed back at her like a madman, the force of his voice shoving her out of the bathroom, striking fear into her heart.

About twenty minutes passed and then Monroe came into the living room, saying he had given Amber a bath and put her to bed. After they watched television for a while, she decided to check on Amber. She kissed Amber goodnight, but Amber didn't react in the usual manner. She hadn't been feeling well during the severe cold spell, according to Stephanie, so she didn't think much about her lackluster behaviour. Some time later Stephanie decided to go to bed and she checked on Amber again as she undressed in the bedroom. The child was still lying motionless on her right side, staring straight ahead, with her covers still on her. They hadn't been moved or even pushed about.

'Stephanie,' I interrupted, 'didn't you realize that Amber was dead? Didn't you realize a child would toss and turn? That her covers were still on her, that her eyes had not moved? Didn't you realize your little girl was *dead*?'

For a moment, the room was silent, save for the echo of my voice as the questions hung in the air. Everyone watched Stephanie, waiting for the answer growing inside of her like a spring thunderstorm. Her eyes welled with tears and she fought back the sobs that began convulsing in her before she let go.

Yes, Mr Dear! *Yes! I knew* . . . Amber was dead!'

Stephanie's face twisted in horror and pain. She began to cry uncontrollably, saying 'My baby's dead!' over and over again. For the first time since the incident reality flooded into her mind.

It took a while to settle her. Some of the family wept softly, others sat stone-faced in shock. After a period of time, I don't know how long, we continued talking. It was as hard for me as it was for them.

She told me she had not been awakened by Monroe, but woke up on her own at approximately ten thirty a.m. She noticed that Monroe had not slept in the bed but rather on top of the covers. For some reason she didn't check on Amber; she walked into the living room and sat on the couch a moment before lighting a cigarette. Monroe then walked calmly in from the kitchen and sat down beside her and said Amber was missing.

'What? You're joking,' Stephanie recalled saying to Monroe. Stephanie said she jumped up and ran to the crib. Amber was gone.

'I reached for the portable phone in our bedroom. I noticed it was on 'talk' which meant no calls could come in and wake me. I then dialled my mother and my sister, Lynn.'

The women were both frantic, telling Stephanie to call the police while they drove to Monroe's house.

That was when Monroe first called the police. Stephanie remembered how calm he was about it; how he told her of the walk he took with Amber and the Doberman that morning and then the trip they allegedly took to the store. I asked her, as I had Monroe the first day I met him, if it didn't seem strange that he would take Amber for a walk in eighteen-degree weather, with a chill factor below zero, without her mittens. Stephanie looked at me oddly.

'Stephanie,' I said, 'we found her little mittens at Lynn's apartment.'

Stephanie went on to tell me she went into the laundry while waiting on the police and her family to arrive. She knew there were more clothes to wash and thought it would be best to stay busy. But when she opened the machine, the load of colored clothes left from the night before was in the washer, still wet and waiting to be dried. They had been washed while she was sleeping.

Monroe had never done the wash before. Stephanie noticed that Amber's nightclothes and her bedsheets and pillowcase were in the wash, a stain of vomit still holding to the toddler's night clothes despite the washing. She emphasized, 'There had been no need to wash the bedsheets because they were clean when I put Amber to bed . . . ' Her voice trailed off, then she looked up at me and corrected herself, '. . . when Britt put her to bed.'

I asked if this was the first time Monroe had hurt the child. She said, no, she had seen him push her head into the toilet before as a form of punishment. Her relatives sobbed quietly, or simply stood staring with their mouths open at the revelations unfolding before them.

Then Mrs Hughes recalled the incident of December 31st, involving Monroe and Marcom, and wondered if the two of them had then actually gone to move the body of little Amber to another location so she couldn't be found.

I picked up the phone and called Captain Gentry of the Dallas Police Department and asked him to meet me at the police headquarters to allow Stephanie to give a statement.

A couple of reporters were waiting in the Missing Persons Division of the Dallas Police Headquarters when we arrived. I'm not sure how they found out, though the media has a collective media office at headquarters. Their office was near CAPERS

(Crimes Against Persons Division), so I'm sure with all of the attention this case was getting, they could smell the story about to break.

Stephanie and I met with the Captain and Investigator Paul Ronyak, and Stephanie gave a detailed statement of the events surrounding the case. When she was directly asked if she believed James Britt Monroe murdered Amber Crum, she said quietly, 'Yes, there is no doubt in my mind.'

I was able to take Stephanie back to her sister's house, but under the provision she return Sunday to talk with Captain Gentry.

In the meantime, Gentry called Sergeant Billy Parker, one of the toughest men in the business. On Sunday Stephanie and I went back to Headquarters. Parker met us, and again Stephanie was advised of her rights. She then retold her story to Parker and me. It didn't vary at all. After she finished her story, Parker began hammering at her as if she was the murderer. He worked to pull apart everything in her story. I knew what he was doing, though Stephanie didn't. In fact, she was feeling like the accused rather than the victim. After two hours of hard interrogation, Parker and I walked out for a break.

'Let's spend another hour with her,' he said, 'then I'll make a determination.'

We walked back in. Stephanie was one big bundle of nerves, which is what Parker wanted. If there was going to be a discrepancy, a change in her story to reveal she was hiding something or trying to lay blame for protection, it would come out during that last hour. It was hard questioning. Never abusive, but direct and unrelenting; going over and over and over and over the same thing time after time after time after time until Parker felt he was at the bottom of it. At the end of the third hour we left the room again. Parker looked at me and said, 'What do you think?'

'Monroe did it,' I said. 'No doubt in my mind.'

'I agree. I think you're right,' Parker replied.

'Stephanie has been covering up for the child abuse. That's common in these situations. It's usually out of fear of retaliation. And maybe, knowing what you tell me about this guy, she's got good reason for concern. But I don't think she's hiding anything about this murder. She might be hiding the fact she probably abused the child herself, as well. But I don't think she's covering for a murder. It just took a little help to get it out of the dark reaches of a shocked mother's mind.'

'I do think,' Parker added, 'That she did drugs that night and that's why she slept so late the next day without hearing anything. I also think after Monroe took the drugs back into the bathroom that night, Amber got a hold of them. That's probably why there was vomit on her nightgown. He probably tried to make her throw up and it was either too late or he beat her to death in a fit of rage.'

I had absolutely no respect for Stephanie Hughes in any way. As far as I was concerned, she was just as guilty as Monroe was when it came to the death of Amber. What really got me was thinking of all the abuse that precious little girl had gone through all that time.

We went back inside. Stephanie signed the statement and I drove her back to her family. I told her family that a murder warrant was going to be issued against James Britt Monroe. The trouble now was that we still had not located the child's body. A search was made of the trailer and the surrounding area. Dallas Police called out its entire tactical force along with several detectives and we combed the area for a full day trying to find any evidence that would lead us to Amber's body. Nothing was found.

I knew the only people who could tell us where to find the body were Monroe and Marcom. On Monday, January 16, 1984, Dallas Police arrested James Britt Monroe for the murder of Amber Nichole Crum.

It was only the second time the Dallas Police had ever arrested a murder suspect without having located the body first. In 1978, a suspect was arrested and convicted in the case of one John Alan McGraw, and sentenced to thirty years in prison. McGraw's body was never found. We were still hoping to find Amber's body. As I stared at that bastard while he was being arrested and processed, I felt rage well up inside me. I knew he had the location of Amber's body stuck down deep in that twisted brain of his.

On Wednesday morning, February 18, 1984, a hearing was held

in Dallas. Stephanie, her family and I arrived to meet Assistant Dallas District Attorney Mary Ludwick. Ludwick and Stephanie went into a room to talk alone. She went over the signed statement that Stephanie had given Dallas Police and me a month earlier. When they emerged from the room, Ludwick looked at me and with a stone face of determination said, 'We're going to put this guy away.'

I felt good about this case for the first time since I took it. The fire in Ludwick's eyes gave me cause to believe we were going to see Monroe fry for Amber's death.

When the hearing was called to order, I kept watching Monroe. He would look at Stephanie, who looked down or away. She was scared. I had figured Stephanie was hardened to rough probing questions by now. But Monroe was there this time. And this time it made all the difference in the world.

Monroe's father had hired attorney Kevin Clancy to defend his son. Clancy left no stone unturned. He worked to pick apart every bit of evidence we had. But his job was made easy for him when Stephanie took the stand. She took another look at Monroe, sitting at his lawyer's table, and completely changed her story. Despite what she told me and the police on several occasions over the period of a month, despite the fact that her story had never changed once, and despite the fact she was under oath and could be charged with perjury, Monroe still scared her. So she lied to protect him and very possibly herself.

She said that Amber had not moved that night when she went to check on her and kiss her goodnight. She also admitted Amber was cold when she kissed her, but she would not admit she thought Amber was dead then. Instead, she said she didn't think anything was out of the ordinary, and she felt Amber was still alive. I couldn't believe what was happening! That bastard had Stephanie so intimidated she wouldn't cross him no matter what. Amber's life meant nothing.

Once that occurred, it was downhill all the way. Clancy got me on the stand and kept yelling, 'But where's the body, Mr Dear! Can you produce the body, Mr Dear?' I wanted to deliver *his* body to the bench, but I knew he was doing what Monroe's father was paying him to do, get Monroe off the hook for murder. Oh, family members were called and they each testified to noticing evidence of child abuse. I tried as best I could to introduce more evidence which pointed directly at Monroe, but it did no good. I wondered who else would stand up for Amber. It was obvious Stephanie was not going to testify against Monroe. The judge promptly dismissed the case for simple lack of evidence. There would be no justice for Amber in this world.

On February 20, 1984, the Dallas County Grand Jury convened and No Billed James Britt Monroe in connection with the disappearance and alleged murder of Amber Nichole Crum. So, the charges were officially dropped.

I had occasion a few weeks later to meet with Monroe once more. He got into my car when I asked to speak with him privately. I turned in my seat and looked him square in the face. I said, 'Monroe, you and I both know you killed Amber.'

He stared back at me for a moment, no emotion showing on his drawn face framed by stringy, dirty hair. 'You may know it. And I may know it. But until you can prove it, you can't do anything about it.'

It took all of the self-discipline I could muster to keep from reaching over and breaking his neck with my bare hands. It would have been as easy as breaking a matchstick. And so rewarding.

About a year later, Monroe moved in with another lady who had a child. The horrible irony was, her child was also two years old at the time and named Amber. Fortunately, she moved out, but only after Monroe abused her baby as well.

Monroe walks the streets a free man to this day, and I worry about the children he happens to meet. But he's not alone. I keep in contact with those who know him and all of the witnesses who harbor the memories of what he has done. Every time he moves to a new location, I make a point of showing up, usually with a photographer to film his comings and goings at his new residence. I always make sure he sees that I'm there and still watching after all of the years. I hope I've become his worse nightmare.

In the meantime, may Amber rest in peace.

BILL DEAR'S NOTEPAD: Crossed Wires

I don't do phone taps, at least not any more. Years ago a man wanted to know if his wife was cheating on him. He asked that I come to his Dallas mansion and install an elaborate bugging device on the line so it would automatically start recording when the receiver was picked up. Now, this was before the development of micro-anything. The devices, by today's standards, were bulky and poor quality. You also had to go to a lot of trouble to install them. So, I told the man it would probably take a few hours. He arranged for his wife to be gone one bright afternoon, but warned me that they would both be back by four p.m.

I arrived on the afternoon we agreed, and like he promised, the back gate to the property was unlocked and no one was around. I found the phone box in the attic, set down my tools and started to work. Now, normally, the wiring in a house has plenty of slack, whether it's electrical or phone wiring. It makes it easier come time for repairs. But this was a stately old Dallas mansion. I would guess that phone lines were added as an afterthought by some young upstart in the family who was intrigued by the new fad of having a telephone in the house. At any rate, once I tore into the box, I found years of adaptations and repairs had left very, very little slack. Besides, the wiring appeared to have been installed as Alexander Graham Bell sat waiting on hold one day at the dawn of the phone age. Each time I bent the wires to secure a connection, they broke. I saw the four o'clock deadline looming closer and closer and . . . damn, broke the wire, again!

I was beginning to get worried, realizing that they would be home any minute, and a telephone repairman in casual street clothes wouldn't add up. Another wire broke. I felt like a bomb expert with only seconds to decide which wires to cut and how to cut them.

I kept stripping wire back until I realized I had run out of wire and was flush with the back wall of the box. If I didn't make this twist gently, I would be out of time, off a simple domestic case and the people living here would be without phone service.

I slowly twisted the remaining fraction of an inch of wire to the connector leading to the tapping device. It held! Then I connected the other wires to the device, each one barely hanging on, but it worked! They were in place.

I slammed the box lid shut as I heard them pull up at the front. Fortunately, I had enough sense not to park in front, but a few blocks away through the alley. As I heard them reach the front door, I dashed past a big picture window that would have provided a clear line of sight to my covert handyman work, was out the rear gate and down the alley like a phantom. At least I wasn't left under the bed like Richard Dreyfuss in the movie *Stakeout*.

I had to stop when I got to my car and catch my breath before I could get in and drive off. I had faced danger before, but for some reason I was mortified over the idea of being caught at the phone box. I guess it was the prospect of embarrassment at being nailed on such an easy, routine job. But my client had his tap and I had a fee coming.

We soon found out that the lady wasn't having an affair at all. She was simply a gossip with a lot of friends and a lot of seedy stories.

CHAPTER 10
An Offer I Couldn't Refuse

On a bright May morning, a young couple in Fort Worth played with their newborn daughter, as they had each morning since little Cherie Ann had been born seven weeks before. Andy and Penny Kennedy were in awe of their little miracle. Cherie Ann embodied the love Penny and Andy shared and their dream for the future of their family. Andy was always reluctant to leave for work, and that sunny spring morning was no different. Something about this heavenly gift made it tough for the hard-working man to walk out the door and concentrate on the day ahead. At the same time, Cherie Ann seemed to give him a better reason to work harder. Penny, a demure and loving young mother, knew what her husband felt as she kissed him goodbye and held Cherie Ann up for her kiss on the forehead from Daddy.

Penny played with Cherie Ann a little while longer before getting her child ready for the routine doctor's visit at John Peter-Smith Hospital in Fort Worth, Texas, where Cherie Ann was born. JPS, as staff and locals call it, is similar to Parkland Hospital in Dallas in many ways. Though they provide premier health care in the region, both are county-run facilities that take in indigent patients and injured criminals. Every manner of human is carried, wheeled or raced through that hospital in situations ranging from minor care and preventive medicine to life-threatening emergencies. A shift in the emergency room can make an observer either dedicate his life to medicine or seek psychiatric help to deal with the unspeakable things he has seen. Penny arrived at JPS about twenty minutes after she left her house. They were right on time for the doctor's visit.

Penny had only been practising for seven weeks, but already had the balancing act down to a fine art; seeing her holding Cherie Ann in one arm and signing in at the reception area with the other, one would have considered her an old pro. She took a seat in the waiting area and was entertaining her daughter when she noticed a smiling, overweight nurse talking with some of the other mothers. Just leave me alone to play with my baby, Penny thought, but suddenly the large smiling nurse was standing above her.

'What a beautiful child,' the nurse said with a hint of a Texas accent.

'Thank you.' Penny beamed.

The two women cooed and clucked over the child. Penny felt a little selfish, having had a mean thought about not wanting this nice nurse to interrupt her time with Cherie Ann; after all, the nurse was here to help. After a few moments the nurse pleaded, 'Oh, let me hold her.'

Naturally Penny was a bit reluctant, as any mother would be. I'm just being a silly mom, she told herself. So she handed over her bundle of love. The nurse held Cherie Ann, rocking her gently in an experienced manner.

'Can I take her down the hall to show some of the other nurses?'

A pang of foreboding raced up Penny's spine. It made her cold and hot at the same time, but she knew she was being too protective.

'Sure,' she replied with a smile. And down the hall went the nurse, baby-talking all the way around the corner.

A few minutes passed. Penny walked to the water fountain for a drink of water, then glanced down at her watch to see how long she had been separated from her little girl. Ten minutes. She imagined seeing the chubby nurse's smiling face any moment. But as the minutes dragged on she began to worry.

She looked at her watch again. It had been almost twenty minutes since the nurse left with her baby just to go down the hall. Penny walked down the hall and turned the corner, but no one was there. Something snapped into raw fear and Penny quickly ran back to the reception area.

'I can't find my baby.' She tried to explain calmly, but it was difficult. The receptionist's forehead furrowed in shared fear. A couple of nurses, hearing what Penny was saying gathered anxiously.

'One of the nurses took my baby to show to the other nurses and she hasn't come back.'

A nurse behind the desk grabbed the phone and called the head nurse to the desk. By then, Penny was beginning to cry as she felt her life starting to crumble. The head nurse arrived and more nurses surrounded the reception area while Penny described the nurse and what happened. The head nurse paged all of the nurses to the reception area but sorrowfully told Penny, 'Mrs Kennedy, I'm afraid that we don't have a nurse fitting that description.'

The head nurse was right. Penny didn't see the nurse in the group. Her heart sank as she shook and cried. Security had been alerted and was searching each floor and the parking lot of the hospital. But the chubby nurse had disappeared, with Cherie Ann Kennedy.

It wasn't long before Andy made it to the hospital and tried to calm his frantic wife. He was just as scared, but knew he had to be strong for Penny. The young couple could only cling to each other and the hope that the police would find their little baby.

The Fort Worth Police Department and the FBI had been notified and soon investigators from both agencies were there. An APB, All Points Bulletin, was issued for the nurse and child. The nurse was described as overweight, perhaps 190 pounds on a five-foot-seven-inch frame. She appeared to be about forty-five years old, perhaps a bit older or younger. The weight made it hard for Penny to decide. It was hard for her to think clearly. All she could see was the chubby nurse's receding back as she walked away with her baby. Each time she saw the vision in her mind, she cried even more. The nurses and hospital staff did what they could to ease her tension; but all, especially those with children of their own, could only stand by and feel the pain. After a while, it was obvious

Cherie Ann was not going to be found immediately, and the Kennedys were advised to go home and rest. It was a tall order. Leaving the hospital meant admitting that Cherie Ann was really gone; resting would be impossible.

The story made quick emotional headlines the next morning. It gave me a hollow feeling inside to read the young couple's appeal to the kidnapper for their baby's safe return. I clipped the article and had a file made on the case that would soon contain other media accounts. I often have files made on cases I'm not hired for. It's easier to go back to my own files from the beginning, than to try and develop a file sometimes a year of more after the case began. Besides, this one hit home to me as a father. I was more than interested in the outcome.

Several days passed and there was more and more coverage on the story in the media, including radio and television interviews with the Kennedys asking that their baby be returned. The likelihood of finding the child, much less finding the child alive, grew dimmer with each passing day. After one of the interviews had aired, I turned off the television in my office and reached for the phone. I called a friend on the inside and asked if they had anything new on the Kennedy kidnapping. He told me they hadn't but that he was just about to call me.

'Several people have called me,' he said, 'asking if you'd take the case.'

I didn't ask him who they were. Looking at my calendar, I could see it had been ten days since Cherie Ann Kennedy had been kidnapped.

'I don't know,' I replied, 'the police and the FBI seem to be working pretty hard on it.' Ten days, I kept thinking.

'You know better than that, Bill,' he chuckled, 'they have a tendency to put in a nine-to-five-day on things and you don't.'

He was right. Ten days, I thought again!

Another week passed without so much as a clue as to the whereabouts of Cherie Ann Kennedy. The media was still hitting the story, but not as hard. Other stories, like the Texas State Legislature considering a pari-mutuel horse-racing bill, as well as the early inklings of a scandal in Texas Attorney General Jim

Mattox's office, were beginning to surface and take headline space and TV and radio news minutes.

I was sitting in my office on the second level of my home near Dallas on a Saturday morning, when the telephone from the front gate rang. There were three people to see me. I buzzed them in and walked out to greet them.

One of the visitors was a former Fort Worth cop who told me, 'Rumor has it that Fort Worth P.D. screwed the case up.'

'How so?'

'Seems they had a suspect with a child on two occasions and let her get away.'

'You're kidding.'

'Nope.' He continued, 'The last time, they even had them in the police station. They were going to make fingerprints of the suspect and footprints of the child. But they smudged the child's footprints. Apparently, one of the lieutenants then had to check something and walked down the hall. The suspect and the baby were gone when he got back.

'They're quite embarrassed over this,' he added, 'and I can assure you it won't hit the newspapers. But what it gets down to is, they just plain screwed up.'

I couldn't believe it. Mistakes happen, but this was ridiculous. I agreed to meet the Kennedys and take the case. It seemed the child wasn't going to be found by the Fort Worth Police or the FBI. And she was still too young to come crawling home on her own.

It isn't that I hate police departments or the FBI, but there are some stupid people with badges running around. Then people like me are left to clean up the mess. Naturally it embarrasses them and they start pointing the finger whenever they can. About a year earlier, the Texas Board of Private Investigators had filed a fourteen-count complaint against me. The charges weren't true, but I had made the mistake of investigating two important members of the Board of Private Investigators. It goes to show someone's always trying to get you when you're doing well. But that's another story.

I decided to handle the Kennedy case. When I visited the Kennedys in their modest Fort Worth home, I made another decision. I told Andy and Penny that the fee would be one dollar and I wanted no part of a $10,000.00 reward being offered for Cherie Ann's safe return. I knew they would have sold their souls to get their daughter back. I knew how they felt. As I've said, you have to be a parent to understand. Cherie Ann Kennedy became my top priority. My staff felt the same way.

The Fort Worth Police Department wouldn't help with any information. So I tried the FBI, with the same results. I was going to get the federal bureaucratic run-around, I could smell it coming. I ran into Daryl Shaver, the FBI agent in charge of the investigation. He and I had worked together at Retail Credit Company, and had both moved on to bigger and better things. Shaver promised to keep me informed, but that's not the way it worked out.

My associate, Dick Riddle, visited with the Fort Worth Investigators. Dick, a former police lieutenant, knew how to schmooze his way into the hearts and minds of the police. I had no tolerance for their lackluster and sloppy work; Dick sort of overlooked it and maneuvered his way right in.

In the meantime, I started going back to John Peter-Smith Hospital. Penny told me she went back many times to see if the woman returned. She knew she would recognize her. I made myself familiar with the hospital. I wanted to see everyone going in and out of the pediatrics area and I wanted the nurses to get to know me and tell me of anything suspicious.

All the time, the police said they had nothing, and kept quiet about the suspect and baby that got away – twice. But my involvement became known through media accounts and I began to receive calls with bits and pieces of information, some useful, some not. We started to put together a profile of the woman. Dick and I felt she was a former nurse or nurse's aide, perhaps at JPS. The hospital is huge, with numerous entrances. She had to know where to go, how to gain the confidence of a mother and where to exit. Quickly.

Then one day in June, I took a call. Cherie Ann Kennedy had been missing most of a month. The man on the line wouldn't identify himself but said he and a business associate might have something useful in the case of the missing baby. I agreed to meet them.

You run down a lot of leads until they turn out to be dead ends. But this looked different. The informant told me that he and his associate had been traveling south on Main next to John Peter-Smith the day of the kidnapping. He said they almost hit a heavyset nurse running across the street with a baby on her shoulder; they had to slam on the brakes to keep from hitting her. He said they were both startled and thought it looked a little funny so they watched her. She headed for an older, powder-blue car that they thought was a 1975 Buick Electra suffering from heavy rust, a damaged left headlight and a missing left rear hubcap. The engine was running as the chubby lady and baby got in on the passenger side. The car sped away, heading north toward downtown Fort Worth. The time was within twenty minutes of the kidnapping of Cherie Ann Kennedy.

Under hypnosis our witness was able to give us enough information to provide a detailed composite drawing of the suspect and the driver of the vehicle. The nurse was described as about forty-five years old, standing five foot seven inches, weighing between 170 and 190 pounds and wearing what appeared to be a blonde wig. The driver, perhaps a woman, was Hispanic, about thirty-five or forty years old, with a slender build, straight black hair and a hook nose.

The composite drawing of the nurse was shown to Penny Kennedy, who immediately recognized her as the person who took her daughter. As we left the hypnotist's office, FBI agents, who had obviously followed us there, went in to talk with him. They learned exactly what I would have told them had they just walked up and asked. I have a lot of friends in the Bureau, but the animosity between police and private investigators seems never to let up. We released the information during a news conference and passed out copies of the drawings to everyone including the police and FBI. But when I would call to see if *they* had learned anything, they were vague.

We checked with nurses' registries and hospitals all over the area, showing the drawings thousands of times. I held another news conference on June 27th, six weeks after Cherie Ann was kidnapped. We released another set of drawings, better composites, of the suspects and discussed the interviews we had with hospital officials, current and former employees and security at JPS. We were of the opinion that the suspect was very familiar with the hospital. If not a nurse or nurse's aide, she could have been in housekeeping. She probably hid in a vacant office until she thought the search of the halls and corridors was complete before leaving through the lower levels of the hospital to the waiting car. I had found that the hospital buildings were interconnected on the basement level and could have given her easy access to any building and the street without being detected. We were getting close to finding the kidnapper. But more important, I felt Cherie Ann Kennedy was alive.

I told Andy and Penny the suspect was probably someone who loved babies and would care for her, possibly unable to have children of her own. The woman had actually inquired about Cherie Ann's health and had been told the baby was in excellent health. I assured the nervous young couple, exhausted from lack of sleep, that we would find Cherie Ann and bring her home. And I truly believed that. But the time seemed to drag as July and August passed, yielding slowly into September. And a phone call.

It was a Dallas firefighter named Chuck Bratton. Arrangements were made for me to meet Chuck at a baseball park in Irving. I had an optimistic feeling as I drove up and parked my car. Chuck walked over, we introduced ourselves and shook hands.

'I tried to call the FBI and the police,' he said. 'I left my name and number. Even my number at the fire station. When nobody called back, I decided to call you. I read you have been working on the case.'

He told me his mother lived in Fort Worth, next door to a woman named Linda Gomez. He described Gomez as a very large woman in her forties who suddenly came up with two babies. Bratton said he first saw the children in June or July while visiting his mother. He became suspicious when he realised that the babies were too close in age to have been born of the same mother. His mother was also suspicious. She said she had once seen Gomez, through a window, lifting her dress and pulling a pillow from underneath. She remembered that Gomez had told the neighbors she was pregnant. It was shortly after this, that the baby Bratton felt might be Cherie Ann Kennedy appeared. It was early to mid-May, according to Bratton's mother. Not long after, *another* newborn appeared. According to Bratton's mother, Gomez claimed the child was adopted. The story seemed very flimsy. Then his mother saw the evidence we needed: Gomez in a nurse's uniform. I had found Cherie Ann Kennedy and her kidnapper. Bratton's information was exactly the break I had needed.

We immediately set up surveillance on the Gomez residence. But she had moved, and only her mother remained. Her maiden name was Linda Ashmore. She was now married to a Juan Gomez, who was about thirty-three years old. Her husband, younger than she, was working in Las Cruces, New Mexico. She had passed several bad checks in Fort Worth and El Paso, including one for a used car. There was a warrant for her arrest for auto theft. I figured if she had hot checks in El Paso and was related to a family in Mexico, it would be a matter of time before she would be across the border . . . with the babies and possibly in the stolen car.

I alerted friends of mine with the U.S. Border Patrol. I wanted to go there myself, but knew it would be like looking for a needle in a haystack. So now I could only wait. I didn't bother to call the Fort Worth police or the FBI, since they hadn't returned my calls. Besides, I wanted to have everything in line before I did call.

On November 2nd, my phone rang. Linda Ashmore Gomez had been arrested trying to cross the border into Mexico at El Paso in the blue car. The child matching the description of Cherie Ann Kennedy was also in the car. The Border Patrol had taken the baby to a nearby youth home for a doctor to examine. I called the doctor and described Cherie Ann, but he wanted a better description. So I called the Kennedys and told them what had happened. As you might expect, they were screaming with joy, laughing and crying, all at the same time. Penny managed to tell me of a birthmark that had not been previously disclosed. I quickly called the doctor. A nurse answered the phone and I described the birthmark. When she returned, she said, 'Mr Dear, that birthmark is on this baby.'

I told her of the kidnapping and to hold the baby there and not let Cherie Ann out of her sight. I called the Fort Worth police, but everyone was out, even when I told them it was an emergency. When I called the FBI office, I got an answering machine, so I left word for Daryl Shaver to call me concerning an emergency with Cherie Ann Kennedy.

Several hours passed without a word from either agency. Meanwhile, I was on the phone with the Kennedys. They were anxious to see their child, as anyone missing a child for six months would be. But you have to remember, with a lot of police investigators, five o'clock means it gets done tomorrow. But we weren't waiting for tomorrow. I called my pilot, Frank Lambert, and told him to ready the plane for the four of us to fly to El Paso. As I left for the Kennedys' home, Penny called and told me, 'Bill, Daryl Shaver of the FBI and a Lieutenant T.C. Swan of the Fort Worth police have called and said if you show up in El Paso, they'll have you arrested for obstruction of justice.'

Those sorry sons of bitches wanted to get the credit for finding Cherie Ann and were now bullying their way into the picture. All I wanted was to get Cherie Ann Kennedy back home. Once I was at their house, the Kennedys convinced me not to go.

'Bill,' Penny pleaded, 'I don't want anything to happen to you.'

Their family had all come over to be with them. There were probably fifteen or twenty people there, and together we waited all night. The phone seemed to ring constantly, but it was never the right call. All night we waited, and most of the next day, until Shaver called to say they would be in that night on a commercial flight, with Cherie Ann. Shaver said they would bring her to the house, but after I hung up, Andy and Penny insisted we go to D-FW Airport.

Late that afternoon, we left in a long convoy for the airport, where we were greeted by hundreds of people who heard that Cherie Ann had been found alive and was coming home. The media had shown up in force. Had we waited at home, we would have been the only ones not at the airport. I knew that Swan and

Shaver were not going to be happy to see me. But I didn't care.

As the silver American Airlines jet pulled up, Penny began to cry. She and Andy asked that I meet the law enforcement officials and have them hand Cherie Ann to me. I stood in the jetway and held out my arms to take Cherie Ann. Surprisingly, Shaver handed her over without hesitation. Cherie Ann and I walked into the cheering crowd and cameras and microphones. I walked straight over to Penny and Andy and said, 'Penny, Andy, here's your baby.' They were both crying, in fact, everyone in the concourse was crying.

Airport security and my staff helped us get through the crowd that followed all the way out to my car. Reporters and photographers from all over huddled around us as I put the elated parents and their baby in my car and drove them home for the happiest night since the birth of Cherie Ann. Before I left the hugs and handshakes of the family, I bent over and kissed little Cherie Ann on the forehead and told her, 'I love you.'.

Linda Ashmore Gomez was extradited to Fort Worth and held under bonds totaling a half million dollars. Eventually she went to jail.

That Sunday, in the Fort Worth *Star-Telegram*, the truth came out. There was a big article on how the police had held Gomez and Cherie Ann at the station, and when the lieutenant's back was turned Gomez took Cherie and left. To cover his embarrassment, Swan was quoted as saying he did receive a tip a couple of weeks before the child was located, concerning Gomez and another child living in Fort Worth. That was the attempt by Bratton to talk with the Fort Worth police and the FBI. He never got a return call. The reporter who wrote the article contacted Bratton after I had told him who the firefighter was. Bratton was quoted in the article and explained how he had contacted me after not getting anywhere with the police or FBI. He also repeated what he and his mother had seen.

Swan claimed I never contacted the police or the FBI about the case. I would have loved to have seen his message box stuffed with memos from me. Swan also said that his department and the FBI would have filed obstruction charges had I flown to El Paso to pick up the child. Who cares? Cherie was back home.

The final paragraph of the article made me very happy. Andy Kennedy was quoted as saying how pleased he was with my investigation and diligence in finding their baby. In fact, they were both so happy, they were going to ask me to be Cherie Ann's godfather, an offer I couldn't refuse. It would take special permission from the priest, since I wasn't Catholic, but that didn't seem to be a problem.

A couple of weeks later, the Kennedys called and asked me to meet them at the church. I knew what was taking place, but it didn't really sink in until the priest met me at the front door and said, 'Mr Dear, it's been approved. You're going to be the godfather of Cherie Ann Kennedy.'

We walked down the aisle and met the rest of the family. All of us, Penny and Andy, their parents and I stood facing the priest as Cherie Ann was christened. Then the priest handed Cherie Ann to me and made me her godfather. It was a wonderful moment.

Outside, as we all started to leave, the Kennedys gave me a gift. I got in my car and as everyone else drove away, I unwrapped the small gift. It was a plaque that read:

Bill Dear
Private Investigator

In appreciation for your time-consuming
efforts to locate our baby,
Cherie Ann Kennedy

Joe and Jean Walker
and
Andy and Penny Kennedy
1983

Lt Swan may have received his reward when he was made Police Officer of the Year for his work in the Cherie Ann Kennedy case, but I had a much greater reward.

BILL DEAR'S NOTEPAD: My Kingdom For a Plane!

I received a call one day from a woman whose fourteen-year-old daughter had run away to be with her father in Florida. The mother had a court order to bring the teenager back to Texas, because she had strong evidence to indicate the father was dealing in narcotics in Florida. I flew to St Augustine, Florida, with my associate, Major Don Tucker. We found the teenager, confronted her with the court order, put her in a car and drove twenty miles to the Jacksonville Airport to catch our flight back to Dallas. I was surprised at how well things were going, given the fact that the mother warned me about the father, who was a very powerful man in the area. There could be trouble. But so far things were going just fine. Or so I thought.

I had let the girl call her aunt to tell her we were taking her back to Dallas to be with her mother. I had also asked her girlfriend to let the family in St Augustine know she was fine. But when we got to the Jacksonville Airport, things just didn't feel right.

To begin with, our plane to Dallas had been delayed for forty-five minutes. That sometimes happens and I didn't think much about it. What I didn't know was that the family had called the St. Augustine authorities to report a kidnapping! The police called my client in Dallas and asked if she had ordered me to kidnap her daughter. She got scared by the implications and denied that she had.

Meanwhile, back at the airport, I suddenly heard an announcement over the public address system that *all* planes had been delayed. I saw police and airport security, guns drawn, racing through the crowded terminal. I got a sick feeling in my stomach. Something is amiss, I told myself, and methinks it's thee, Bill Dear. I told Don to stand with the girl while I made a call to the mother.

'What in the hell did you do?' I asked her. 'The cops are all over the place.'

180

'I just got mixed up, Bill,' she blubbered, 'I thought if I lied it would give you more time.'

'Lady, they're gonna kill me!'

'Oh, Bill, I'm so sorry . . . '

'Look,' I interrupted, 'I've got to go!'

I hung up and called the District Attorney's office to try to explain. But it was no use.

'Listen to me, Dear,' he blurted when he heard my voice, 'you're dead! Your life isn't worth crap, do you hear? You might as well give yourself up 'cause you're going to jail, or we'll shoot you on sight for kidnapping.'

Hey,' I said, 'I know who your friend is and just how powerful he is, but I've got a court order . . . '

'We don't recognize no Texas court order in this state . . . '

'So even if I turn myself in and give you back the girl . . . '

He interrupted me again. 'That's right, you're dead! Your ass is mine!'

I hung up the phone and ran back over to Don. 'We've got to get out of here!'

I took the girl over to the ladies' restroom, pushed her inside, and said, 'Don't you come out of here for anything!'

I then placed a tall heavy free-standing ashtray in front of the door. I found a 'Restroom out of order' sign from a cleaning lady's cart and hung it on the door of the restroom. I rested my foot on the ashtray and leaned over like I was smoking a cigarette; waiting impatiently, like thousands of other passengers, for the planes to start taking off again. I couldn't believe this guy had so much power he could shut down an international airport, but I had been warned.

I casually looked around at that moment to see twenty-five or thirty armed police coming through the terminal. Don was close by, but acting like he didn't really know me. We were just a couple of guys waiting in a crowded airport for a plane. Then I overheard one of the police say, 'We're gonna get this sonofabitch. We're gonna kill 'em.' Poor Don's eyes widened as he looked at me. Having been through World War II and Korea he had probably figured that at his age his life was finally out of danger. Now, armed men were looking to kill him.

'Look,' I ordered Don quietly, 'you get your ass downstairs and out of this airport. Then get home. I'll stay here and see what I can do. If you look back and see me raise my hands and they start to shoot me, you'll know they were ordered to shoot.'

He hesitated for a moment at the thought of leaving me behind. But I urged him to go. Just then, the girl stuck her head out of the restroom. I quickly pushed it back in.

'You stick your head out one more time,' I spat, 'and I'll knock it right off!'

The cops looked me over suspiciously. I knew they were looking for a man and a teenage girl, and I could only hope she would not stick her nose out again.

I said, 'Sure will be glad when you guys get through. We gotta plane to catch.' They had already heard the complaint dozens of times. I was just another disgruntled passenger.

The police moved on. Once they were clear of me I dumped the briefcase I had been carrying, ran down the stairs and made my way to the airport tarmac. There weren't any planes taking off and only a few landing, so I ran across the runways to the other side of the airport and into the woods.

It was getting dark and I found myself crawling through woods and marshlands in a suit and tie. Soon there were helicopters overhead, their spotlights shining down into the woods, trying to find a so-called kidnapper. I ducked beneath underbrush and stayed still until they had left. My coat was dark and I had my hands in my coat to keep the light from reflecting off my rings and watch. After a while the choppers passed on by, and I was able to make my way out and to a nearby airport hotel.

I slowed my run to a casual walk as I went into the hotel like I belonged and headed straight for a restroom. I knew they would soon search the surrounding hotels and buildings, so I went into a stall and perched myself up on the cistern. I felt like an overgrown buzzard. Before long some cops burst into the restroom. They never opened any of the stalls; they just glanced under them to see if any feet were showing, and left.

But I wasn't taking any chances on coming out and walking right into a trap. So I waited. I sat perched on that toilet for three and a half hours. Finally, I came down from my roost, went to a phone and made a call to the District Attorney, who informed me they had the girl back. I figured they had by now.

'Well, I want you to know,' I said, 'I didn't do anything wrong. I had a court order. You've got the girl back.'

'Give yourself up, Dear,' he said, 'You're dead meat. I've already told you that once.'

'Go to Hell,' I yelled, and hung up. I went back and hid in that restroom all night.

The next morning I eased out of the restroom again and quietly walked down the hall. It was still very early and not much was going on. I needed to look like I had a purpose in life, so I picked up a couple of empty shirt boxes someone had left outside their door. I tucked the boxes under my arm like they were mine. As I continued down the hall, I noticed scraps of food left from various room-service dinners the night before. By this time I was starving to death. So as I walked I selected a few pieces of bread that looked like they had not been touched and ate my breakfast.

Once outside, I hailed a cab and had the driver take me to another airport in the vicinity. I knew now that they had the girl and the heat was off, but I didn't want to take my chances with the Jacksonville Airport again.

I made it home. Eventually we managed to bring the girl back to Texas, regardless of the politics.

I also developed a new policy: never use the Jacksonville, Florida Airport.

CHAPTER 11
The Desperate Search for Christie Meeks

In January 1985 I was living on twenty-eight acres of land spread out across the North Texas countryside, south of Dallas. Three gates, electronically controlled and watched by remote television cameras, separated my staff and me from the outside world. The drive wound along half a mile of road from the first gate, past the guests' quarters, stables and tennis court, through the second gate and over a bridge that spanned a small creek, to the third gate that provided the entrance to my home and offices. It was a beautiful and captivating approach that embraced the lay of the land and the grove of trees that hid my residence. Many who visited, noting the helipad and facilities for an array of automobiles, said the combination of nature, beauty and unobtrusive, though effective, high-tech security would have made Howard Hughes green with envy.

There were times when I simply enjoyed the place and other times when I really needed its seclusion. The heartbreak I felt following the Amber Crum investigation resulted in one of those times of need. My home gave me sanctuary as well as access to my work, as little or as much work as I wanted during such times. It hadn't been too long after the Amber Crum investigation when my phone rang one morning. A man was asking me to consider helping someone else, someone whose child was missing. I get emotional about such cases. If they turn out all right, I get a high that can't be matched. If they don't . . .

'This fellow,' the voice on the phone told me, 'isn't Mr Personality, but he cares about his children just like you do. He's also trying to raise his children like you've raised Michael.'

I had gained custody of Michael when he was two years old, following my divorce. That was about the same age as Christie when Mike Meeks got custody of his daughter.

I had been following the case of Christie Meeks since she had last been seen several days before at her mother's apartment in Dallas. I had noted that the five-year-old had disappeared about fifteen miles from Amber Crum's home, and I was wondering if my suspect had struck again. I guess I just couldn't put little Amber Crum out of my mind.

My friend told me he knew Mike Meeks simply could not afford my fee. I knew any father would gladly pay any price for his little girl's return. But there are times when fees just don't matter. This would be one. I agreed to meet with Mike Meeks and his second wife Lisa.

The couple were hard-working people, living on the east side of Dallas in Mesquite. This working man, racked with pain that grew with each passing moment his daughter's whereabouts remained a mystery, had pulled together his entire life savings of $5,000 to put up a reward for her safe return. Within a few days, the fund had grown to $25,000 through the generosity of people in the area. But I assured Mike I wasn't interested in the money, I wanted to find Christie. I said, 'Don't pay me whether we find her or not. Use the money for a trust fund for Christie and her brother.' Like my friend said, Mike Meeks was a gruff fellow, but he readily agreed to the plan.

I left the Mesquite home with a rather pessimistic feeling about ever finding the five-year-old these two people loved so much. I did think there was a remote possibility of a link between the disappearance of Christie Meeks and that of Amber Crum. If I were to find the same man had abducted both, I could solve two cases at once. And if that person happened to be James Britt Monroe, his ass would be mine.

The first thing I noticed, as I drove to visit Linda Peacock, Christie's mother, was how hard it was to find the apartment complex even though it was visible from Interstate 20. If you knew which building you were looking for, located between two exits on the interstate, you could easily see it. But most of those apartment buildings looked the same, and I actually had to drive to Town East Boulevard, some distance from the apartment, to find a exit to turn around and get there. It was a convoluted drive, but a simple walk from the highway. To kidnap the child and speed away in a car would draw attention and require the motorist to know the complex entrances and exits. It would also slow the getaway tremendously, and could bring the car back into view of any witnesses for a second look as it drove down the interstate.

I pulled into the complex, which was called Charter Oaks. I never understood why they bothered to name these cookie-cutter apartment buildings. Except for the paint, they looked alike. Why didn't they call them Beige, Mud Brown or Off-White Apartments instead of these meaningless names?

I had the distinct feeling as I parked my car that the job wasn't going to be easy. Most of the residents were transients, perhaps with children, perhaps not. They never saw anything, didn't hear anything, didn't know anything except what went on inside their little five-hundred-square-foot box; not the kind of people to talk to the police. Hell, most were probably wanted for some violation or other; parking or traffic tickets that remained unpaid, maybe even a little drug dealing. They lived off the dreams of other people; championship high-school football teams or the escapades of Jerry Hall, the Mesquite native who is married to Mick Jagger. The Mesquite Championship Rodeo and its owner Don Gay, well known in the country, did very well with the locals. They could escape lives of quiet desperation in the lives of their heroes in the arena. Of course, not everyone in the town of 85,000 is like that. Most of the people in Mesquite are hard-working, family people who go to church and raise their kids to be strong, upstanding adults. They take pride in their town, as they should. But Charter Oaks people, unfortunately, take up a lot of space in Mesquite.

I noticed that the layout of open space in the vicinity of the buildings would make it hard for someone to kidnap a child without *anyone* seeing or hearing anything. I was surprised how quickly Linda opened the door when I knocked. Her husband, Eddie, was standing behind her. By this time, perhaps because I had had a chance to mull the case over in my mind or perhaps because I have a sense of these things, I had developed a feeling that Christie Meeks was already dead. I wasn't about to tell Linda or Mike. Though my experience in these cases taught me when to face reality, I knew never to let the parents have reason to give up hope. Most of the time, it's all they have.

The apartment had seen better days. Linda told me about the day Christie disappeared. The day had started out beautiful, but a fast-moving cold front had turned the sunny morning into a more typically gray January afternoon. Christie had been playing with friends. She had worn a pair of skates most of the day, but sometime during the afternoon she came back to the apartment and traded the skates for a pair of Cabbage Patch tennis shoes. She still had on the bluejeans and T-shirt with which she started the day. When Christie went missing, approximately 5.45 p.m., Linda had gone to the store. Eddie had just come home from work, so Linda didn't worry about leaving Christie.

Something wouldn't let me warm up to Eddie. I took an instant dislike to him the moment we met, but I tried not to let it interfere with my work. Through the back door was a four-foot square fenced patio, with a little gate leading to an area beyond with another solid fence about five feet farther which defined the property line. It was an area where the kids could play, or people could walk, behind the apartments.

I talked with some of the children playing there, as well as with their parents. I got more details than the police had; some thought they remembered a man, others remembered what Christie was wearing. I was still finding it hard to believe no one saw anything, but it was obvious from the surroundings that people just didn't care. There were wadded-up chip bags, beer cans, cigarette butts, garbage and old furniture scattered everywhere in the little fenced-in alleyway. I even picked up a dime. I passed out my business cards and told them I would keep any information confidential, the same speech I've made ten thousand times. But many of the parents said they didn't want to get involved and none of my conversations produced anything in the way of hard evidence.

I did learn during another talk with Linda that Christie came home from school one day with a little necklace. When Mike Meeks asked her about it she hemmed and hawed and finally said that one of her little girlfriends had given it to her. Neither the police nor the teachers had ever mentioned a necklace, and I wondered if an adult had given it to her. Apart from the necklace clue, very little in the case changed, except for the carnival atmosphere.

The media had really become involved in the story, and everything from Saturday search parties to psychics was being tried in the hopes of finding Christie Meeks. It was time to separate the speculation from fact. As I saw it:

1. The abductor had to live there, or know someone who lived there, to be in the area on more than one occasion without raising suspicion.

2. Christie didn't resist or make a lot of noise when she was taken. That would have aroused some suspicion, even here. Therefore she probably knew her abductor.

3. Someone noticed a man in the area with a mug of beer. The fact he had it in a mug and not a can indicated that he probably lived in the complex or nearby.

Apart from this we had nothing. Then, one day, a break.

One of the children remembered hearing someone yell to Christie, just before she disappeared, 'Come to Daddy' or 'Come to Danny' or even 'Come to Teddy.' Linda said she didn't know anyone named Danny or Denny or Teddy. But a little girl told me of an uncle with whom Christie spent some time. I asked Linda and she said, she had a brother named Robert Anthony. He was twenty-three and lived in another complex in Mesquite.

Mike Meeks didn't know much about Anthony, other than the fact that Linda had lived with him for a while. It wasn't much, but I called in a few favors to run down a Robert Anthony. What I received was a Robert D. Anthony, living in Mesquite. He had no criminal record.

I also discovered, in a subsequent interview, that Linda had just scolded Christie, not twenty minutes before she disappeared, about going outside the area in which she was allowed to play. I felt that if she knew the person who abducted her she might have thought it okay. In fact, if that person was a relative, she wouldn't have hesitated.

It was time to call Robert Anthony. I had a hunch about his middle initial. When he answered the phone I said, 'Yes, is Danny there?'

'This is Danny,' he replied.

I said, 'Well, I'm looking for Danny Davis.'

'Sorry,' he replied. 'My name is Robert Anthony.'

I decided it was time to visit the very lovely Cascade Apartments.

After assuring his apartment manager that everything I was told would be in the strictest of confidence, she opened up. It seems there had been a complaint in 1984. Anthony had exposed himself to small children as they passed by his apartment on their way from school. The manager said she never called the police because she felt it would be too difficult to prove Anthony had exposed himself. However, I was able to find a witness in the complex who had seen the event, and had made the original complaint.

The manager pulled her file on Anthony and gave me the make and model of Anthony's car, a 1971 Pontiac. Dick began surveillance on Anthony and his car. The vehicle registration told me that Anthony had previously lived at the New West Apartments in Dallas, no doubt another garden spot in the Metroplex.

At the New West the manager told me Anthony had lived with a divorcee with a child. The woman's name was Debra Houseman. Another source who lived at the apartment told me that Houseman's bedside table held a notepad with the names Robert Anthony and *Jimmy* Anthony next to corresponding phone numbers. I talked to Mike Meeks who confirmed that Linda had *another* brother named Jimmy, who worked for him at his shop. A further check revealed that Debra's maiden name was Brown. Then I discovered that Mike Meeks had taken out a marriage license in 1973 with a woman named Trema Brown, but the marriage never occurred. It's so easy to be thrown on to the wrong track by similar names. You have to be very meticulous in background searches to avoid an embarrassing mistake.

Unlike Robert, Jimmy Anthony had a criminal record. In 1981 he was charged with possessing a dangerous drug. In 1982 he was charged with driving while intoxicated. The paperwork indicated that Jimmy had shown his employer to be Mike Meeks.

Several of the witnesses I talked with thought they recalled a small gray or yellow vehicle in the area before the disappearance of Christie Meeks. I found that Debra Houseman drove a yellow 1980 two-door Toyota. She had received the car as part of her divorce settlement from her ex-husband George Houseman.

Through further investigation I obtained the name of a Mrs Sammy Spillman, who lived about three blocks from the Charter Oaks Apartments. It took some persuasion to get Mrs Spillman to open up; like most people in the area, she didn't want to get involved. But once she knew we were seriously trying to locate Christie, she started to talk.

On the day of Christie's disappearance she had driven by the apartments on her way home from shopping at around 5.30. It was time to fix supper for her husband. That's why she recalled the time, because she always had supper ready for her husband at 6 p.m.

She noticed a man and a little girl fitting Christie's description walking hand-in-hand along the street, and when he opened the car door for her, the girl gladly hopped in. Mrs Spillman didn't pay much attention until her son, a police officer with the University Park Police Department, arrived at approximately 8 p.m. and asked what all the police cars were doing at the Charter Oaks Apartments. A phone call to the Mesquite Police Department gave Mrs Spillman the explanation. A little girl was missing and possibly kidnapped.

We presented Mrs Spillman with photographs of several young men and asked if she recognized any of them. We didn't tell her who they were. She stopped at one and asked, 'Isn't this Robert Anthony?'

'Why?'

Mrs Spillman, who worked at a local bank, said she knew on a casual basis one of the regular customers, a bookkeeper with a frozen foods company in Dallas. When she told the customer about living near the apartments where Christie Meeks was abducted and how the police and reporters were everywhere, her friend told her that one of Christie's uncles worked with her at the frozen foods business. According to the bookkeeper, Christie was his favorite niece and he was her favorite uncle. His name was Robert Anthony. Mrs Spillman recognized him as a bank customer.

A few days after her conversation with the bookkeeper, Mrs Spillman received a call from an inquisitive Robert Anthony, wanting to know what she had seen the evening Christie disappeared. After she had told him what she saw, which seemed to her like nothing much, he told her that if she remembered anything else she was to call the police. She thought it awfully strange he called, but she figured her conversation with Anthony wasn't of any consequence. That's usually the way cases are solved, by some tucked-away piece of information people don't realize they have. -

By phone I confirmed that Robert Anthony worked as a truck-driver for Country Pride Foods.

On April 3rd, J.A. 'Les' Owens and his fishing partner, Toby Evans, were trolling in their boat along the edges of Lake Texoma trying to snag the whopper that would make up their next fishing lie for the buddies back home. They didn't know they were about to snag the biggest fishing story of their lives.

Lake Texoma is a popular boating and fishing lake in Eisenhower State Park, about fifty miles north of Dallas on the Texas-Oklahoma border. As the two men drifted quietly across the smooth cool lake in the early spring morning one of them saw something floating in the water. They swung in as close as they could to some submerged brush. Tangled in its dead branches were the remains of a child. They fired up the outboard and lunged for the shore. They called the Grayson County Sheriff's Department, who called the Justice of the Peace.

It seemed only minutes before four deputies and the Justice of the Peace Charles Olde were on the scene. The J.P. could tell that the body was badly decomposed, and a special pallet had to be used to pull the remains from the lake. It appeared that the child was a small boy wearing bluejeans and a t-shirt with the words *Color Me The Rainbow* written across the front. On one of the little feet was a Cabbage Patch tennis shoe. The J.P. didn't recognize the significance of this; he was unaware that Christie had been wearing Cabbage Patch tennis shoes.

Grayson County does not have a medical examiner, so the child's body was taken to the Dallas County Medical Examiner's Office. Dr William Roe, Associate Pathologist, examined the severely-decomposed remains and concluded that probably the child was a young boy and that the cause of death was an accidental drowning. But what didn't make the examiner's report, or for that matter, any police dispatches, was the fact the body had panties on it, the type a little girl would be wearing, even in bluejeans.

It was two weeks, until April 17th, before the complete description of the child made the wires and cleared the teletype of the Mesquite Police Department. When someone saw bluejeans, t-shirt and one Cabbage Patch tennis shoe, it dawned on everyone this little boy might have been Christie Meeks.

Two investigators from Mesquite drove to the Medical Examiner's office and demanded a re-examination of the remains. This time, under more careful scrutiny, it was discovered the body was not that of a five-to-seven-year-old boy, but a five-year-old girl. It was Christie Meeks.

The police called Mike Meeks and asked that he bring Christie's dental charts for verification. Though it had been three months, and he had had time to realize she was probably dead, Christie's father now had to face the stark reality of it. I got the call right after Mike and was on my way to the M.E.'s office in a second. I had been afraid of this all along. In my mind, it was only a matter of time.

When the dental records were checked, the identification was positively made. It was, without a doubt, Christie. Mike's grief turned to rage aimed at the Medical Examiner.

'You mean to tell me,' he screamed, 'that she's been lying here for two weeks in panties and you thought all along it was a little boy! How could you do that? How could you be so stupid?'

I couldn't blame him. My staff and I had been in contact with every police department in Texas and several in the surrounding states on the chance they may have come across something that would lead us to Christie, and her body had lain in the M.E.'s office for two weeks, misidentified as to its sex! I would have some serious run-ins with the Chief Medical Examiner, Dr Charles Petty, on other occasions, but this one took the cake. To inflict a screw-up of this magnitude on the parents after what they had already gone through was unforgivable. Had I been the Dallas County Judge, I would have fired Petty and Roe on the spot!

I reserved my rage for the privacy of my office, trying to be supportive of Mike. Besides, the case was not over. I had to find Christie's killer. Unlike in the case of Amber Crum, there was a body to work with, and I knew there was a killer on the street. I had an idea where to start.

I worked closely with the Mesquite police, giving them what I had. Of course, as is usually the case with a police department embarrassed at having not found the killer, we got very little in return. I didn't let that stop me. I decided to interview Anthony. His middle initial, I discovered stood for Daniel not Danny, although his family called him 'Danny.'

At the same time a TV producer I knew in California called to ask me what cases I was working on. He and I had become friends after the publication of my book *The Dungeon Master*. I told him I was trying to close in on the killer of Christie Meeks. He had heard about the case and asked if he could do a television show. I had already decided to interview Danny, and the producer asked that I wait until he had a camera crew there. I thought about it and decided a few more days wouldn't matter. I couldn't do anything for Christie now.

On the day of the interview I was wired for sound by a remote, wireless tie-tack microphone. The camera crew and the producer set up our surveillance van at Country Pride Foods and shot the interview from across the road. I found Danny's truck and waited nearby. At five o'clock he came out and I walked up behind him.

'Hi, Danny.'

He immediately turned and acknowledged me. I told him who

I was, and we sat down on the lowered tailgate of his truck. I noticed his rod, reel and other fishing tackle in the back of the truck. He told me his whole family called him Danny. Funny, I thought, his sister Linda, Christie's mother, said she didn't know a Danny.

Danny told me the disappearance and murder of Christie had really taken its toll on him and he couldn't understand why someone would hurt her. He also said he and Christie, whom he called Chrissy, had been very close; he told me about an occasion when he took Christie and another little girl to an amusement park. He said he had gone to Lake Texoma on one occasion and was planning another trip with his girlfriend. I was also able to get him to say the Lake Texoma area was part of his route for the frozen food company.

Later he offered the story of the company bookkeeper talking with the woman at the bank about Christie's favorite uncle. It didn't surprise me he was relating this. Most suspects will offer some information they think will check out and make it look as if everything they say is the truth. I asked him if he ever talked with the woman at the bank. At first he said no. Then when I asked, 'Are you sure?' he looked rather startled and suddenly recanted.

'Oh, yeah,' he replied nervously, 'talked with her once on the phone.'

I asked him if he knew of anyone who would want to hurt Christie. He said there was a guy by the name of Arnold Fox from Fort Worth.

'He once threatened to kill me,' Danny said, 'but I don't think Fox would kill Christie just to get at me.'

I finally asked if he knew of anyone in his or Mike's family who had ever been in trouble for sexual abuse or exposing themselves to children. He said no. Knowing better, I simply smiled.

He did say he had used drugs in the past, and had received them from Arnold Fox. But he claimed he had not used them in quite some time. He confirmed a few other items of interest, like his brother Jimmy's employment with Mike Meeks. He said he lived alone, except for the time when his sister Linda lived with him briefly.

As we shook hands and I walked away, the hidden camera stayed on Danny. I had obviously struck a nerve by the way he watched me leave. Later, the camera crew and I agreed we had hit paydirt.

I went back to my office and made some notes as to what I knew so far:

1. Linda didn't acknowledge knowing a Danny, even though Danny was her own brother.

2. Danny had been caught exposing himself to children. I later confirmed that through several other witnesses at his apartment complex.

3. Danny was about the same size and build as the man seen in the area just before Christie disappeared.

4. Danny had been growing a beard at the time, a key part of the suspect's description. He shaved it off right after Christie disappeared, as everyone was searching for a bearded kidnapper.

5. Danny first denied he ever called Mrs Spillman, but then changed his story.

6. He mentioned 'degrading' himself when using drugs, but never told me what that meant.

7. Fishing gear in his truck. Lake Texoma is a favorite fishing spot.

8. Danny's route took him to the Lake Texoma area, though he would later tell me his route didn't quite make it there. Christie's body was discovered at Lake Texoma.

9. His girlfriend owned a yellow Toyota which looked like the car Spillman saw the evening Christie disappeared.

10. Danny seemed to evade the tough questions I had about Christie and her disappearance, and his face would flush when I asked if he had any idea who killed Christie.

11. When I mentioned Eddie Peacock, Linda's husband, Danny seemed very protective of him, pointing to a cover-up.

12. Danny said he had a friend named Robert in the Lake Texoma area. Later he would change the name of the friend to William Jack Greer, a supermarket manager in Denison.

13. Danny had a beer mug in the window of his apartment with Christie's picture on it. He seemed extremely close to the child. It

often made me wonder about the kind of relationship they had.

14. Christie was wearing a necklace she was very secretive about. She had apparently received the necklace around Christmas 1984, during the time she and her mother stayed with Danny.

15. Danny lived about three or four minutes from Christie's mother's apartment.

16. As a truck driver for Country Pride Foods, Danny would have been able to place Christie's body in his refrigerated truck and take it to Lake Texoma unnoticed.

All of these might add up to coincidence, but I doubted it. I decided to dig a bit deeper, namely with his friend Bob in Denison. Danny seemed to have trouble with names and it turned out Bob was actually named William Jack Greer and was the assistant manager of a supermarket where Danny delivered for Country Pride. When I talked with Greer, he told me Danny was off the week following Christie's disappearance. He said Danny was very emotional about the whole affair, mentioning that even though he had been to Eisenhower State Park the year before, he couldn't go back knowing Christie's body had been found there.

Texas Park Ranger Julian Means told me that from what he had seen of the site where Christie's body was found, whoever put it in the cove had to know where they were going and what they were doing, because the water's current wouldn't have washed the body into the cove. Debra Houseman told me she and Danny had gone to Lake Texoma in July of 1982. I searched the park records and found they stayed in Shelter Site #7 in the park, near where Christie's body was found in the spring of 1985.

When I went to pick Danny up for a little fact-finding trip up to the lake, he volunteered that he had mistakenly referred to Jack Greer as Bob and that his route for Country Pride did not include the area near Lake Texoma. He said he hadn't been to the lake in years, contrary to what Greer and Houseman said. He also said he wanted Greer and his brother Jimmy with him for the trip. Then he decided not to go, so we rescheduled the trip for the next morning. But the next day, a Sunday morning, he told me he had been advised by Captain Kyle Hale and Chief Grayson of the Mesquite police not to go with me. Captain Hale was a deacon at the church Danny attended. I checked with the church to find that Danny had walked down the aisle the week after Christie's body was found, become a Christian and joined the church. Danny told me that all of his sins had been cleansed away.

Though Danny denied having gone to Linda's apartment the day Christie was kidnapped, Debra Houseman said Danny phoned her to get Linda's address. There were a host of other contradictions surrounding Danny, like telling people he intended to have children, though he believed he was sterile due to a football injury or a car accident, depending on who you talked with; the fact he had trouble remembering the last name of the girl he was currently dating. These things are minor when standing alone, but together indicate a tendency toward lying.

I decided to take my information to the Mesquite Police. The TV producer asked to film the reaction of the police department. They were understandably reluctant, but finally gave in and allowed him to film.

After my presentation to the Chief of Police and his staff, the producer turned to the Chief and asked, 'On a scale of one to ten, how does Mr Dear's investigation rate?'

'A nine,' the Chief replied. His staff agreed.

I walked out of the Mesquite Police Headquarters feeling I had done as much as I could to bring the killer of Christie Meeks to justice. I looked back to a conference table scattered with more evidence and photographs than they needed to finish this investigation. But I still couldn't figure why Chief Grayson and Captain Hale had told Danny not to talk with me any more, despite how close I was to a confession from Danny regarding his involvement. I had noticed a lieutenant leave the room a few times during the meeting. I later learned he had apparently called all my witnesses and told them not to speak with me; just as the department had done with Danny.

It wasn't long after that Eddie and Linda Peacock moved out of the Charter Oaks Apartments. I went over and, while looking through their trash, came across a map of nearby Lake Ray Hubbard. I recalled how Mike Meeks said that Linda called the day they began searching, saying she had two flat tires and no money to buy new ones. Danny and Jimmy replaced them for her, then threw the old tires behind Mike's building. It turned out that huge thorns, the kind found in the wooded areas near Lake Ray Hubbard, had punctured the tires. Had Danny killed Christie? Or had Eddie killed Christie in an unknown fit of rage when he came home that day? Had he and perhaps Linda taken the body of the child to Lake Ray Hubbard? Had Danny moved the body to Lake Texoma to help protect his sister?

The Mesquite Police have shut down my investigation into the Meeks case, so we may never know. To this day, no one has been indicted and brought to trial for the kidnapping and murder of Christie Meeks.

However, I have not yet given up.

BILL DEAR'S NOTEPAD: Just Sit Up and Take Notice!

Police officers are always taking off-duty jobs to earn a little extra cash. Most of the time these jobs consist of turning up in uniform as a deterrent to violence at rock concerts or football games. Not much happens outside of a few 'drunk and disorderly' arrests, if that much, and it's usually easy money and good public relations. Of course, I do things the unusual way: when I was a trooper of the Florida Highway Patrol, my off-duty job was hauling dead bodies for funeral homes.

I don't really know why the funeral homes would come to us for part-time help, but they did. And for twenty-five bucks all I had to do was put on a dark suit and drive the dear departed from the hospital to the funeral home. It was easy, quiet work, at least most of the time.

It was, naturally, a dark and stormy night in South Florida. One of the garden-variety thunderstorms was passing over the lower half of the peninsula and putting on a light show that would rival any Fourth of July display at the White House. I had gone home after working my shift and put on the only dark suit I owned, in fact the only suit I owned of any colour.

I picked up the hearse from the funeral director and drove a hundred miles north to a hospital in Fort Meyers. It was going to be a simple run up the coast, pick up the body and bring it to the funeral home in Miami. As always we were very careful and respectful when placing the body in the hearse and making sure the gurney was locked down. Then, in the driving rain and pulsating lightning, I jumped in the hearse and headed south.

As I headed toward Miami, I had the radio on for a little music and some news on the storm. It wasn't letting up at all, it was getting worse. Lightning strikes became more frequent and much more intense as I drove through the rain-soaked night. I had almost forgotten about the body in the back, because I was

199

watching the road and the explosions of lightning all around me. The windshield wipers were barely keeping up with the torrential downpour. It was a night out of a Stephen King thriller. My skin crawled and the little hairs on the back of my neck stood up. I hoped it was fear and not the static electricity building up in my body that would lure a bolt of death my way.

Then, very quietly, between the rolls of thunder I heard something. I couldn't quite make it out. It was a low rumble . . . no, more like a moan. I couldn't make it out. Probably the old hearse creaking with age, I thought. But then I heard it again.

Suddenly, a flash of lightning lit everything up around me. I looked in my rearview mirror to see the corpse rise straight up into a sitting position on the gurney!

'Holy—!'

I didn't even finish the exclamation before I found myself in a struggle to keep the hearse out of the ditch. The body in my rearview mirror swayed with each jerking turn of my wheel. I fought against the slick highway and the weight of the hearse until I came to a sudden stop.

The car hadn't rolled. I was safe. But that damned body was still sitting up. I jumped out of the car, visions of old horror movies running through my mind. My intelligence told me that the body had not been strapped down at the chest and a combination of nerves not yet dead and gases not yet expelled made the corpse both moan and sit up. It was natural and quite common. As I stood there getting soaked, I decided to finish the job. I walked to the back of the hearse, hoping Bela Lugosi wouldn't jump out as I opened the door. There sat the body, straight up on the gurney, looking right at me.

Yes, I told myself, the eyes are still partly open because the mortician had not permanently fixed them closed; the body had not even been embalmed.

Reluctantly, I climbed into the hearse and gently pushed the body back down. Then I made sure it was strapped down this time. I got out of the rear of the hearse, and for some reason, wiped my hands on my soaked suit. I calmly walked back to the front of the hearse like it wasn't even raining, got in and resumed my trip. It was the last trip I made for a funeral home. This kind of excitement I didn't need. I could earn twenty-five bucks at a rock and roll concert.

CHAPTER 12
The Great Impostor

Of all the people I've met during my career in law enforcement or as a private investigator, none compare to the mysterious personality who called himself by many names. I knew him as Jack Eubanks.*

I had just left police work for good to work for the Retail Credit Company of Dallas. The name was misleading. I didn't investigate credit reports or anything like that. I investigated people for insurance companies to determine if their claims were valid. But all of us at the company had about twenty reports, each containing around three personal interviews to type up every day. The insurance companies paid Retail Credit about $15.00 for each report and the investigators were paid a salary. It didn't take long to realize that each person could not get through that much work per day and honestly say each case was thoroughly investigated. I began to feel the same slipshod situation developing as in Miami and Grand Prairie. The difference was the contacts I was making.

My boss at Retail Credit asked me to join the Toastmaster Club in Dallas along with his two assistants. Retail Credit thought I had great management potential and wanted me to learn the skills of public speaking; Toastmaster was a club that helped promote good public-speaking habits as well as good fellowship. That is where I met a man by the name of Tom Hight, who helped me get started as a private investigator. I also met a fellow by the name of Thomas A. P. Krock, son of Pulitzer Prizewinning New York columnist Arthur Krock. Thomas Krock was a stately gentleman with a mustache, who reminded me of an old Kentucky colonel. He was usually with another man by the name of Jack Eubanks.

In 1962 Eubanks was in his mid-forties and looked like a very successful Texas businessman, or perhaps a high-ranking military officer in civilian clothes, or maybe a top surgeon. With his lean looks and educated manner he could have been all three at once; impersonating other people was what Jack Eubanks could do better than anyone else in the world.

Eubanks had a dynamic way of speaking, with a command of the English language other club members could only wish for. I heard him speak on many occasions and was awestruck by his talents at communicating with his audience. He was the kind of speaker Retail Credit Company wanted me to learn from. I watched him at meetings, noticing how he met people and how he handled himself.

The original Great Impostor was a man by the name of Walter Demara. He had successfully impersonated military leaders, captains of industry, even doctors, without getting caught. Tony Curtis had played him in a movie. But Jack Eubanks was a better actor than Demara *or* Curtis. Of course, I had no way of knowing it at the time. No one had.

At the same time Tom Hight, a prominent Dallas lawyer, was beginning to ask me about my long-term plans. Over the course of several meetings, as I watched Eubanks out of the corner of my eye, Hight and I talked about my future. Then one night Hight took me aside.

'You don't seem to be too happy about your future at Retail Credit.'

'Well, not really, Tom,' I replied.

'Tell you what,' he said, 'why don't you go to work for me?'

'Doing what?' I knew the answer, I was just surprised.

'You will be my investigator.'

I couldn't believe what I was hearing. I jumped at the chance. I would be working real cases for an attorney for a change, cases that required a skill at finding clues good enough to hold up in a court of law. It was exactly the break I was looking for.

The next day I walked into the offices of Retail Credit, past the other slaves chained to their jobs. I picked up the twenty-odd cases laying on my desk, threw them straight into the air and let them scatter across the room. It was probably the most excitement that salt mine had seen in years, until the manager was charged with embezzling company funds.

I began with civil cases. Tom taught me how to take statements from officers and witnesses, how to have all of the paperwork, pictures and diagrams in order, complete with the properly signed and filed statements. Tom taught me how to prepare everything for admission into court. I was enjoying the job, in fact, I loved it. I worked night and day. I couldn't get enough. I soaked in information and procedures like a sponge. I did everything I could to learn all I could from Tom. Then one day, Tom called me into his office.

'Bill, I'm letting you go.'

My heart fell and I sank in the chair. 'Have I not done a good enough job?'

'Oh, you've done just the opposite,' he said. 'You've done a great job. That's why I think it would be unfair for me to keep you on exclusively. I've recommended you to work for several other lawyers I know, as well as continue to work on all of my cases. So, go get your license and open your own company; you're going to have plenty of work.'

That night was Toastmaster night and I walked in with a newfound confidence and a gleam in my eye. Bill Dear was going to be self-employed. From that point on I was the head of William C. Dear and Associates, Private Investigators. My dream had come true.

I shared my good news with the members of the Toastmaster Club that night. Jack Eubanks was the first one to jump up and come forward with an outstretched hand of congratulation, followed by Tom Krock. Later, a member pulled me aside and asked if I knew much about Eubanks and Krock.

'No,' I said, 'except for what I know of them here at the club.'

'Well,' the member said in a hushed tone, 'they're both federal prisoners at the Seagoville Federal Prison just east of Dallas.

They're brought here by the prison officials on the nights we hold the meetings, then picked up and taken back. It's part of some kind of a rehab program we're involved with.'

I stood in shock as he continued.

'Krock was sent to prison for representing a foreign government without registering with the United States State Department. I'm not exactly sure what Eubanks is doing time for. But they will both be freed in a few years.'

I couldn't believe what I was hearing. But Eubanks and I stayed in touch after he got out of prison.

Eubanks worked in his brother's paint store in Dallas. I would visit him often, when I wasn't playing detective, and pick his brain. He had a wealth of great stories about his life, but he was also a tremendously smart man and helped me figure out things about some of my cases. He stayed with the Toastmasters long after prison. Finally, he decided to run for Toastmaster International Director. I helped him because I believe everyone deserves a second chance.

One day another member of the club came to me and suggested there was something more to Eubanks and I should check him out. By then Eubanks was well connected in the organization, traveling over the country making speeches as he rose through the ranks toward the position he sought of International Director.

I had noticed how he could always manage to drive a new car, yet make virtually no money except what little his brother paid him for working at the paint store. I would watch him on the phone at the paint store, when his brother wasn't there, putting down bill collectors. It was amazing to see him put them off so successfully.

So, I decided it was time to pay the FBI a visit. I took another member of the Toastmaster Club with me to the Dallas office of the FBI. I told the agent I had made friends with a guy by the name of Jack Eubanks, but some things didn't seem to add up. The agent excused himself for a moment. When he returned he had an eighteen-inch-thick file which made an unmistakable slap when it hit the agent's desk.

'This is your Jack Eubanks,' he told me, 'alias Jack Kenneth

Ritchie, alias this and alias that.' The list of names could fill a football team roster. And the coach was the only player.

The agent said, 'You guys in the Toastmaster are rather gullible, aren't you?'

'What do you mean?' I asked.

'Jack Eubanks has conned his way into everything you can imagine,' the agent continued as he sat back down. 'He has been in and out of prison so many times they had to put a revolving door on his cell. Hell, he even took over a military base using papers he forged himself; of course, he made himself the base commander. The truly amazing thing is, he could fly every plane we had in the Air Force and he never had any formal training.

'And if that wasn't enough, I watched him beat us in court, systematically taking apart each charge we had against him, while representing himself. And he ain't a lawyer, gentlemen.'

We sat flabbergasted at what the agent was telling us.

'You fellows remember Judge Sarah Hughes? The one who swore in President Johnson on board Air Force One when Kennedy was killed?'

We nodded and waited for the punchline.

'Eubanks, if that's his name, took us apart in her court. He represented himself so well we couldn't pin anything on him. In fact, Judge Hughes told us it was the best preparation of a defense she had ever seen. Now can you beat that?'

We sat in silence for a moment. Finally, I said to the agent, 'Look, he's done his time, and I think he deserves a second chance.'

The agent look back at me with cold eyes. 'He deserves, Mr Dear, to be dead.'

That night, we contacted the president of the Toastmaster and reported our findings from the FBI. We also mentioned the fact that Eubanks was a karate expert and had recently taken out several people who tried his skill in a bar. He finished the fight unscathed, but left injured men lying all over the smoky barroom. The president suggested we confront Eubanks about what we had found. I didn't want to confront him because he had become my friend. He had never really lied to me, he just didn't tell me everything.

That night, the president and several members went out to the parking lot as Eubanks drove up. I had asked that they let me talk with him because he was my friend, but I was outvoted. As Eubanks got out of his car, all smiles and waves, the president said, 'Eubanks, if that's your name, you're a fake.'

Eubanks unleashed a lightning-fast karate kick at the president, barely missing him. From my angle I could see he could have hit him, but he intended the kick as a warning.

'I don't have to take this from any of you,' he yelled. Then, as everyone stood still, unsure of what to do next, Eubanks slowly turned and walked toward me. I didn't know if he was going to hit me or kick me or put his arm around me. I stood still. He reached up and laid his arm around me.

'Bill,' he said seriously, 'maybe it's time I leave the Toastmasters.'

I said, 'Yeah, Jack, I think it is. But you've always been my friend and I wish you the best. Sounds like you've lived the best from what I can tell.'

I didn't hear of Jack Eubanks again until several years later, when a magazine published an article entitled *The Magnificent Obsession of Colonel Brown*. There was a picture of the man I knew as Jack Eubanks, standing by a tree overlooking the Air Force base he had taken over as commander via forged paperwork.

In the piece he talked about how he had given up that line of work; how he quietly donated all of his uniforms, complete with brass and clusters, by way of a janitor to the cadet program at Southern Methodist University in Dallas. But I knew better. Eubanks didn't stop. He became a chaplain at a prison and then repeated a few old impersonations; a doctor and a couple of military commanders. In 1990, I decided to find him. After a lot of searching, and numerous phone calls, I got a call one day at my office. It was Jack Ritchie, alias Jack Eubanks. Or vice versa. Who knows for sure? To keep it simple I always call him Jack.

'I hear you've been trying to reach me.' I could hear the smile in his voice.

'I just wanted to see you. How are you doing?'

'I'm well,' he replied in his cordial, gentlemanly manner, 'where would you like to meet?'

I said, 'I understand you're not living in Texas.'

'No, I'm not.'

'Then how can I get in touch with you?'

'You can't. So just tell me where to meet you.'

We decided on breakfast at a place in the Dallas suburb of Irving, not far from the D-FW International Airport. I figured I would arrive early and maybe see how Jack arrived. He figured better and arrived earlier.

He was sitting at a table and stood when he saw me. Jack was the same tall, lean Texan with the same sandy hair and bald spot as before. He hadn't aged a day. He extended his hand and smiled. 'Hi, Bill. How are you doing?'

We sat down over breakfast, pulling up some great old memories. He had more than I; impersonating military officers since 1948 with great skill, serving prison time in Leavenworth for the offenses, then doing it again. The funny thing, he learned to fly legitimately as a teenager and even joined the Civil Air Patrol. But once he began impersonating officers in the military and flying all over the world on Uncle Sam's tab, he couldn't stop.

One of the few times he was caught, they simply removed him from the base. Eubanks figured they thought he was an intelligence officer trying to breach their security and they weren't even going to let him have the pleasure of causing a big commotion.

We laughed about a lot of the things he did. We talked about some of the times we had together in the Toastmaster Club. Then it was time to go.

As we left, walking out together, I said, 'You're going to leave *before* me.'

'It doesn't matter, Bill,' he answered. 'I don't lead that sort of life any more.'

I watched him as I got into my car. I drove around a corner and used my best surveillance techniques to observe him from afar.

He made his way through the row of cars, winding between them at random. Finally, he dropped down into the driver's seat of a white sedan. And waited. I waited to see what was going on.

Several minutes passed, and as I was ready to leave, the passenger door opened and out stepped Eubanks. He looked to his left, then to his right, and nonchalantly walked across the parking lot. He slipped between the restaurant and a motel building and disappeared. I've not seen him since, but I know somewhere on this earth, Jack Ritchie, alias Jack Eubanks, remains the Great Impostor. Just one last impersonation from prison.

BILL DEAR'S NOTEPAD: The Tamperproof Bottles

Every time I come across a medicine bottle which claims to be 'tamper-resistant' or 'childproof,' I have to laugh. It reminds me of the so-called 'tamper-proof' urine specimen bottles in a Canadian courtroom, a few years back.

I had finished an investigation into a death; the authorities claimed it was suicide, but my findings strongly indicated murder. It was a celebrated case in Canada, and the effects of the case are still being felt in both the United States and Canada. But on this particular day the focus was on a group of urine specimen bottles introduced into evidence. I sat at the table of attorney John Murray, who was representing the deceased man's family, watching the testimony.

The witness on the stand was Dr Pierre Beaumier, the Chief Chemist at Mann Testing Laboratories. There was debate over some drug testing. The deceased was a jockey, and therefore subject to drug testing by examination of urine samples. The doctor claimed that the bottles, duly introduced into evidence, were tamperproof. Well, I had my doubts.

They were standard-issue dark plastic specimen bottles, sealed with the usual plastic band around the top to demonstrate how no one could tamper with them without disturbing the seal. John continued questioning the doctor as he passed the bottles to the jury, then to the attorney seated with me at the counsel table. I picked up three of the six bottles and let the rest continue to the opposing attorneys. I began to look at the bottles as the doctor answered John's question.

'Doctor, are these bottles tamperproof?'

'Absolutely.'

'Is there any way anyone can contaminate the contents once sealed inside the bottles?'

'Not without breaking the seal, no.'

'Your honor,' John concluded, 'I pass the witness.'

I half listened to the opposing attorney's re-examination of his own witness. It was boring rhetoric needed to 'lay the predicate', as attorneys say, for future testimony I really didn't care to pay attention to. Instead, I began fidgeting with the bottles; I could see how the seal worked and it seemed to be adequate. As I thumbed the seal, I noticed a couple of jury members watching me, wondering what I was doing under the table with my hands in my lap.

A warm feeling came over me as I felt the seal move a little. I leaned to John and asked for his business card. He looked at me oddly. But he gave me the card anyway. I took one of my own and kept playing with the bottles. After a while, thank goodness for small miracles, we broke for lunch and I pulled John off to the side and whispered in his ear. Then I turned to the court bailiff and said, 'I want you to secure these bottles.' I gave him the three bottles and made sure he understood they were not to leave his sight.

After lunch we all filed back into the courtroom and took our respective places. The judge called the proceedings to order, then called to the bailiff and dispatched him to retrieve the good doctor. He was reminded of his oath and seated. John reiterated his early question.

'Dr Beaumier, did you not say that the bottles here on the table are tamperproof?'

'I did.'

'Are you *absolutely* sure of that, Doctor?'

'I am.' The doctor drew himself up, insulted by the question.

John brought the three bottles to the doctor at the witness stand.

'Doctor, would you demonstrate how the seal is broken and the bottles opened once your lab is ready to test the specimens?'

Beaumier was puzzled, and a little hesitant. He cautiously reached for one like it contained the last remnants of the Black Death, broke the seal and opened it, holding it toward John to indicate the simple procedure was complete.

'Doctor Beaumier, is there anything *in* the bottle?'

'Well, of course not, these bottles were sealed to . . . ' Beaumier looked inside and went white, then red.

211

John, a smirk on his face, turned away from the witness and slowly walked toward me while directing his question to the doctor.

'What's wrong, Doctor? Is there something in the bottle?'

'Yes,' the doctor whispered, still staring in disbelief into the bottle.

'Doctor, the jury can't hear you, would you speak up and repeat your answer?'

'I said, "Yes".'

There was a pause for emphasis before John pressed the obvious question.

'Well, what is it, Doctor?'

Beaumier dislodged a business card from the bottle.

'What does it say?' John asked as he turned to face the witness.

Beaumier cleared his throat. 'It says, "William C. Dear and Associates, Private Investigations". And on the back' – he glanced at me with daggers as he flipped the card – 'it says, "I have just opened this bottle that is supposed to be tamperproof" and it's signed, "William C. Dear, June 15, 1988".'

John smiled politely at the doctor. 'Would you open the second bottle in this group of three, please?'

The flustered doctor fumbled with the second bottle, afraid of what he would discover.

'This one is empty,' he replied.

'And what about the third?' John asked as he leaned against the witness stand and gazed knowingly toward the jury.

Beaumier pulled the seal from the third bottle. He unscrewed the cap but didn't wait to be instructed to retrieve the contents. With a disgusted sigh, the Chief Chemist pulled another business card from the third bottle like a reluctant magician pulling the wrong rabbit from the wrong hat. He cleared his throat and read the card.

'"John Murray, Attorney at Law,"' he intoned. '"Beckon Case, June 15, 1988".'

'Well, Doctor,' John stabbed as he walked away, 'I'm glad you didn't stake anything important, like your reputation, on these bottles being tamperproof. We have no further questions.'

A host of reporters leaped from the courtroom, making up headlines as they ran for the phones. I looked toward the couple of jury members who had watched me fidgeting with something under the table. They had not been able to see how I could slowly work the seals up and off the bottle, slip the business cards in and return the seals without breaking them. It was just a matter of using slow and easy pressure on the plastic seals.

It was a helluva story in the morning papers.

CHAPTER 13
'Please Help Her . . . She's Only Six'

'Dick, I want you to come with me,' I said to Dick Riddle as I strode quickly down the hall and past his office.

'Where are we going?' Dick came out of his chair and followed. A stout man who would make a lot of men think twice about a confrontation, Dick is more than my Chief Investigator, he's the closest thing I have to a brother. I'd trust my life to him and have on several occasions.

'Let's just take a drive,' I answered vaguely, 'over to Arlington. We'll discuss it in the car.' Dick and I slid into my black Corvette. It's a great car, but its low-slung profile and imposing front end makes me feel like I'm riding in a coffin half the time.

Arlington is a sizable town in its own right, halfway between Dallas and Fort Worth. Dick didn't ask anything. He knew I'd tell him what was on my mind when I'd had a chance to mull it over. Finally I blurted out the thoughts running through my head, as though Dick had been privy to everything leading up to the moment. But he was used to that.

'If what the letter says is true, Dick, then time is of the essence. So I think it's worth the drive to check it out.' Dick's face had the expression of someone who had arrived at the theater in the middle of the play, but he probably figured it was important or I wouldn't be burning up the highway.

I said no more during the half-hour trip, concentrating instead on what I had read in the letter, dated March 4, 1989:

Dear Mr Dear,

My mother and I are extremely worried about the welfare of my sister's child, Guinevere Ackels*. My sister was born Agnes Mary Thompkins* on May 14, 1957. She died under questionable circumstances on August 31, 1982, in a small Texas town called Paint Rock. At the time of my sister's death, she was married to Fred Kenneth Ackels*. She was only 25 years old at the time. Little Guinevere was born just a couple of months before she died. (Guinevere was born June 4, 1982.) The problem is that when my sister died, they couldn't or wouldn't tell us just how she died. In fact we flew all the way from Connecticut and New York for the funeral, only to be told we couldn't go in to view the body.

Her husband, Fred, and his father had a deputy sheriff there barring us from going in. The deputy was kind enough to let us stick our heads in to look inside. But that was as close as we could get. We weren't even allowed to go to the graveside services. It seems that Ackels's father had a lot of power and control in this small Texas town.

My mother wrote letters to everybody trying to find out what happened to my sister. She finally obtained the services of a lawyer in Carmel, New York. Richard Al Mayer corresponded with a law firm in Ballinger, Texas, not far from Paint Rock, and received back some paperwork dated October 12, 1982.

That letter is painted in my mind, Mr Dear. Addressed to my mother, Catherine Thompkins, the overnight express letter contained a copy of the final report provided by the Department of Public Safety lab in Austin, Texas stating that Agnes had apparently been poisoned. It further indicated that Fred 'Tex' Ackels had moved to Arlington to live with his mother. There was no hard evidence, though, to proceed in court, so the letter offered the opinion that my sister had been the victim of 'the perfect crime'. It went on to suggest we try to maintain whatever contacts we have with the Ackels in an effort to stay in touch with Guinevere.

The Perfect Crime. It seemed to me that I had heard that one before. No doubt, from the information I had already obtained and gone over before Dick and I left the office, this Tex Ackels guy might have thought he had committed the Perfect Crime. But that wasn't going to stop me.

I had studied the autopsy report I had received on Agnes Mary Ackels, dated September 1, 1982. She had been admitted to Ballinger Memorial Hospital in a comatose condition. An exploratory laparotomy was performed which indicated extensive necrosis of the stomach, with clinical history of multiple lacerations at the time of surgery. She had died shortly after she had been hospitalized.

I noticed that the pathologist, Dr Joe B. Hall, found hemorrhagic necrotizing gastritis of the stomach, along with acute tubular necrosis of the kidneys. The pathology, the physician pointed out, would be consistent with the ingestion of toxic material.

So Agnes Mary Ackels had probably been poisoned.

Ackels had told everyone Agnes died from drinking some bad water. I wondered exactly what kind of water would have substances to cause these stomach lacerations and leave toxins in the body. I thought about strychnine. Arsenic leaves a residue that can be detected in an autopsy. But strychnine is washed through the system, leaving no telltale tracks in its wake of death.

I had discovered that Ackels had left Paint Rock and moved home to Arlington less than a month after Agnes's death. Maybe I'm suspicious, but it didn't seem long before he went back home to Momma. Something told me he wasn't the grieving kind.

Bradley Lane in Arlington seemed blue collar; affordable houses mortgaged to hardworking people happy to have their single-level homes in which to raise their families. Then the neighborhood suddenly turned into a haven for mobile homes. But these houses weren't going anywhere; they were just cheaper, anchored-down habitats on parcels of land that were lower priced than the homes we had just driven by. I slowed down as I looked for 4600 Bradley. The moment I spotted it I saw a burly man about five foot five or six, weighing about two hundred pounds, standing in front of the house with a little girl. He sported a big beard and looked like one of those survivalists. He was throwing his hunting knife into the ground. The little girl looked to be about six years old with a round little face and glasses. Strapped on her hip was a knife.

As we passed slowly by I saw a very large pentagram, a symbol of great significance to Satan worshippers, painted on the driveway.

'No doubt in my mind,' Dick offered, 'this guy's involved in the occult.' Out of curiosity, Dick had been involved in occult activities in college – fortunately, he came away unharmed and with a greater insight into the phenomenon than I. I've used his first-hand knowledge on many occasions. 'Let's pull around the corner and see what's going on,' I said.

The bearded wonder with the knife, the little girl with her own knife and the pentagram added up to a bad situation. I decided we had to get going on this case. Now.

For a couple of hours we watched from afar, staring through binoculars at Tex Ackels, a man with the eyes of a Charles Manson. With the exception of the knife-throwing in the front-yard, there wasn't much to see. Until dark.

At dusk, Tex left with Guinevere and began walking toward a wooded area on the edge of the neighborhood. As they disappeared into the underbrush I got out and told Dick to stay with the car. Keeping well back of Tex and Guinevere as they entered the deepest part of the woods, I followed, trying not to make any noise. It was pretty hard, despite my Indian blood. My ancestors wore moccasins and little else, not ostrich-skin boots with a coat and tie.

I came to realize I was in the middle of two or three hundred acres of dirt trails, underbrush and makeshift neighborhood dumps. There were definitely other places I'd rather be. Finally Tex and Guinevere stopped on a knoll in a clearing.

I eased my way in as close as I could and saw two other people join them. The little girl just stood there. She obviously hadn't taken a bath in quite some time, but still she looked sweet and innocent. I could tell why her uncle and her grandmother wanted to make sure she was all right. I wondered what twisted role this man made her play. I was damned sure going to find out. For now, I decided to retreat for the night and talk with the client.

I brushed the grass and dirt from my clothes as I opened the car door.

'We're going to take this one, Dick,' I said as I pulled a twig from my hair. 'No matter what, we're going to get to the bottom of this. I don't like what I see.'

Joe Villanueva, Shawn Dunnahoe and Dick Riddle immediately began staking out Tex around the clock. Back at the office we hit the computers to find anything we could on him. A standard driver's license check indicated he hadn't had a current license in ten years and his last address was Paint Rock, Texas. But further probing told us he didn't have a job either, only the $600 per month in Social Security paid on behalf of Agnes's death benefits. The money was intended to raise and care for Guinevere. But it was obvious he wasn't using the money on soap or clothes for the child.

A check on Tex's mother, Charlene Walker*, told me she owned the mobile home from some kind of inheritance or divorce. She was supposedly only fifty-four years old. I had seen her briefly during our surveillance and I would have guessed her to be in her seventies. She was a bad-looking woman who appeared to have been rode hard and put up wet more than a few times.

Walker apparently owned the old gray Lincoln in the driveway of the mobile home. A blue Buick, bearing expired Oklahoma plates from several years back, appeared to belong to Tex. We also found out that Walker's sister had filed on Ackels and her several times in a dispute over some property. We located the sister, Mary Lou Hopkins.

She told us she couldn't care less about Fred, but she was very worried about the health and welfare of Guin. She said the inside of the house was absolutely filthy and the neighbors tried to watch out for Guin, but couldn't watch at all times and were worried. Mary Lou had heard of Guin being taken into the woods for hours late at night, along with men. Fred and Charlene were believed to be involved in the occult. She said the two of them believed in the healing power of crystals and would often go into the woods to receive their instructions from whatever or whomever they worshipped.

We then went to visit some of the neighbors Mary Lou had told us to talk with. They all confirmed the same things about Tex; that he smelled like he hadn't taken a bath in some time and was usually dirty, with dried food matted in his beard, and that they feared for Guin's safety. It was also rumored that the child was sharing a bed with her father.

Fred was thought to have belonged to a number of supremacy groups, including the Ku Klux Klan. He didn't have a job and seemed to occupy himself with making knives. He and his mother appeared to stay very close together; much more so than most mother-son relationships. Charlene had been married and divorced several times.

Guin was not allowed to play with other children. Even when wearing just shorts and no top, Guinevere carried a knife strapped to the wide leather belt she wore.

The question of how Tex was raising Guin, and the habits of Tex and his visitors, during all hours of the night, didn't just center around Arlington. We received similar responses from people in Paint Rock, were Guin was born and where her mother died. Tex's survivalist tendencies, meeting with supremacy groups and use of cryptic symbols came up in both places. There was the suspicion of child molestation. I worried about the damage this animal had already inflicted on his daughter. Enough was enough, it was time to get down to business.

I decided to follow Ackels back into the woods. Like before, Dick and I waited in the car until we could see the two of them leave the house and walk in to the wooded area. Just as before, I kept a safe distance as I dissolved into the brush, dressed in dark clothes.

I walked through, over and under bushes, weeds and tree limbs for five or six minutes at a slow but steady pace. Soon, a clearing opened up before me, containing the old back seat of a car and something that looked as if it were some kind of altar. Trying to hear what was going on, I got down on my hands and knees and crawled as close as I could. Guin was sitting next to her father as he talked with two others, the three men kneeling down.

Suddenly, something landed on my neck. I grabbed for it and

pulled back my hand to see a big Brown Recluse Spider. James Bond might have let that spider crawl all over him without moving, but I sure as hell wasn't about to. I knew what these big spiders could do with one bite. Just as I slapped the spider with my other hand, a small dead limb moved in between my hands and snapped. In the eerie silence, it was just loud enough. I saw Ackels and his fellow cult worshippers jump. Two ran in my direction. I lay as still as possible, hoping they would suspect it was an animal. I didn't know if others were to arrive for the nocturnal meeting. The last thing I needed was for a bunch of devil worshippers to discover me there in the woods. If there was to be a sacrifice, I hoped it wasn't going to be me.

Slowly I exhaled, lying silent and motionless. Suddenly, my eye caught a movement. My heart raced. I glanced up to see the silhouette of a tree limb blowing across the face of the full moon. A perfect night for cult rites. I knew I had been lying there only moments, but it seemed like hours.

Finally, I saw Ackels and Guin make a hasty retreat. I was relieved. After a few minutes, to let the adrenalin dwindle and my breathing slow, I got up and quietly made my way back to the car, where Dick was waiting.

Dick chuckled as I got in the car. 'Well, I guess they didn't sacrifice your body tonight.'

'No,' I answered, sliding into the passenger seat with a sigh, 'and they ain't going to get the chance tomorrow night, either! I think it's time we tell the client what's going on.'

The next day, I called Catherine Thompkins in Connecticut and told her it was time to take action. I explained I felt we had enough evidence to get court action to protect Guin from the harmful conditions; the filth, lack of guidance and apparent abuse she suffered. We contacted Dallas attorney Kathy Kinser, who filed a court action in Judge Bryan Carper's Court in Tarrant County on behalf of Guin, with her grandmother Catherine Thompkins as the complainant. This resulted in the judge issuing a writ of attachment ordering the Tarrant County Sheriff's Office to pick up Guinevere immediately. But I wasn't taking any chances. We kept the residence on Bradley Lane under surveillance until Deputies J. D. Walker and Charles W. Washington arrived at the house. They were unaware we were watching nearby.

We watched Ackels walk out of the house to meet the deputies. They presented him with the papers ordering Guin be turned over to them, and the three men talked for several minutes.

'Where the hell is Guin?' I said to Dick as we sat watching the meeting through binoculars.

The men continued to talk in the front yard, nodding at each other and making mild gestures until the deputies shook hands with Ackels, walked back to their cars and left!

I couldn't believe they had left without Guin. I grabbed the car phone and called Kinser. She made a call and then phoned me back. She was hot! She said the two deputies had been assured by Ackels he would have Guin in court on Monday morning at nine o'clock. But today was Friday. Ackels had two whole days in which to run!

We saw a lot of activity that night around the house, a great deal of moving about, but we were unable to see what was actually going on. The next day there was no sign of Ackels or Guin. Then on Sunday night, seventeen large garbage bags were placed out on the curb for the next morning's garbage pick-up. I wanted what was in those bags.

That was the last activity we saw from the mobile home. The next morning, nothing. No sign of life at all. When nine o'clock arrived and passed, Kinser called to say that Ackels failed to show up in court and the judge had issued a warrant on grounds of interfering with child custody. I knew it!

This time two deputies from the Sheriff's Office would be replaced by Constable Jim Palmer and his men. They knew what they might be dealing with thanks to the information we provided from our investigation. If Ackels had indeed killed his wife just to have a newborn baby to himself, for whatever reason, then there was no telling what he might do.

Within two hours of the warrant being issued, five cars from the Constable's Office rolled up to the mobile home on Bradley Lane. The men and women deputies under Palmer's command dispersed around the house, armed and wearing bulletproof vests.

Palmer himself went to the door and called for Ackels to come out. No response. A couple of minutes passed, then the door was opened and Palmer was allowed inside. A few minutes later he emerged with Charlene Walker. The child and Ackels were gone. But because of a brief career change on our part that day, from P.I.s to garbage men, we managed to get a few clues anyway.

While we waited for Palmer and the warrant to arrive, Shawn paid the garbage collectors $20.00 to ride the truck to the house and help collect the seventeen bags of garbage left on the curb. Then he put the bags in his pick-up truck. It wasn't the first time I had worked to solve a case by sifting through garbage. It wasn't the most fun part of my work, but it could be effective, especially if Ackels had left like I suspected he might have.

Sure enough, as Palmer's men searched the house, he told me that Ackels had apparently left during the night.

'And Bill,' he added, 'you won't believe the filth in that house! It smells of urine and excrement. What looks like blood is dripping down the inside of the refrigerator.'

Dick confirmed that some of the items found in the refrigerator, bloody bones and the like, were used in devil worship. Palmer called Kinser and told her to inform the judge.

'We'll find her, Bill,' Palmer told me. 'We'll find her.'

Back at my office, while a team of investigators watched the mobile home in case Ackels returned, Dick, Shawn and I went through the garbage.

It took hours to go through everything, and it was even worse than we had anticipated. There was so much filth, so many lice and roaches, we had to fumigate the garbage before going through it. We couldn't believe what we were finding. Articles on child incest, Satanism and child pornography as well as various articles used for deviate sexual gratification were mixed throughout the trash. We found a picture of the Goat of Mendes having sex with a virgin. Was Tex planning to use Guin as a virgin sacrifice? I know it's hard for some people to believe this kind of outrageous activity goes on, but it does. I also found an envelope from a Carrie Burton* addressed to Tex. It had been ripped in half, but

222

we could still read that the letter inside invited Tex to the February full moon ritual at her house. Another note read:

Just a note to let you know of the celebration of the anticipated full moon on Monday, March 20th at 7.30 p.m. at my place. I hope you can make it. I would enjoy seeing Guin again, too.

Carrie

Another scrap of paper, drawn by Ackels, was a diagram of how to disembowel a human and then cut him up into little pieces to be devoured. I found a license issued by a supremacy group that supposedly gave Ackels 'the right to kill niggers'. Then at the bottom of a bag of the trash, I came across the ripped remnants of a photograph. I collected all of the pieces and worked them like a jigsaw puzzle until the picture was complete. It was a picture of Agnes the day she and Ackels were married. If he really had cared for her, why had he ripped the picture? *Had* he poisoned her? Unbelievably, I even found a list of chemicals Ackels had purchased just a short time before Agnes died!

The media picked up the story that occult literature had been discovered in the home of a missing child. Cult experts pored over the material we had and reaffirmed our suspicions of Ackels. We turned our findings over to the judge, who issued an arrest warrant and called for an All Points Bulletin nationwide for Fred 'Tex' Ackels.

I followed up on all Ackels's visitors during our surveillance, and pushed them hard about where Ackels might have gone. I couldn't believe the people we were meeting, people from all walks of life, who would finally admit to their involvement in the occult. They said they felt Ackels was trying to take a little information from each cult he was involved with, perhaps to start his own cult, just as Charles Manson had.

We received a tip from a computer hacker that a network of cultists was using computers to stay in touch and shuffle Ackels from place to place in the underground network. The one good thing that came from tapping into the network was the fact that

Guin was still alive. We were also able to discover that Ackels and Guin had boarded a Greyhound bus headed for Nebraska. That rang a bell in my mind.

By computer to the Schuller Institute in Washington, D.C., I pulled up a number of articles on ritualistic child abuse. According to the Schuller Institute, a group of Nebraskans was working to uncover and destroy a network of satanic child abusers in their state. The group, including highly placed government officials, members of law enforcement and political party leaders, had children who had been abused and/or killed by the satanic network, which was part of a larger national organization. Damn, I thought, this stuff spreads like a cancer. I figured that Ackels was en route to join his friends in Nebraska. The media put me on TV so I could plead for any information to help save the life of Guin.

In the meantime, Walker was picked up and jailed for contempt of court after refusing to tell us where her son had fled. After several days in jail, the judge allowed her to go home to think it over. I went by her house with Constable Palmer that night. This time I saw it all for myself. I couldn't believe little Guin had to live in such hideous conditions.

The floor was covered with a matted and filthy carpet. Dog excrement was everywhere; the couch, the chairs, the beds. Everywhere. The stench was unbearable. You couldn't find a place to sit that wasn't filthy. In the refrigerator, bones, blood and herbal concoctions dripped all over everything. It made you want to throw up. She said the items were something to do with what her son was involved with, but she didn't know what it was or anything about it. We looked in her bedroom; it was nearly impossible to walk around inside because of the junk. Then we looked in the other bedroom where Ackels and, allegedly, Guin slept. There wasn't even a sleeping bag. I felt nothing but hostility toward Walker; she was just as guilty of the abuse of Guin as her son. To allow her granddaughter, a gift from God, to be treated like this was inhuman. I also wondered about the relationship between her and her son. I could only imagine. She was again arrested after refusing to say where her son was. For weeks, our men and Palmer's men staked out the Walker home in case Ackels returned. We staked out the post office as well, in case he came to pick up the monthly $600 check.

On May 12th, five weeks after Ackels left with Guin, I received a phone call telling me that Ackels was definitely in Nebraska. I flew to Freemont, Nebraska, hoping finally to come face to face with this bastard.

I found that Ackels had been staying in a two-story frame house. It didn't take long to find, but Ackels had skipped about a week earlier. Stories of the search and the missing child trapped in the jaws of a devil-worshipping network were everywhere.

It was back to Freemont Airport and my next stop, Lincoln, Nebraska, where I had been told I might find Ackels. As I walked through the terminal I was paged.

Sheriff's Deputy Randall Walters of Saline County, Nebraska, had just called my office from Lincoln. Fred Ackels had been arrested and booked into the Saline County Jail.

'Is Guin with him? Is she okay?' I blurted.

'She's okay, Bill,' my secretary answered, 'but she's a mess.'

I called Palmer and told him to get up to Lincoln. Then I boarded the plane and flew to Lincoln, where Deputy Sheriff Walters met me. He told me Ackels and a guy named Brad Kovar had stolen the Kovar family car, a brown 1980 Mercury Monarch. Ackels, Kovar and Guin were asleep outside the car in some woods when Nebraska Game Wardens spotted the car and realized by the tag number that it was stolen. They surrounded the men and handcuffed them, then gathered up little Guinevere and put her in their car. She had been eaten up by mosquitoes and chiggers. She wasn't wearing panties and had been living rough with those two men. Her hair was greasy and matted, and her body was caked with mud and dirt. I wanted to rip Fred Ackels's head off with my bare hands.

Within a few hours Palmer and one of his assistants arrived, then the four of us rode to the Sheriff's Office with Walters. On the way we stopped by the Kovar home.

His parents told us they weren't allowed in their son's room. But when he and Ackels stole their car, the Kovars went into his room. They found that Brad had material on Dungeons and

Dragons and the occult. Brad Kovar had been working as an armed security guard. Ackels's bag contained pornography, cult material and the papers the Tarrant County Deputies had served ordering him to bring Guin to the court.

According to the Kovars, Ackels and Guin were dropped off by a woman named Eva about three days before the arrests. Their son had told them Ackels and Guin were friends of his. Mrs Kovar asked Guin if she was hungry. The child replied, 'I haven't eaten in two days.' She fixed Guin a hot-dog and potato chips, and before she could fix a second hot-dog, Guin had gobbled the food and was waiting for more. The child was filthy. Her greasy hair had been dyed black and parted down the middle. The Kovars said they felt the child had her appearance changed, perhaps because she had been kidnapped. They felt that something was seriously wrong.

We found out the two men had already made plans to go to Canada with Guin by way of the network's underground. That's where they were headed when arrested. We caught up with them just in the nick of time.

Warrants for Ackels's arrest were faxed to the Saline County Sheriff's Office in Lincoln, and an immediate hearing was called. Guin had been taken into the protective custody of Evonne M. Foust of Nebraska's Department of Social Services.

Foust and one of her assistants were going to try to clean Guin up, but it was no easy job.

'Mr Dear,' she told me, 'you wouldn't believe what we saw.'

I asked her to put it on paper for the child custody case back in Texas.

According to Foust, Guin wore a little summer outfit and tennis shoes, but no panties. The stench of urine and body odor from the child was so intense her assistant threw up while Foust herself gagged repeatedly. Every part of Guin's exposed body was covered in layers of mud and dirt and it took several baths before the child was clean. They also found a caked-on muddy substance on the inside of Guin's glasses where the frames rested on the child's cheek, the residue of tears and dirt on her face.

After the bath, they talked a great deal and had lunch. Guin told

226

Foust her mother had died when she was a little baby, and asked, 'Would you be my mother?'

The social worker fought back the tears.

Guin began telling Foust about the bad men looking for her and her father back in Texas, and that they couldn't go back there. In particular, there was a man named 'Cookie' who lived in Grand Prairie. This was a new one on me, but I intended to find out who 'Cookie' was and what he had done to her.

Then Guin laid on the floor and asked Foust to rub her stomach like her father, whom she called 'Tex', did all the time. Foust, who has a lot of experience in these cases, asked Guin to point to the area of her stomach her father had rubbed. She did. Then Foust asked if her father rubbed her anywhere else, to which Guin said as she squirmed on the floor, 'You know where else. Tex and I have a lot of secrets and you know some of them, don't you?'

Foust asked where Guin slept. But Guin said that was a secret and told Foust she already knew those secrets too. Then Guin jumped up and said she wanted to play.

The next day, in court, we were told we could take Guin back to Texas. I walked over to Foust's office to get her. Standing on the upper level of the office for a few minutes, I watched Guin play in a small area below. I kept thinking about everything she had gone through. Tears began to well up in my eyes as I watched her play so innocently in this haven. Slowly I walked down the steps, looking forward to taking little Guin home. Ms Foust extended her hand as I approached.

'I'm glad you'll see that she'll have a second chance.'

She turned and called to Guin to come over as Palmer joined us.

'Guin,' she said, 'meet Mr Dear and Mr Palmer. They're going to take you home.'

I think I heard Palmer trying to clear his voice as the precious little girl gazed up with a smile that melted our two old hearts simultaneously. Then she reached up and took my hand tightly and trustingly.

As we left the building, a camera crew from WFAA-TV News in Dallas was waiting. Reporter Charles Duncan held a microphone. Guin seemed to like the bright lights and attention.

'Mr Dear, how's Guinevere?'

'Time will tell,' I answered. Duncan understood. Then Palmer, Guin and I headed for the airport. I stopped at a drugstore and purchased ointment for Guin's many insect bites. As I paid for the ointment, I saw a blue teddy bear. Little Guinevere would have another friend to carry back to Dallas this day.

Forty years ago, what came out in Ackels's trial about the conditions the child lived in, and the abuse she suffered while living with her father, would have caused a lynch mob to take to the streets with Ackels in tow. But now our judicial system guards against that.

Pity.

Guin is in the custody of her grandmother, Catherine Thompkins; a woman Guin had never met, who had been the catalyst for saving her young life. I receive cards and letters from time to time from them. During the first week of May 1991, I received a card inviting me to join in the celebration of Guin's Baptism and First Communion.

Though I wanted to, I was not able to attend. But that card is still on my desk, right next to her picture.

Tex Ackels went to jail. The sad thing about this story is that he is now out, freely walking the streets. I pray he doesn't find your son or daughter.

BILL DEAR'S NOTEPAD: Bill in One

I had been assigned to watch the comings, goings and general routine of a woman, who lived next to Tennison Golf Course in Oak Cliff, a suburb of Dallas. I found my best vantage point was actually from a tree on the golf course itself, across the street from the house. She couldn't see me from that distance, but with binoculars I could watch everything she did.

So, my first day, with binoculars strapped across my shoulder and a sack lunch, I climbed up my tree. I had been there about an hour, watching the subject go about her day and making notes of what she did, when suddenly, *ping*!

I looked around. It sounded as if something had hit the tree not a foot from my head.

I soon forgot about it and went back to watching my subject, when, *ping*! It happened again. This time I saw the golf ball hit, just about head level. I thought, my God, these guys are professional golfers and they're out here trying to kill me. By the end of the day I had been hit several times by golf balls, and getting pretty pissed off I might add. Then, after a while, it dawned on me that perhaps they weren't as accurate as I was giving them credit for being. I began watching them. They weren't aiming at me, they didn't have a clue I was up there. They were hooking like a dog's hind leg. Had they tried to hit me, they would have probably scored a hole in one.

The funniest was one old duffer who came walking up to the tree moments after his ball had barely missed me and ricocheted straight across the rough at a forty-five degree angle from where he wanted it to go. He looked all around to make sure no one saw him, then reached into his pocket and took out another ball and let it drop beside the tree – with a great lie for the hole. He then turned back to his old partner way across the fairway and yelled, 'Three! I've got three, John!' Lying old geezer. If I'd only been a bird up there perched right above him . . . *splat*!

CHAPTER 14
The Deadly Date

The shrill chirp of the car phone cut through the deep melodic tones of my black Corvette's engine. I was swinging high off Central Expressway on to the Woodall Rogers Freeway north of downtown Dallas on a rainy, overcast day. As I picked up the phone, I noticed how nicely the skyscrapers of downtown reflected the gray clouds above them. I was feeling comfortable here. I was at home.

'Hello.'

'Bill, it's Donna*.'

'Hi, Donna, what's up?'

'Bill, I can't get anyone to go out with me.' Pain and frustration came through in her soft voice, luring my attention from the skyline. 'My divorce isn't final but everyone's afraid of Butch*.'

'I realize that, Donna. I really wish I could help.'

'He keeps coming over to the house.' Her soft voice became angry. 'Banging on my windows. He won't leave me alone. Bill, he got into the house the other night.'

'What?'

'He broke in and came to my bed and grabbed me.' I could hear her voice break a little as she sniffled, 'Then he tied me to the bed and poured water on me. He left me tied up with the baby in the house.'

Anger swelled up inside me. 'Did he hurt you or the baby?'

'No, I'm just a little scared. I guess everyone is scared of Butch.'

230

'I'm not,' I said.

'I know you're not,' she replied, 'you're the only investigator in town who has helped me.'

'What do you want me to do, Donna?'

'Take me out.'

'What?'

'Just take me out. Away.' She sighed. 'I just want to go out for the evening. I've been in the house for so long. I've got to get away for a while.'

'You want to go out? On a date, hunh?' I smiled. 'Well, Donna, I haven't had an offer like that in a long time.'

'Now, Bill, I know that's not true.' We were good friends, and I could tell that just the light-hearted conversation made her feel better. But it didn't last.

'Bill, I've got to get out. I mean even when I go out with the girls to have lunch or something, he shows up and spills food and water on me. They don't want to go anywhere with me, and I don't blame them. But I've got to get out of here. He won't mess with me if I'm with you.'

Donna Spalding*, at twenty-six, was perhaps the most beautiful woman I knew and certainly one of the most lovely in Dallas. Her long, flowing brown hair always seemed to fall down her tall, slender, perfectly shaped body like a cascading fountain. Her blue eyes were always smiling and full of life.

'Donna,' I smiled as I spoke, 'we're going to go out tomorrow night and have the best night you can imagine.'

'Oh, thank you, Bill.' She sounded like a school girl accepting a date to her first prom. 'Oh, it'll be so much fun. I've got just the outfit to wear. You'll love it.'

I figured I would.

The next evening I drove, I have to admit, with some excitement. It *would* be a fun evening. A beautiful woman, a lovely moonlit night and the whole city to play in.

I met her in the parking lot of a shopping center, so her soon-to-be ex-husband wouldn't see us leave her house and try to cause trouble. She jumped from her car and the vision almost took my breath away. She was more beautiful than ever. Dressed to the hilt, she could have paled any starlet on the big screen. She ran over to me, put her arms around me and gave me a sweet kiss. How any man could mistreat this goddess was beyond me.

'Bill, you don't know what this means to me,' she said as her eyes beamed up at me.

'Come on,' I replied, grabbing her hand, 'we're going to have one helluva great night.'

We hit the best nightspots Dallas had to offer: the Black Garter Club, the French Room at the Adolphus Hotel, even a big band that was really sounding great at one of the hotels near the airport. That was our last stop. The romantic melodies and her intoxicating presence made me feel like I was King of the World. Donna was a real joy to spend an evening with. Finally, she looked up at me, as we danced close and slow under the sparkling winks of light that tripped across the room and through her hair, just before she kissed me deeply.

'Bill, this has been a wonderful night. The best night I've had in years. You don't know how good it feels to be out after so many years of being beaten and intimidated and cursed at.'

I held her close as she continued.

'Bill, I used to press charges against him with Justice of the Peace Joe B. Black, Jr*. And he would dismiss them. He did that until. . . .until . . . '

'Until what?' I asked. She had stopped dancing and was looking down. I reached to her chin and gently raised it to see her sparkling blue eyes filled with tears.

'Until what, Donna?'

She took a deep breath and sighed as she looked away. 'Black would make me have sex with him.'

'He what!'

'He would come over, after I filed for divorce.' A tear fell, streaking her precious face. 'And he would tell me that if I had sex with him, he'd keep Butch away.' Her face shriveled as she began to cry. I walked her back to our table.

'I wasn't that kind of person,' she said, as she gained her composure at the table, 'but I had sex with him a number of times because it was filed in his court and he promised to keep Butch

232

away. And every time Butch did something to me and I would file charges against him, they would end up in Black's court. I knew . . . I knew that Black was using me. So, finally, I had enough and I told him that this wasn't right and I wasn't doing it any more.'

I controlled the rage I felt at Butch and Black. 'You don't have to do that, ever again, Donna,' I promised as she leaned over and laid her head on my shoulder. 'If I ever get the chance, I'll have Joe B. Black's butt in jail for this. I promise.'

I had heard that this type of thing went on behind Black's closed office door. I had once confronted Black when he called a woman we were investigating and told her what we had on her. He begged me not to bring charges that would remove him from office, saying he had only made a mistake. I should've taken him out then and there.

I held her for a while, and soon began making a few little jokes to make her laugh again. After a while, she was coming out of her shell of painful memories into a new world of hope. Before long, Donna was having a good time again, and the night continued its magical ride.

On the way from our last spot, she called her home and talked with the babysitter. During a couple of previous calls, the babysitter had reassured her that her child was fine and that she should just have a good time for a change. But this call was different.

'Donna,' the sitter told her, 'don't come home tonight. We've seen Butch prowling around. Don't come home. '

She told me what her sitter had said as she hung up the phone. 'Bill, can I spend the night with you?'

'Sure you can,' I replied as we sped through the streets of Dallas, the bright lights of the skyscrapers reflecting in our wake.

After a brief tour of the house, I indicated where the bedroom was and Donna soon disappeared. I made sure the lights were out and the doors and alarms were secured, then I walked into the bedroom, dark save for the moonlight. Donna stood near the window, with moonlight bathing her soft form. I watched as her dress fell gently from her silhouette. Her body was perfect and I stood for a moment, captured by its sheer beauty. It was one of the most passionate nights of my life. She came alive as the fears and troubles of her world faded away with each kiss and caress.

As the Sunday morning sun woke me, I eased myself up on one arm and just laid there quietly for a while and watched Donna sleep. She finally opened her eyes, looked up at me and smiled.

'I haven't had a night like that in years,' she said, then she cuddled close and kissed me. She seemed very happy, and I was happy for her.

'Bill,' she suddenly blurted, 'did I tell you I have a job? Starting tomorrow?'

'No,' I smiled, genuinely happy for her.

After she got out of the shower, wrapped in a towel, she told me about landing the job. The conversation ended when she dropped the towel, put her arms around me and kissed me.

'I hope this is the first of many mornings like this,' she said after the kiss.

'I do too,' I answered.

I insisted on following her to her house in Oak Cliff, despite her claims that everything would be fine. She had called her house-keeper to see if everything was okay.

'Yes, Mrs Spalding,' she replied, knowing exactly what Donna meant, 'everything is just fine.'

As she got out of her car, she waved to let me know she was okay, then blew me a kiss to let me know she had had a good time. So had I.

Later that Sunday evening, I called to make sure she was all right.

'I'm fine, Bill.' Her joy-filled voice made me feel warm inside. 'I'm getting ready for my job. I have all of my clothes laid out. Everything is ready. I'm going to make a new life for me and my baby, Bill.'

'I know you will, Donna. I'm really proud of you.' I hung up the phone and pondered the wonderful weekend as I laid back in my bed, reflecting on the memories of the night before.

The next morning, after getting up bright and early, Donna dressed, then got her little three-year-old daughter ready to take to daycare. Once they were both ready to go, Donna took her child and walked out of the house into the garage and hit the garage door opener. Then she put her little girl in the car and fastened her seatbelt. The garage door slowly rose as Donna sat behind the wheel.

She started the engine and began to back out of the garage. Suddenly, in her rearview mirror, she saw a sight that sent a cold rush down her spine. Butch Spalding was running toward her. With a gun!

Donna grabbed her child, jumped out of the car and ran back to hit the garage door opener, screaming, 'NO! . . . NO!' The door began its slow descent and just as it was about to seal against the floor of the garage, Butch rolled underneath and into what was now a closed and locked garage. Donna was shaking and crying at the vision of her nightmare coming back to haunt her. He fired at her, then grabbed the child and took her into the house. Spalding returned to the garage and, without emotion, grabbed Donna's long beautiful hair, twisted it in a knot and pulled her up to him. Then he raised the gun to her head and pulled the trigger. The loud explosion was somewhat muffled by the closed garage. He looked up from her bloody body, lying limp on the floor, to see their child standing outside the door.

Spalding walked past his daughter, into the house, picked up the phone and called his mother.

'Momma,' he said, 'I've just killed Donna. Now I'm gonna kill myself. Call the police.'

Spalding then hung up the phone, walked out to Donna's body, placed the gun to his side and pulled the trigger. He fell next to Donna's body, though the wound did not kill him. In fact I'm of the opinion that he shot himself in the side in the hopes of *not* dying; a premeditated plan for murder.

The police came to find Spalding lying next to Donna in a pool of blood. The child was crying and screaming. Spalding was placed under arrest for murder, then taken to the hospital for treatment.

I heard about it on the radio and stopped dead in my tracks. I couldn't believe it. I was in shock. I was enraged. I drove to Donna's house and jumped out of my car about the time they wheeled her body out of the garage. I learned they had just found Spalding's truck several blocks away. I overheard a couple of officers say they saw a note and a high-powered rifle with a scope in the locked truck, so they were going to open the vehicle. I figured it was a suicide note. I wished he had told me he wanted to die. I would have been happy to arrange it. At least a beautiful woman would be alive and her child would not be scarred for life. After he was released from the hospital, he was charged with the murder of Donna Spalding.

I contacted the District Attorney and told him about Donna and me spending the evening together. He sent a couple of his men over to talk with me. I told them everything that happened and everything Donna had told me, including the story about Joe B. Black forcing Donna to have sex with him in exchange for protection from Spalding. And even that didn't help. I told them I thought that in a sense Black was directly responsible for Donna's death.

After the D.A.'s investigators left, I called Black and told him what I had told the D.A.'s office.

'And if there's any way to get you disbarred, you sonofabitch,' I screamed, 'I'm going to do it.'

'Bill! Bill,' he begged, 'I've got a wife and children. I feel bad about this.'

I got tired of listening to the weasel so I hung up to let him worry.

In the meantime, Spalding was processed into jail awaiting trial and the child was taken to Spalding's mother who received temporary custody.

Later, at Donna's funeral, we were all stunned as Spalding's brother, himself a convicted felon, jumped up on top of the casket and took a picture of Donna's body. I found out he sent it to Spalding in jail, at Spalding's request.

I was ready to testify in court and watch Spalding fry for killing Donna, but there was no need. About as quickly as Spalding had ended Donna's life, a jury convicted Spalding and sent him to the Texas State Prison in Huntsville.

Then, a few months later, a motion to dismiss was granted by the judge for illegal search and seizure. The officers had apparently broken some law, according to some liberal precedent, by breaking into Spalding's truck and retrieving the suicide note. After a year in jail, Spalding was set free. On top of that, Spalding obtained full custody of the child. Today Spalding owns a chain of restaurants and is walking around a free man. All because of a suicide note and a technicality.

The weird thing was, the contents of the note. Spalding wrote that he had waited all night in the bushes near Donna's home on the evening of our date with a high-powered rifle. He said he had every intention of killing Donna and the man she had gone out with, no matter who he was. I only wished he had tried. Maybe I would be dead, too. Or maybe Donna would be alive and Spalding would be where he belongs, carried by six instead of judged by twelve.

237

CHAPTER 16
What Are You Doing Now, Mr Dear?

My speech before the Texas Corrections Association, which had centered around *The Dungeon Master* and several other cases, was concluded, as always, with questions from the audience, many wanting more details. (Those readers of this book who want more details about the Dungeon Master case are referred to my book of the same name.) Many want to know if so and so was really that mean, or so and so was really that beautiful, or if I would really kill someone if faced with no other choice. The questioner usually wants some stereotype reinforced or dispelled. I do what I can and usually make some joke about those questions, followed by an example of what it is really like.

But there's one question someone always asks. Today was no different.

'Yes, Ma'am.' I pointed to a lady a few rows back from the podium.

'What are you doing now, Mr Dear?' she asked. 'Are there any more cases in the works?'

'Actually,' I smiled, 'I'm working on a book about the murder of a corporate president in Ohio and the subsequent arrest of eleven people, the largest number of arrests and convictions for a single murder case in the history of the United States.'

'What happened?' came a voice from the audience.

'The butler did it,' I joked as everyone laughed. 'No,' I

continued, 'I don't want to spoil it for you, but suffice to say, it will keep you on the edge of your seat.'

'Aw, come on,' said someone else. 'What happened?'

'Okay,' I raised one hand in the air and began counting off fingers. 'One . . . the victim is found lying near his front door wearing boxer shorts on backwards, fatally shot. Two . . . there's a sofa pillow with a bullet hole through it over his head as he lay face down, and two spent cartridges lying nearby. Three . . . there's no sign of a struggle. Four . . . a blank telegram lying next to his feet. And five . . . his mouth is stuffed with cotton.'

The ladies cringe.

'During the case, I hid in the trunk of a car, listening to two killers in the front seat. I posed as a doctor at a hospital to arrest the trigger man. I spent two months in jail, living with our informant to keep him alive during the trial. As a result, we arrested eleven people and helped convict them.' As they shook their heads in disbelief, I added, 'There should've been two more arrested and convicted if you want to know the truth. It would have made it a baker's dozen. As a matter of fact, I've just been inducted into the Police Officer's Hall of Fame for my work on this murder case.'

The crowd broke into applause. As it faded, I continued, 'Right now, I am dealing with the fallout from a very difficult case in Canada. A jockey was found dead a few miles from his home. It was initially ruled suicide. After a year of working on the case, I obtained enough hard evidence to justify one of the longest and most probing inquests in Canadian history. Despite the odds stacked against me from sources such as the Ontario Provincial Police and the Ontario Jockey Club, I was able to produce evidence of corruption and payoffs involving key characters in the case. Three weeks after the inquest, I met with the man who drove the car the murderer rode in, and he identified those involved in the death of the jockey, Dan Beckon. The driver admitted Beckon was murdered. As a result of our investigation, the Coroner's ruling was overturned, the first time that had ever happened in Canada.

'It also set the stage for my final run-in with the mystery woman, Barbara Russo. And, Ladies and Gentlemen, that's a story in itself. Sherlock Holmes had his Professor Moriarty, I've got Barbara Russo. In fact, I intend to write a book just on the Russo case and another on the Beckon murder.'

A question rose anonymously from the audience. 'What about this high society lady I read you were checking on?'

'I'm glad you asked that.' The crowd laughed. 'Most of you have seen or heard of the motion picture, *The Black Widow*, starring Teresa Russell as the Black Widow and Debra Winger as the FBI agent. It was a fantastic story written by Ron Bass, who later won the Academy Award for writing *Rainman*. The truth is, I feel that was *my* case. In my crime scene area at my offices in DeSoto, I have the vehicle the last husband/victim was found in. I had either the pleasure, or the misfortune, to be involved with this lady, who hired me to solve the death of her husband. She turned out to be my prime suspect. Three of her husbands and one woman had died under strange circumstances, and until I became involved in the case, no one had tied the events together. In the movie, the Black Widow went to prison. In real life, the Black Widow still crawls about, spinning a web for her next victim. I just hope I can bring her to justice before another man falls prey to her bite.

'You may also have seen, on the show *Unsolved Mysteries*, the case of the Wax Museum murder in Grand Prairie, Texas. I wasn't brought into the case until two and a half years after the owner of the museum, Patsy Wright, died. The death certificate showed the cause of death as "undetermined". Within two months of my involvement in the case, her death was changed to murder.

'Patsy and her sister, Sally Horning, were the joint owners of the museum that had been started by their father. In 1987, on Halloween to be exact, Patsy was found dead in her home, after making an emergency call to her sister. An autopsy was performed, but before the results were available Patsy's body was cremated. Later, the results would show the NyQuil cold medicine she took the night of her death had been laced with strychnine just below the level of crystallization. This was similar to the events leading to the death of Patsy's executive secretary, Lori Williams, two years earlier. What's more, one year after Patsy's death, the Wax Museum mysteriously burned to the ground.

'Despite the complexities of the case, after years of study and investigation I believe I know who killed Patsy Wright and why. Ladies and gentlemen, the story becomes more bizarre and intriguing the deeper I go. The case now involves other countries, and possibly twelve other deaths. The case has become so big, and has now stepped on so many influential toes, that a major effort is under way to discredit me and have my license revoked. This attempt is to keep me from exposing the truth about the deaths surrounding the case of the Wax Museum and those involved.'

The room was silent, save for a voice in the crowd. 'Sounds like a pretty good movie.'

Epilogue

On Tuesday, December 18, 1990, I returned to Dallas from Chicago after a particularly tiring trip. I opened the door to my home and stepped inside, dragging my bags behind me, and promptly tossed them into my bedroom. I made my way into my bathroom and proceeded to wash my face. I was looking forward to relaxing at home for a while. No work, no calls. Just relaxing. Perhaps a dip in the pool.

As I stood at the sink in the bathroom splashing cool water in my face, I felt something under my feet. I grabbed a towel, dried my face and looked down. I couldn't really see what it was, so I stooped down to find broken glass on the floor. I looked up to the window above and saw two bullet holes in the window pane. One was about head level to me, the other was about chest level. The shots had come, I discovered, from outside my property, past the security fence surrounding my home. The shots were obviously meant as a warning.

It wasn't the first time that something like this had happened, nor, I'm sure, will it be the last. I figure it proves I'm doing something right.

I walked back into my bedroom and picked up some mail on my dresser, which included a letter from the Texas Attorney General's Office advising me that the A-G was filing suit against the Irving Police Department on my behalf, under the Freedom of Information Act. They were refusing to give me information their department had obtained when two of its officers flew to Canada to meet with mystery woman Barbara Russo. They were trying to build a case against me. The Irving Police Department has an axe to grind: I had exposed their department's sloppiness and subsequent cover-up in the Courson murder case. But I expect to get my day in court in the lawsuit I'm preparing against them for harassment against me and my firm.

At the same time, I've filed a six-million-dollar lawsuit against Russo for trying to discredit me. When you're at the top, it's easy for people to take shots at you from afar, just as they had through my bathroom window. I expect both cases will make for interesting reading, once all's said and done. We'll see . . .

ACKNOWLEDGMENTS

I would like to thank all the people who have been involved in my life, but the list would be too long. However, I would like to acknowledge some very special friends and associates who have stuck by me in the good times as well as the bad. I know, as I sit at this typewriter, that I will surely forget some who are as important as those I have mentioned; I hope they will forgive me.

To Victoria Bogner, my secretary and friend, without whose help and understanding this book would not have been possible.

A special thank you to Joann Daughety, who has spent many hours working with me and helping to bring the project to its fruition.

To Randy Wyles who collaborated with me in the preparation of the manuscript.

To my friends who have given me their encouragement and support: Lt Larry Momchilov, Doug Jenny, Marianne Courson, Malcolm, Erica, Faye and Alexander Brinkworth, Dr C. Miller Ballem, Joe Villanueva, Andy Dixon, Chris Stewart, Teresa Whitaker, Janice Swanson, Arlene Line, Paul and Maureen Arnold, Dr and Mrs French Anderson, Tom Apple, Richard and Diane Eubanks, Dr Joe and Barbara Phipps, Roberta Goodwin, Amy and Mark Coker, Tommy and Patricia Fallin, Larry and Tommy Price, Sally Foster, John and Joanne Ritchie, Lynn and Laura Ferguson, Jerry and Sandy Forrester, Aileen Foster, Aubrey and Judith Golden, Sandy Goroff-Mailly, Ruth Hapgood, David Nerman, Dave and Sandra Salyers, Suzanne Haddad, Dr Joann Houts, John Iacoviello, Kathy James, Betty Kisor, Sue Kollinger, Kathy Kinser, Tom Hight, Sr, Bob Loving, Carl Lilly, Barbara Lowe, Willard Green, Paul Leech, Debbie Lockhurst and Ron Woods, Allie Martin, Marge McGill, Betty Sue May, Marla Messersmith, Danny and Jerri McBride, Wanda Stoll, Harvey Davisson, Wyatt Carr, Kay McNabb, Jim Proudfoot, Richard

244

Russell, Richard and Kathleen Stallings, Paula Snoga, Keith Vinsonhaler, Beverly VonHelms, Jean Winzeler, Kristi Wester, Tanya Lucas, Rita Wong, Linda Wurzbacher, Zach Watson, Chris Hykel, Mrs Eli Momchilov, Nancy Dixon, Blue and Helen Clark, Bill and Judy Hoffman, Bob France, Shelley and Yael Elnekave, Manny and J. P. Snapps, Kathleen and Tommy Thompkins, Russell and Shirley Albury, Gregg Happ, Mike and Donna Phipps, Donna, Danny, Barbara, Mark, Shane and Julie Cockerham, Chad Beckon, Jim Palmer, Kay and Floyd Fisher, Terri and Joe Bauer, Mike and Nancy Furlich, Mr and Mrs John Isbell, Harry Tinnerella, Bud and Judy Isenhart, Stu Bonnett, Detective John Bailey, Cheri Ann Kennedy.

And last, but not least, to my very special friend and associate, John McCready.